Data Science from Scratch

Joel Grus

Beijing · Cambridge · Farnham · Köln · Sebastopol · Tokyo

Data Science from Scratch

by Joel Grus

Printed in the United States of America.

Published by O'Reilly Media, Inc., 1005 Gravenstein Highway North, Sebastopol, CA 95472.

O'Reilly books may be purchased for educational, business, or sales promotional use. Online editions are also available for most titles (*http://safaribooksonline.com*). For more information, contact our corporate/institutional sales department: 800-998-9938 or *corporate@oreilly.com*.

Editor: Marie Beaugureau	**Indexer:** Ellen Troutman-Zaig
Production Editor: Melanie Yarbrough	**Interior Designer:** David Futato
Copyeditor: Nan Reinhardt	**Cover Designer:** Karen Montgomery
Proofreader: Eileen Cohen	**Illustrator:** Rebecca Demarest

April 2015:   First Edition

Revision History for the First Edition
2015-04-10:   First Release

See *http://oreilly.com/catalog/errata.csp?isbn=9781491901427* for release details.

978-1-491-90142-7

[LSI]

Table of Contents

Preface

Data Science

Data scientist has been called "the sexiest job of the 21st century," (*http://bit.ly/1Bqe1WY*) presumably by someone who has never visited a fire station. Nonetheless, data science is a hot and growing field, and it doesn't take a great deal of sleuthing to find analysts breathlessly prognosticating that over the next 10 years, we'll need billions and billions more data scientists than we currently have.

But what is data science? After all, we can't produce data scientists if we don't know what data science is. According to a Venn diagram (*http://bit.ly/1EQNZ4A*) that is somewhat famous in the industry, data science lies at the intersection of:

- Hacking skills
- Math and statistics knowledge
- Substantive expertise

Although I originally intended to write a book covering all three, I quickly realized that a thorough treatment of "substantive expertise" would require tens of thousands of pages. At that point, I decided to focus on the first two. My goal is to help you develop the hacking skills that you'll need to get started doing data science. And my goal is to help you get comfortable with the mathematics and statistics that are at the core of data science.

This is a somewhat heavy aspiration for a book. The best way to learn hacking skills is by hacking on things. By reading this book, you will get a good understanding of the way I hack on things, which may not necessarily be the best way for you to hack on things. You will get a good understanding of some of the tools I use, which will not necessarily be the best tools for you to use. You will get a good understanding of the way I approach data problems, which may not necessarily be the best way for you to approach data problems. The intent (and the hope) is that my examples will inspire you try things your own way. All the code and data from the book is available on GitHub (*https://github.com/joelgrus/data-science-from-scratch*) to get you started.

Similarly, the best way to learn mathematics is by doing mathematics. This is emphatically not a math book, and for the most part, we won't be "doing mathematics." However, you can't really do data science without *some* understanding of probability and statistics and linear algebra. This means that, where appropriate, we will dive into mathematical equations, mathematical intuition, mathematical axioms, and cartoon versions of big mathematical ideas. I hope that you won't be afraid to dive in with me.

Throughout it all, I also hope to give you a sense that playing with data is fun, because, well, playing with data is fun! (Especially compared to some of the alternatives, like tax preparation or coal mining.)

From Scratch

There are lots and lots of data science libraries, frameworks, modules, and toolkits that efficiently implement the most common (as well as the least common) data science algorithms and techniques. If you become a data scientist, you will become intimately familiar with NumPy, with scikit-learn, with pandas, and with a panoply of other libraries. They are great for doing data science. But they are also a good way to start doing data science without actually understanding data science.

In this book, we will be approaching data science from scratch. That means we'll be building tools and implementing algorithms by hand in order to better understand them. I put a lot of thought into creating implementations and examples that are clear, well-commented, and readable. In most cases, the tools we build will be illuminating but impractical. They will work well on small toy data sets but fall over on "web scale" ones.

Throughout the book, I will point you to libraries you might use to apply these techniques to larger data sets. But we won't be using them here.

There is a healthy debate raging over the best language for learning data science. Many people believe it's the statistical programming language R. (We call those people *wrong*.) A few people suggest Java or Scala. However, in my opinion, Python is the obvious choice.

Python has several features that make it well suited for learning (and doing) data science:

- It's free.
- It's relatively simple to code in (and, in particular, to understand).
- It has lots of useful data science–related libraries.

I am hesitant to call Python my favorite programming language. There are other languages I find more pleasant, better-designed, or just more fun to code in. And yet pretty much every time I start a new data science project, I end up using Python. Every time I need to quickly prototype something that just works, I end up using Python. And every time I want to demonstrate data science concepts in a clear, easy-to-understand way, I end up using Python. Accordingly, this book uses Python.

The goal of this book is not to teach you Python. (Although it is nearly certain that by reading this book you will learn some Python.) I'll take you through a chapter-long crash course that highlights the features that are most important for our purposes, but if you know nothing about programming in Python (or about programming at all) then you might want to supplement this book with some sort of "Python for Beginners" tutorial.

The remainder of our introduction to data science will take this same approach — going into detail where going into detail seems crucial or illuminating, at other times leaving details for you to figure out yourself (or look up on Wikipedia).

Over the years, I've trained a number of data scientists. While not all of them have gone on to become world-changing data ninja rockstars, I've left them all better data scientists than I found them. And I've grown to believe that anyone who has some amount of mathematical aptitude and some amount of programming skill has the necessary raw materials to do data science. All she needs is an inquisitive mind, a willingness to work hard, and this book. Hence this book.

Conventions Used in This Book

The following typographical conventions are used in this book:

Italic
    Indicates new terms, URLs, email addresses, filenames, and file extensions.

`Constant width`
    Used for program listings, as well as within paragraphs to refer to program elements such as variable or function names, databases, data types, environment variables, statements, and keywords.

`Constant width bold`
    Shows commands or other text that should be typed literally by the user.

`Constant width italic`
    Shows text that should be replaced with user-supplied values or by values determined by context.

This element signifies a tip or suggestion.

 This element signifies a general note.

 This element indicates a warning or caution.

Using Code Examples

Supplemental material (code examples, exercises, etc.) is available for download at *https://github.com/joelgrus/data-science-from-scratch*.

This book is here to help you get your job done. In general, if example code is offered with this book, you may use it in your programs and documentation. You do not need to contact us for permission unless you're reproducing a significant portion of the code. For example, writing a program that uses several chunks of code from this book does not require permission. Selling or distributing a CD-ROM of examples from O'Reilly books does require permission. Answering a question by citing this book and quoting example code does not require permission. Incorporating a significant amount of example code from this book into your product's documentation does require permission.

We appreciate, but do not require, attribution. An attribution usually includes the title, author, publisher, and ISBN. For example: "*Data Science from Scratch* by Joel Grus (O'Reilly). Copyright 2015 Joel Grus, 978-1-4919-0142-7."

If you feel your use of code examples falls outside fair use or the permission given above, feel free to contact us at *permissions@oreilly.com*.

Safari® Books Online

Safari Books Online is an on-demand digital library that delivers expert content in both book and video form from the world's leading authors in technology and business.

Technology professionals, software developers, web designers, and business and creative professionals use Safari Books Online as their primary resource for research, problem solving, learning, and certification training.

Safari Books Online offers a range of plans and pricing for enterprise, government, education, and individuals.

Members have access to thousands of books, training videos, and prepublication manuscripts in one fully searchable database from publishers like O'Reilly Media, Prentice Hall Professional, Addison-Wesley Professional, Microsoft Press, Sams, Que, Peachpit Press, Focal Press, Cisco Press, John Wiley & Sons, Syngress, Morgan Kaufmann, IBM Redbooks, Packt, Adobe Press, FT Press, Apress, Manning, New Riders, McGraw-Hill, Jones & Bartlett, Course Technology, and hundreds more. For more information about Safari Books Online, please visit us online.

How to Contact Us

Please address comments and questions concerning this book to the publisher:

O'Reilly Media, Inc.
1005 Gravenstein Highway North
Sebastopol, CA 95472
800-998-9938 (in the United States or Canada)
707-829-0515 (international or local)
707-829-0104 (fax)

We have a web page for this book, where we list errata, examples, and any additional information. You can access this page at *http://bit.ly/data-science-from-scratch*.

To comment or ask technical questions about this book, send email to *bookquestions@oreilly.com*.

For more information about our books, courses, conferences, and news, see our website at *http://www.oreilly.com*.

Find us on Facebook: *http://facebook.com/oreilly*

Follow us on Twitter: *http://twitter.com/oreillymedia*

Watch us on YouTube: *http://www.youtube.com/oreillymedia*

Acknowledgments

First, I would like to thank Mike Loukides for accepting my proposal for this book (and for insisting that I pare it down to a reasonable size). It would have been very easy for him to say, "Who's this person who keeps emailing me sample chapters, and how do I get him to go away?" I'm grateful he didn't. I'd also like to thank my editor, Marie Beaugureau, for guiding me through the publishing process and getting the book in a much better state than I ever would have gotten it on my own.

I couldn't have written this book if I'd never learned data science, and I probably wouldn't have learned data science if not for the influence of Dave Hsu, Igor Tatarinov, John Rauser, and the rest of the Farecast gang. (So long ago that it wasn't even called data science at the time!) The good folks at Coursera deserve a lot of credit, too.

I am also grateful to my beta readers and reviewers. Jay Fundling found a ton of mistakes and pointed out many unclear explanations, and the book is much better (and much more correct) thanks to him. Debashis Ghosh is a hero for sanity-checking all of my statistics. Andrew Musselman suggested toning down the "people who prefer R to Python are moral reprobates" aspect of the book, which I think ended up being pretty good advice. Trey Causey, Ryan Matthew Balfanz, Loris Mularoni, Núria Pujol, Rob Jefferson, Mary Pat Campbell, Zach Geary, and Wendy Grus also provided invaluable feedback. Any errors remaining are of course my responsibility.

I owe a lot to the Twitter #datascience commmunity, for exposing me to a ton of new concepts, introducing me to a lot of great people, and making me feel like enough of an underachiever that I went out and wrote a book to compensate. Special thanks to Trey Causey (again), for (inadvertently) reminding me to include a chapter on linear algebra, and to Sean J. Taylor, for (inadvertently) pointing out a couple of huge gaps in the "Working with Data" chapter.

Above all, I owe immense thanks to Ganga and Madeline. The only thing harder than writing a book is living with someone who's writing a book, and I couldn't have pulled it off without their support.

## CHAPTER 1

Introduction

"Data! Data! Data!" he cried impatiently. "I can't make bricks without clay."
—Arthur Conan Doyle

The Ascendance of Data

We live in a world that's drowning in data. Websites track every user's every click. Your smartphone is building up a record of your location and speed every second of every day. "Quantified selfers" wear pedometers-on-steroids that are ever recording their heart rates, movement habits, diet, and sleep patterns. Smart cars collect driving habits, smart homes collect living habits, and smart marketers collect purchasing habits. The Internet itself represents a huge graph of knowledge that contains (among other things) an enormous cross-referenced encyclopedia; domain-specific databases about movies, music, sports results, pinball machines, memes, and cocktails; and too many government statistics (some of them nearly true!) from too many governments to wrap your head around.

Buried in these data are answers to countless questions that no one's ever thought to ask. In this book, we'll learn how to find them.

What Is Data Science?

There's a joke that says a data scientist is someone who knows more statistics than a computer scientist and more computer science than a statistician. (I didn't say it was a good joke.) In fact, some data scientists are—for all practical purposes—statisticians, while others are pretty much indistinguishable from software engineers. Some are machine-learning experts, while others couldn't machine-learn their way out of kindergarten. Some are PhDs with impressive publication records, while others have never read an academic paper (shame on them, though). In short, pretty much no matter how you define data science, you'll find practitioners for whom the definition is totally, absolutely wrong.

Nonetheless, we won't let that stop us from trying. We'll say that a data scientist is someone who extracts insights from messy data. Today's world is full of people trying to turn data into insight.

For instance, the dating site OkCupid asks its members to answer thousands of questions in order to find the most appropriate matches for them. But it also analyzes these results to figure out innocuous-sounding questions you can ask someone to find out how likely someone is to sleep with you on the first date (*http://bit.ly/ 1EQU0hI*).

Facebook asks you to list your hometown and your current location, ostensibly to make it easier for your friends to find and connect with you. But it also analyzes these locations to identify global migration patterns (*http://on.fb.me/1EQTq3A*) and where the fanbases of different football teams live (*http://on.fb.me/1EQTvnO*).

As a large retailer, Target tracks your purchases and interactions, both online and in-store. And it uses the data to predictively model (*http://nyti.ms/1EQTznL*) which of its customers are pregnant, to better market baby-related purchases to them.

In 2012, the Obama campaign employed dozens of data scientists who data-mined and experimented their way to identifying voters who needed extra attention, choosing optimal donor-specific fundraising appeals and programs, and focusing get-out-the-vote efforts where they were most likely to be useful. It is generally agreed that these efforts played an important role in the president's re-election, which means it is a safe bet that political campaigns of the future will become more and more data-driven, resulting in a never-ending arms race of data science and data collection.

Now, before you start feeling too jaded: some data scientists also occasionally use their skills for good—using data to make government more effective (*http://bit.ly/ 1EQTGiW*), to help the homeless (*http://bit.ly/1EQTIYl*), and to improve public health (*http://bit.ly/1EQTPTv*). But it certainly won't hurt your career if you like figuring out the best way to get people to click on advertisements.

Motivating Hypothetical: DataSciencester

Congratulations! You've just been hired to lead the data science efforts at DataSciencester, *the* social network for data scientists.

Despite being *for* data scientists, DataSciencester has never actually invested in building its own data science practice. (In fairness, DataSciencester has never really invested in building its product either.) That will be your job! Throughout the book, we'll be learning about data science concepts by solving problems that you encounter at work. Sometimes we'll look at data explicitly supplied by users, sometimes we'll look at data generated through their interactions with the site, and sometimes we'll even look at data from experiments that we'll design.

And because DataSciencester has a strong "not-invented-here" mentality, we'll be building our own tools from scratch. At the end, you'll have a pretty solid understanding of the fundamentals of data science. And you'll be ready to apply your skills at a company with a less shaky premise, or to any other problems that happen to interest you.

Welcome aboard, and good luck! (You're allowed to wear jeans on Fridays, and the bathroom is down the hall on the right.)

Finding Key Connectors

It's your first day on the job at DataSciencester, and the VP of Networking is full of questions about your users. Until now he's had no one to ask, so he's very excited to have you aboard.

In particular, he wants you to identify who the "key connectors" are among data scientists. To this end, he gives you a dump of the entire DataSciencester network. (In real life, people don't typically hand you the data you need. Chapter 9 is devoted to getting data.)

What does this data dump look like? It consists of a list of users, each represented by a `dict` that contains for each user his or her `id` (which is a number) and `name` (which, in one of the great cosmic coincidences, rhymes with the user's `id`):

```
users = [
    { "id": 0, "name": "Hero" },
    { "id": 1, "name": "Dunn" },
    { "id": 2, "name": "Sue" },
    { "id": 3, "name": "Chi" },
    { "id": 4, "name": "Thor" },
    { "id": 5, "name": "Clive" },
    { "id": 6, "name": "Hicks" },
    { "id": 7, "name": "Devin" },
    { "id": 8, "name": "Kate" },
    { "id": 9, "name": "Klein" }
]
```

He also gives you the "friendship" data, represented as a list of pairs of IDs:

```
friendships = [(0, 1), (0, 2), (1, 2), (1, 3), (2, 3), (3, 4),
               (4, 5), (5, 6), (5, 7), (6, 8), (7, 8), (8, 9)]
```

For example, the tuple (0, 1) indicates that the data scientist with `id` 0 (Hero) and the data scientist with `id` 1 (Dunn) are friends. The network is illustrated in Figure 1-1.

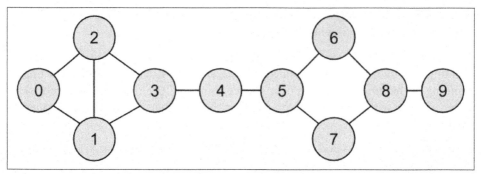

Figure 1-1. The DataSciencester network

Since we represented our users as dicts, it's easy to augment them with extra data.

> Don't get too hung up on the details of the code right now. In Chapter 2, we'll take you through a crash course in Python. For now just try to get the general flavor of what we're doing.

For example, we might want to add a list of friends to each user. First we set each user's friends property to an empty list:

```
for user in users:
    user["friends"] = []
```

And then we populate the lists using the friendships data:

```
for i, j in friendships:
    # this works because users[i] is the user whose id is i
    users[i]["friends"].append(users[j]) # add i as a friend of j
    users[j]["friends"].append(users[i]) # add j as a friend of i
```

Once each user dict contains a list of friends, we can easily ask questions of our graph, like "what's the average number of connections?"

First we find the *total* number of connections, by summing up the lengths of all the friends lists:

```
def number_of_friends(user):
    """how many friends does _user_ have?"""
    return len(user["friends"])                    # length of friend_ids list

total_connections = sum(number_of_friends(user)
                        for user in users)         # 24
```

And then we just divide by the number of users:

```
from __future__ import division          # integer division is lame
num_users = len(users)                   # length of the users list
avg_connections = total_connections / num_users  # 2.4
```

It's also easy to find the most connected people—they're the people who have the larg-est number of friends.

Since there aren't very many users, we can sort them from "most friends" to "least friends":

```
# create a list (user_id, number_of_friends)
num_friends_by_id = [(user["id"], number_of_friends(user))
                     for user in users]

sorted(num_friends_by_id,                        # get it sorted
       key=lambda (user_id, num_friends): num_friends,  # by num_friends
       reverse=True)                             # largest to smallest

# each pair is (user_id, num_friends)
# [(1, 3), (2, 3), (3, 3), (5, 3), (8, 3),
#  (0, 2), (4, 2), (6, 2), (7, 2), (9, 1)]
```

One way to think of what we've done is as a way of identifying people who are some-how central to the network. In fact, what we've just computed is the network metric *degree centrality* (Figure 1-2).

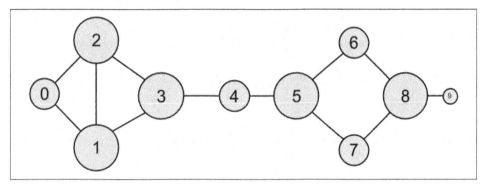

Figure 1-2. The DataSciencester network sized by degree

This has the virtue of being pretty easy to calculate, but it doesn't always give the results you'd want or expect. For example, in the DataSciencester network Thor (id 4) only has two connections while Dunn (id 1) has three. Yet looking at the network it intuitively seems like Thor should be more central. In Chapter 21, we'll investigate networks in more detail, and we'll look at more complex notions of centrality that may or may not accord better with our intuition.

Data Scientists You May Know

While you're still filling out new-hire paperwork, the VP of Fraternization comes by your desk. She wants to encourage more connections among your members, and she asks you to design a "Data Scientists You May Know" suggester.

Your first instinct is to suggest that a user might know the friends of friends. These are easy to compute: for each of a user's friends, iterate over that person's friends, and collect all the results:

```
def friends_of_friend_ids_bad(user):
    # "foaf" is short for "friend of a friend"
    return [foaf["id"]
            for friend in user["friends"]     # for each of user's friends
            for foaf in friend["friends"]]     # get each of _their_ friends
```

When we call this on users[0] (Hero), it produces:

```
[0, 2, 3, 0, 1, 3]
```

It includes user 0 (twice), since Hero is indeed friends with both of his friends. It includes users 1 and 2, although they are both friends with Hero already. And it includes user 3 twice, as Chi is reachable through two different friends:

```
print [friend["id"] for friend in users[0]["friends"]]  # [1, 2]
print [friend["id"] for friend in users[1]["friends"]]  # [0, 2, 3]
print [friend["id"] for friend in users[2]["friends"]]  # [0, 1, 3]
```

Knowing that people are friends-of-friends in multiple ways seems like interesting information, so maybe instead we should produce a *count* of mutual friends. And we definitely should use a helper function to exclude people already known to the user:

```
from collections import Counter                      # not loaded by default

def not_the_same(user, other_user):
    """two users are not the same if they have different ids"""
    return user["id"] != other_user["id"]

def not_friends(user, other_user):
    """other_user is not a friend if he's not in user["friends"];
    that is, if he's not_the_same as all the people in user["friends"]"""
    return all(not_the_same(friend, other_user)
               for friend in user["friends"])

def friends_of_friend_ids(user):
    return Counter(foaf["id"]
                   for friend in user["friends"]      # for each of my friends
                   for foaf in friend["friends"]      # count *their* friends
                   if not_the_same(user, foaf)        # who aren't me
                   and not_friends(user, foaf))       # and aren't my friends

print friends_of_friend_ids(users[3])                 # Counter({0: 2, 5: 1})
```

This correctly tells Chi (`id` 3) that she has two mutual friends with Hero (`id` 0) but only one mutual friend with Clive (`id` 5).

As a data scientist, you know that you also might enjoy meeting users with similar interests. (This is a good example of the "substantive expertise" aspect of data science.) After asking around, you manage to get your hands on this data, as a list of pairs (`user_id, interest`):

```
interests = [
    (0, "Hadoop"), (0, "Big Data"), (0, "HBase"), (0, "Java"),
    (0, "Spark"), (0, "Storm"), (0, "Cassandra"),
    (1, "NoSQL"), (1, "MongoDB"), (1, "Cassandra"), (1, "HBase"),
    (1, "Postgres"), (2, "Python"), (2, "scikit-learn"), (2, "scipy"),
    (2, "numpy"), (2, "statsmodels"), (2, "pandas"), (3, "R"), (3, "Python"),
    (3, "statistics"), (3, "regression"), (3, "probability"),
    (4, "machine learning"), (4, "regression"), (4, "decision trees"),
    (4, "libsvm"), (5, "Python"), (5, "R"), (5, "Java"), (5, "C++"),
    (5, "Haskell"), (5, "programming languages"), (6, "statistics"),
    (6, "probability"), (6, "mathematics"), (6, "theory"),
    (7, "machine learning"), (7, "scikit-learn"), (7, "Mahout"),
    (7, "neural networks"), (8, "neural networks"), (8, "deep learning"),
    (8, "Big Data"), (8, "artificial intelligence"), (9, "Hadoop"),
    (9, "Java"), (9, "MapReduce"), (9, "Big Data")
]
```

For example, Thor (`id` 4) has no friends in common with Devin (`id` 7), but they share an interest in machine learning.

It's easy to build a function that finds users with a certain interest:

```
def data_scientists_who_like(target_interest):
    return [user_id
            for user_id, user_interest in interests
            if user_interest == target_interest]
```

This works, but it has to examine the whole list of interests for every search. If we have a lot of users and interests (or if we just want to do a lot of searches), we're probably better off building an index from interests to users:

```
from collections import defaultdict

# keys are interests, values are lists of user_ids with that interest
user_ids_by_interest = defaultdict(list)

for user_id, interest in interests:
    user_ids_by_interest[interest].append(user_id)
```

And another from users to interests:

```
# keys are user_ids, values are lists of interests for that user_id
interests_by_user_id = defaultdict(list)
```

```
for user_id, interest in interests:
    interests_by_user_id[user_id].append(interest)
```

Now it's easy to find who has the most interests in common with a given user:

- Iterate over the user's interests.

- For each interest, iterate over the other users with that interest.

- Keep count of how many times we see each other user.

```
def most_common_interests_with(user):
    return Counter(interested_user_id
        for interest in interests_by_user_id[user["id"]]
        for interested_user_id in user_ids_by_interest[interest]
        if interested_user_id != user["id"])
```

We could then use this to build a richer "Data Scientists You Should Know" feature based on a combination of mutual friends and mutual interests. We'll explore these kinds of applications in Chapter 22.

Salaries and Experience

Right as you're about to head to lunch, the VP of Public Relations asks if you can provide some fun facts about how much data scientists earn. Salary data is of course sensitive, but he manages to provide you an anonymous data set containing each user's salary (in dollars) and tenure as a data scientist (in years):

```
salaries_and_tenures = [(83000, 8.7), (88000, 8.1),
                        (48000, 0.7), (76000, 6),
                        (69000, 6.5), (76000, 7.5),
                        (60000, 2.5), (83000, 10),
                        (48000, 1.9), (63000, 4.2)]
```

The natural first step is to plot the data (which we'll see how to do in Chapter 3). You can see the results in Figure 1-3.

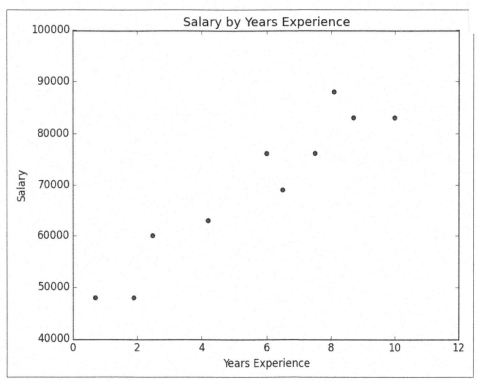

Figure 1-3. Salary by years of experience

It seems pretty clear that people with more experience tend to earn more. How can you turn this into a fun fact? Your first idea is to look at the average salary for each tenure:

```
# keys are years, values are lists of the salaries for each tenure
salary_by_tenure = defaultdict(list)

for salary, tenure in salaries_and_tenures:
    salary_by_tenure[tenure].append(salary)

# keys are years, each value is average salary for that tenure
average_salary_by_tenure = {
    tenure : sum(salaries) / len(salaries)
    for tenure, salaries in salary_by_tenure.items()
}
```

This turns out to be not particularly useful, as none of the users have the same tenure, which means we're just reporting the individual users' salaries:

```
{0.7: 48000.0,
 1.9: 48000.0,
 2.5: 60000.0,
 4.2: 63000.0,
```

```
    6: 76000.0,
    6.5: 69000.0,
    7.5: 76000.0,
    8.1: 88000.0,
    8.7: 83000.0,
    10: 83000.0}
```

It might be more helpful to bucket the tenures:

```
def tenure_bucket(tenure):
    if tenure < 2:
        return "less than two"
    elif tenure < 5:
        return "between two and five"
    else:
        return "more than five"
```

Then group together the salaries corresponding to each bucket:

```
# keys are tenure buckets, values are lists of salaries for that bucket
salary_by_tenure_bucket = defaultdict(list)

for salary, tenure in salaries_and_tenures:
    bucket = tenure_bucket(tenure)
    salary_by_tenure_bucket[bucket].append(salary)
```

And finally compute the average salary for each group:

```
# keys are tenure buckets, values are average salary for that bucket
average_salary_by_bucket = {
  tenure_bucket : sum(salaries) / len(salaries)
  for tenure_bucket, salaries in salary_by_tenure_bucket.iteritems()
}
```

which is more interesting:

```
{'between two and five': 61500.0,
 'less than two': 48000.0,
 'more than five': 79166.66666666667}
```

And you have your soundbite: "Data scientists with more than five years experience earn 65% more than data scientists with little or no experience!"

But we chose the buckets in a pretty arbitrary way. What we'd really like is to make some sort of statement about the salary effect—on average—of having an additional year of experience. In addition to making for a snappier fun fact, this allows us to *make predictions* about salaries that we don't know. We'll explore this idea in Chapter 14.

Paid Accounts

When you get back to your desk, the VP of Revenue is waiting for you. She wants to better understand which users pay for accounts and which don't. (She knows their names, but that's not particularly actionable information.)

You notice that there seems to be a correspondence between years of experience and paid accounts:

```
0.7  paid
1.9  unpaid
2.5  paid
4.2  unpaid
6    unpaid
6.5  unpaid
7.5  unpaid
8.1  unpaid
8.7  paid
10   paid
```

Users with very few and very many years of experience tend to pay; users with average amounts of experience don't.

Accordingly, if you wanted to create a model—though this is definitely not enough data to base a model on—you might try to predict "paid" for users with very few and very many years of experience, and "unpaid" for users with middling amounts of experience:

```python
def predict_paid_or_unpaid(years_experience):
    if years_experience < 3.0:
        return "paid"
    elif years_experience < 8.5:
        return "unpaid"
    else:
        return "paid"
```

Of course, we totally eyeballed the cutoffs.

With more data (and more mathematics), we could build a model predicting the likelihood that a user would pay, based on his years of experience. We'll investigate this sort of problem in Chapter 16.

Topics of Interest

As you're wrapping up your first day, the VP of Content Strategy asks you for data about what topics users are most interested in, so that she can plan out her blog calendar accordingly. You already have the raw data from the friend-suggester project:

```python
interests = [
    (0, "Hadoop"), (0, "Big Data"), (0, "HBase"), (0, "Java"),
    (0, "Spark"), (0, "Storm"), (0, "Cassandra"),
```

```
        (1, "NoSQL"), (1, "MongoDB"), (1, "Cassandra"), (1, "HBase"),
        (1, "Postgres"), (2, "Python"), (2, "scikit-learn"), (2, "scipy"),
        (2, "numpy"), (2, "statsmodels"), (2, "pandas"), (3, "R"), (3, "Python"),
        (3, "statistics"), (3, "regression"), (3, "probability"),
        (4, "machine learning"), (4, "regression"), (4, "decision trees"),
        (4, "libsvm"), (5, "Python"), (5, "R"), (5, "Java"), (5, "C++"),
        (5, "Haskell"), (5, "programming languages"), (6, "statistics"),
        (6, "probability"), (6, "mathematics"), (6, "theory"),
        (7, "machine learning"), (7, "scikit-learn"), (7, "Mahout"),
        (7, "neural networks"), (8, "neural networks"), (8, "deep learning"),
        (8, "Big Data"), (8, "artificial intelligence"), (9, "Hadoop"),
        (9, "Java"), (9, "MapReduce"), (9, "Big Data")
]
```

One simple (if not particularly exciting) way to find the most popular interests is simply to count the words:

1. Lowercase each interest (since different users may or may not capitalize their interests).
2. Split it into words.
3. Count the results.

In code:

```
words_and_counts = Counter(word
                          for user, interest in interests
                          for word in interest.lower().split())
```

This makes it easy to list out the words that occur more than once:

```
for word, count in words_and_counts.most_common():
    if count > 1:
        print word, count
```

which gives the results you'd expect (unless you expect "scikit-learn" to get split into two words, in which case it doesn't give the results you expect):

```
learning 3
java 3
python 3
big 3
data 3
hbase 2
regression 2
cassandra 2
statistics 2
probability 2
hadoop 2
networks 2
machine 2
neural 2
```

```
scikit-learn 2
r 2
```

We'll look at more sophisticated ways to extract topics from data in Chapter 20.

Onward

It's been a successful first day! Exhausted, you slip out of the building before anyone else can ask you for anything else. Get a good night's rest, because tomorrow is new employee orientation. (Yes, you went through a full day of work *before* new employee orientation. Take it up with HR.)

## CHAPTER 2

A Crash Course in Python

People are still crazy about Python after twenty-five years, which I find hard to believe.

—Michael Palin

All new employees at DataSciencester are required to go through new employee orientation, the most interesting part of which is a crash course in Python.

This is not a comprehensive Python tutorial but instead is intended to highlight the parts of the language that will be most important to us (some of which are often not the focus of Python tutorials).

The Basics

Getting Python

You can download Python from python.org (*https://www.python.org/*). But if you don't already have Python, I recommend instead installing the Anaconda (*https://store.continuum.io/cshop/anaconda/*) distribution, which already includes most of the libraries that you need to do data science.

As I write this, the latest version of Python is 3.4. At DataSciencester, however, we use old, reliable Python 2.7. Python 3 is not backward-compatible with Python 2, and many important libraries only work well with 2.7. The data science community is still firmly stuck on 2.7, which means we will be, too. Make sure to get that version.

If you don't get Anaconda, make sure to install pip (*https://pypi.python.org/pypi/pip*), which is a Python package manager that allows you to easily install third-party packages (some of which we'll need). It's also worth getting IPython (*http://ipython.org/*), which is a much nicer Python shell to work with.

(If you installed Anaconda then it should have come with pip and IPython.)

Just run:

```
pip install ipython
```

and then search the Internet for solutions to whatever cryptic error messages that causes.

The Zen of Python

Python has a somewhat Zen description of its design principles (*http://legacy.python.org/dev/peps/pep-0020/*), which you can also find inside the Python interpreter itself by typing `import this`.

One of the most discussed of these is:

> There should be one—and preferably only one—obvious way to do it.

Code written in accordance with this "obvious" way (which may not be obvious at all to a newcomer) is often described as "Pythonic." Although this is not a book about Python, we will occasionally contrast Pythonic and non-Pythonic ways of accomplishing the same things, and we will generally favor Pythonic solutions to our problems.

Whitespace Formatting

Many languages use curly braces to delimit blocks of code. Python uses indentation:

```
for i in [1, 2, 3, 4, 5]:
    print i                    # first line in "for i" block
    for j in [1, 2, 3, 4, 5]:
        print j                # first line in "for j" block
        print i + j            # last line in "for j" block
    print i                    # last line in "for i" block
print "done looping"
```

This makes Python code very readable, but it also means that you have to be very careful with your formatting. Whitespace is ignored inside parentheses and brackets, which can be helpful for long-winded computations:

```
long_winded_computation = (1 + 2 + 3 + 4 + 5 + 6 + 7 + 8 + 9 + 10 + 11 + 12 +
                           13 + 14 + 15 + 16 + 17 + 18 + 19 + 20)
```

and for making code easier to read:

```
list_of_lists = [[1, 2, 3], [4, 5, 6], [7, 8, 9]]

easier_to_read_list_of_lists = [ [1, 2, 3],
                                 [4, 5, 6],
                                 [7, 8, 9] ]
```

You can also use a backslash to indicate that a statement continues onto the next line, although we'll rarely do this:

```
two_plus_three = 2 + \
                 3
```

One consequence of whitespace formatting is that it can be hard to copy and paste code into the Python shell. For example, if you tried to paste the code:

```
for i in [1, 2, 3, 4, 5]:

    # notice the blank line
    print i
```

into the ordinary Python shell, you would get a:

```
IndentationError: expected an indented block
```

because the interpreter thinks the blank line signals the end of the for loop's block.

IPython has a magic function %paste, which correctly pastes whatever is on your clipboard, whitespace and all. This alone is a good reason to use IPython.

Modules

Certain features of Python are not loaded by default. These include both features included as part of the language as well as third-party features that you download yourself. In order to use these features, you'll need to import the modules that contain them.

One approach is to simply import the module itself:

```
import re
my_regex = re.compile("[0-9]+", re.I)
```

Here re is the module containing functions and constants for working with regular expressions. After this type of import you can only access those functions by prefixing them with re..

If you already had a different re in your code you could use an alias:

```
import re as regex
my_regex = regex.compile("[0-9]+", regex.I)
```

You might also do this if your module has an unwieldy name or if you're going to be typing it a lot. For example, when visualizing data with matplotlib, a standard convention is:

```
import matplotlib.pyplot as plt
```

If you need a few specific values from a module, you can import them explicitly and use them without qualification:

```
from collections import defaultdict, Counter
lookup = defaultdict(int)
my_counter = Counter()
```

If you were a bad person, you could import the entire contents of a module into your namespace, which might inadvertently overwrite variables you've already defined:

```
match = 10
from re import *    # uh oh, re has a match function
print match         # "<function re.match>"
```

However, since you are not a bad person, you won't ever do this.

Arithmetic

Python 2.7 uses integer division by default, so that 5 / 2 equals 2. Almost always this is not what we want, so we will always start our files with:

```
from __future__ import division
```

after which 5 / 2 equals 2.5. Every code example in this book uses this new-style division. In the handful of cases where we need integer division, we can get it with a double slash: 5 // 2.

Functions

A function is a rule for taking zero or more inputs and returning a corresponding output. In Python, we typically define functions using def:

```
def double(x):
    """this is where you put an optional docstring
    that explains what the function does.
    for example, this function multiplies its input by 2"""
    return x * 2
```

Python functions are *first-class*, which means that we can assign them to variables and pass them into functions just like any other arguments:

```
def apply_to_one(f):
    """calls the function f with 1 as its argument"""
    return f(1)

my_double = double              # refers to the previously defined function
x = apply_to_one(my_double)     # equals 2
```

It is also easy to create short anonymous functions, or lambdas:

```
y = apply_to_one(lambda x: x + 4)      # equals 5
```

You can assign lambdas to variables, although most people will tell you that you should just use def instead:

```
another_double = lambda x: 2 * x       # don't do this
def another_double(x): return 2 * x    # do this instead
```

Function parameters can also be given default arguments, which only need to be specified when you want a value other than the default:

```
def my_print(message="my default message"):
    print message

my_print("hello")   # prints 'hello'
my_print()          # prints 'my default message'
```

It is sometimes useful to specify arguments by name:

```
def subtract(a=0, b=0):
    return a - b

subtract(10, 5) # returns 5
subtract(0, 5)  # returns -5
subtract(b=5)   # same as previous
```

We will be creating many, many functions.

Strings

Strings can be delimited by single or double quotation marks (but the quotes have to match):

```
single_quoted_string = 'data science'
double_quoted_string = "data science"
```

Python uses backslashes to encode special characters. For example:

```
tab_string = "\t"       # represents the tab character
len(tab_string)         # is 1
```

If you want backslashes as backslashes (which you might in Windows directory names or in regular expressions), you can create *raw* strings using r"":

```
not_tab_string = r"\t"  # represents the characters '\' and 't'
len(not_tab_string)     # is 2
```

You can create multiline strings using triple-[double-]-quotes:

```
multi_line_string = """This is the first line.
and this is the second line
and this is the third line"""
```

Exceptions

When something goes wrong, Python raises an *exception*. Unhandled, these will cause your program to crash. You can handle them using try and except:

```
try:
    print 0 / 0
except ZeroDivisionError:
    print "cannot divide by zero"
```

Although in many languages exceptions are considered bad, in Python there is no shame in using them to make your code cleaner, and we will occasionally do so.

Lists

Probably the most fundamental data structure in Python is the list. A list is simply an ordered collection. (It is similar to what in other languages might be called an array, but with some added functionality.)

```
integer_list = [1, 2, 3]
heterogeneous_list = ["string", 0.1, True]
list_of_lists = [ integer_list, heterogeneous_list, [] ]

list_length = len(integer_list)     # equals 3
list_sum    = sum(integer_list)     # equals 6
```

You can get or set the *n*th element of a list with square brackets:

```
x = range(10)   # is the list [0, 1, ..., 9]
zero = x[0]     # equals 0, lists are 0-indexed
one = x[1]      # equals 1
nine = x[-1]    # equals 9, 'Pythonic' for last element
eight = x[-2]   # equals 8, 'Pythonic' for next-to-last element
x[0] = -1       # now x is [-1, 1, 2, 3, ..., 9]
```

You can also use square brackets to "slice" lists:

```
first_three    = x[:3]              # [-1, 1, 2]
three_to_end = x[3:]                # [3, 4, ..., 9]
one_to_four = x[1:5]                # [1, 2, 3, 4]
last_three = x[-3:]                 # [7, 8, 9]
without_first_and_last = x[1:-1]    # [1, 2, ..., 8]
copy_of_x = x[:]                    # [-1, 1, 2, ..., 9]
```

Python has an in operator to check for list membership:

```
1 in [1, 2, 3]    # True
0 in [1, 2, 3]    # False
```

This check involves examining the elements of the list one at a time, which means that you probably shouldn't use it unless you know your list is pretty small (or unless you don't care how long the check takes).

It is easy to concatenate lists together:

```
x = [1, 2, 3]
x.extend([4, 5, 6])    # x is now [1,2,3,4,5,6]
```

If you don't want to modify x you can use list addition:

```
x = [1, 2, 3]
y = x + [4, 5, 6]      # y is [1, 2, 3, 4, 5, 6]; x is unchanged
```

More frequently we will append to lists one item at a time:

```
x = [1, 2, 3]
x.append(0)    # x is now [1, 2, 3, 0]
```

```
y = x[-1]          # equals 0
z = len(x)         # equals 4
```

It is often convenient to *unpack* lists if you know how many elements they contain:

```
x, y = [1, 2]    # now x is 1, y is 2
```

although you will get a ValueError if you don't have the same numbers of elements on both sides.

It's common to use an underscore for a value you're going to throw away:

```
_, y = [1, 2]      # now y == 2, didn't care about the first element
```

Tuples

Tuples are lists' immutable cousins. Pretty much anything you can do to a list that doesn't involve modifying it, you can do to a tuple. You specify a tuple by using parentheses (or nothing) instead of square brackets:

```
my_list = [1, 2]
my_tuple = (1, 2)
other_tuple = 3, 4
my_list[1] = 3       # my_list is now [1, 3]

try:
    my_tuple[1] = 3
except TypeError:
    print "cannot modify a tuple"
```

Tuples are a convenient way to return multiple values from functions:

```
def sum_and_product(x, y):
    return (x + y),(x * y)

sp = sum_and_product(2, 3)     # equals (5, 6)
s, p = sum_and_product(5, 10) # s is 15, p is 50
```

Tuples (and lists) can also be used for *multiple assignment*:

```
x, y = 1, 2      # now x is 1, y is 2
x, y = y, x      # Pythonic way to swap variables; now x is 2, y is 1
```

Dictionaries

Another fundamental data structure is a dictionary, which associates *values* with *keys* and allows you to quickly retrieve the value corresponding to a given key:

```
empty_dict = {}                          # Pythonic
empty_dict2 = dict()                     # less Pythonic
grades = { "Joel" : 80, "Tim" : 95 }     # dictionary literal
```

You can look up the value for a key using square brackets:

```
joels_grade = grades["Joel"]              # equals 80
```

But you'll get a `KeyError` if you ask for a key that's not in the dictionary:

```
try:
    kates_grade = grades["Kate"]
except KeyError:
    print "no grade for Kate!"
```

You can check for the existence of a key using `in`:

```
joel_has_grade = "Joel" in grades     # True
kate_has_grade = "Kate" in grades     # False
```

Dictionaries have a `get` method that returns a default value (instead of raising an exception) when you look up a key that's not in the dictionary:

```
joels_grade = grades.get("Joel", 0)   # equals 80
kates_grade = grades.get("Kate", 0)   # equals 0
no_ones_grade = grades.get("No One")  # default default is None
```

You assign key-value pairs using the same square brackets:

```
grades["Tim"] = 99                        # replaces the old value
grades["Kate"] = 100                      # adds a third entry
num_students = len(grades)                # equals 3
```

We will frequently use dictionaries as a simple way to represent structured data:

```
tweet = {
    "user" : "joelgrus",
    "text" : "Data Science is Awesome",
    "retweet_count" : 100,
    "hashtags" : ["#data", "#science", "#datascience", "#awesome", "#yolo"]
}
```

Besides looking for specific keys we can look at all of them:

```
tweet_keys   = tweet.keys()     # list of keys
tweet_values = tweet.values()   # list of values
tweet_items  = tweet.items()    # list of (key, value) tuples

"user" in tweet_keys            # True, but uses a slow list in
"user" in tweet                 # more Pythonic, uses faster dict in
"joelgrus" in tweet_values      # True
```

Dictionary keys must be immutable; in particular, you cannot use `lists` as keys. If you need a multipart key, you should use a `tuple` or figure out a way to turn the key into a string.

defaultdict

Imagine that you're trying to count the words in a document. An obvious approach is to create a dictionary in which the keys are words and the values are counts. As you check each word, you can increment its count if it's already in the dictionary and add it to the dictionary if it's not:

```
word_counts = {}
for word in document:
    if word in word_counts:
        word_counts[word] += 1
    else:
        word_counts[word] = 1
```

You could also use the "forgiveness is better than permission" approach and just handle the exception from trying to look up a missing key:

```
word_counts = {}
for word in document:
    try:
        word_counts[word] += 1
    except KeyError:
        word_counts[word] = 1
```

A third approach is to use get, which behaves gracefully for missing keys:

```
word_counts = {}
for word in document:
    previous_count = word_counts.get(word, 0)
    word_counts[word] = previous_count + 1
```

Every one of these is slightly unwieldy, which is why defaultdict is useful. A defaultdict is like a regular dictionary, except that when you try to look up a key it doesn't contain, it first adds a value for it using a zero-argument function you provided when you created it. In order to use defaultdicts, you have to import them from collections:

```
from collections import defaultdict

word_counts = defaultdict(int)          # int() produces 0
for word in document:
    word_counts[word] += 1
```

They can also be useful with list or dict or even your own functions:

```
dd_list = defaultdict(list)             # list() produces an empty list
dd_list[2].append(1)                    # now dd_list contains {2: [1]}

dd_dict = defaultdict(dict)             # dict() produces an empty dict
dd_dict["Joel"]["City"] = "Seattle"     # { "Joel" : { "City" : Seattle"}}

dd_pair = defaultdict(lambda: [0, 0])
dd_pair[2][1] = 1                       # now dd_pair contains {2: [0,1]}
```

These will be useful when we're using dictionaries to "collect" results by some key and don't want to have to check every time to see if the key exists yet.

Counter

A `Counter` turns a sequence of values into a `defaultdict(int)`-like object mapping keys to counts. We will primarily use it to create histograms:

```
from collections import Counter
c = Counter([0, 1, 2, 0])          # c is (basically) { 0 : 2, 1 : 1, 2 : 1 }
```

This gives us a very simple way to solve our `word_counts` problem:

```
word_counts = Counter(document)
```

A `Counter` instance has a `most_common` method that is frequently useful:

```
# print the 10 most common words and their counts
for word, count in word_counts.most_common(10):
    print word, count
```

Sets

Another data structure is `set`, which represents a collection of *distinct* elements:

```
s = set()
s.add(1)        # s is now { 1 }
s.add(2)        # s is now { 1, 2 }
s.add(2)        # s is still { 1, 2 }
x = len(s)      # equals 2
y = 2 in s      # equals True
z = 3 in s      # equals False
```

We'll use sets for two main reasons. The first is that `in` is a very fast operation on sets. If we have a large collection of items that we want to use for a membership test, a set is more appropriate than a list:

```
stopwords_list = ["a","an","at"] + hundreds_of_other_words + ["yet", "you"]

"zip" in stopwords_list      # False, but have to check every element

stopwords_set = set(stopwords_list)
"zip" in stopwords_set       # very fast to check
```

The second reason is to find the *distinct* items in a collection:

```
item_list = [1, 2, 3, 1, 2, 3]
num_items = len(item_list)              # 6
item_set = set(item_list)               # {1, 2, 3}
num_distinct_items = len(item_set)      # 3
distinct_item_list = list(item_set)     # [1, 2, 3]
```

We'll use sets much less frequently than dicts and lists.

Control Flow

As in most programming languages, you can perform an action conditionally using if:

```
if 1 > 2:
    message = "if only 1 were greater than two..."
elif 1 > 3:
    message = "elif stands for 'else if'"
else:
    message = "when all else fails use else (if you want to)"
```

You can also write a *ternary* if-then-else on one line, which we will do occasionally:

```
parity = "even" if x % 2 == 0 else "odd"
```

Python has a while loop:

```
x = 0
while x < 10:
    print x, "is less than 10"
    x += 1
```

although more often we'll use for and in:

```
for x in range(10):
    print x, "is less than 10"
```

If you need more-complex logic, you can use continue and break:

```
for x in range(10):
    if x == 3:
        continue  # go immediately to the next iteration
    if x == 5:
        break     # quit the loop entirely
    print x
```

This will print 0, 1, 2, and 4.

Truthiness

Booleans in Python work as in most other languages, except that they're capitalized:

```
one_is_less_than_two = 1 < 2      # equals True
true_equals_false = True == False  # equals False
```

Python uses the value None to indicate a nonexistent value. It is similar to other languages' null:

```
x = None
print x == None    # prints True, but is not Pythonic
print x is None    # prints True, and is Pythonic
```

Python lets you use any value where it expects a Boolean. The following are all "Falsy":

- False

- None

- [] (an empty list)

- {} (an empty dict)

- " "

- set()

- 0

- 0.0

Pretty much anything else gets treated as True. This allows you to easily use if statements to test for empty lists or empty strings or empty dictionaries or so on. It also sometimes causes tricky bugs if you're not expecting this behavior:

```
s = some_function_that_returns_a_string()
if s:
    first_char = s[0]
else:
    first_char = ""
```

A simpler way of doing the same is:

```
first_char = s and s[0]
```

since and returns its second value when the first is "truthy," the first value when it's not. Similarly, if x is either a number or possibly None:

```
safe_x = x or 0
```

is definitely a number.

Python has an all function, which takes a list and returns True precisely when every element is truthy, and an any function, which returns True when at least one element is truthy:

```
all([True, 1, { 3 }])   # True
all([True, 1, {}])      # False, {} is falsy
any([True, 1, {}])      # True, True is truthy
all([])                 # True, no falsy elements in the list
any([])                 # False, no truthy elements in the list
```

The Not-So-Basics

Here we'll look at some more-advanced Python features that we'll find useful for working with data.

Sorting

Every Python list has a `sort` method that sorts it in place. If you don't want to mess up your list, you can use the `sorted` function, which returns a new list:

```
x = [4,1,2,3]
y = sorted(x)      # is [1,2,3,4], x is unchanged
x.sort()           # now x is [1,2,3,4]
```

By default, `sort` (and `sorted`) sort a list from smallest to largest based on naively comparing the elements to one another.

If you want elements sorted from largest to smallest, you can specify a `reverse=True` parameter. And instead of comparing the elements themselves, you can compare the results of a function that you specify with `key`:

```
# sort the list by absolute value from largest to smallest
x = sorted([-4,1,-2,3], key=abs, reverse=True)  # is [-4,3,-2,1]

# sort the words and counts from highest count to lowest
wc = sorted(word_counts.items(),
            key=lambda (word, count): count,
            reverse=True)
```

List Comprehensions

Frequently, you'll want to transform a list into another list, by choosing only certain elements, or by transforming elements, or both. The Pythonic way of doing this is *list comprehensions*:

```
even_numbers = [x for x in range(5) if x % 2 == 0]  # [0, 2, 4]
squares      = [x * x for x in range(5)]            # [0, 1, 4, 9, 16]
even_squares = [x * x for x in even_numbers]        # [0, 4, 16]
```

You can similarly turn lists into dictionaries or sets:

```
square_dict = { x : x * x for x in range(5) }  # { 0:0, 1:1, 2:4, 3:9, 4:16 }
square_set  = { x * x for x in [1, -1] }       # { 1 }
```

If you don't need the value from the list, it's conventional to use an underscore as the variable:

```
zeroes = [0 for _ in even_numbers]      # has the same length as even_numbers
```

A list comprehension can include multiple `for`s:

```
pairs = [(x, y)
         for x in range(10)
         for y in range(10)]   # 100 pairs (0,0) (0,1) ... (9,8), (9,9)
```

and later `for`s can use the results of earlier ones:

```
increasing_pairs = [(x, y)                    # only pairs with x < y,
                    for x in range(10)        # range(lo, hi) equals
                    for y in range(x + 1, 10)] # [lo, lo + 1, ..., hi - 1]
```

We will use list comprehensions a lot.

Generators and Iterators

A problem with lists is that they can easily grow very big. `range(1000000)` creates an actual list of 1 million elements. If you only need to deal with them one at a time, this can be a huge source of inefficiency (or of running out of memory). If you potentially only need the first few values, then calculating them all is a waste.

A *generator* is something that you can iterate over (for us, usually using `for`) but whose values are produced only as needed (*lazily*).

One way to create generators is with functions and the `yield` operator:

```
def lazy_range(n):
    """a lazy version of range"""
    i = 0
    while i < n:
        yield i
        i += 1
```

The following loop will consume the `yield`ed values one at a time until none are left:

```
for i in lazy_range(10):
    do_something_with(i)
```

(Python actually comes with a `lazy_range` function called `xrange`, and in Python 3, `range` itself is lazy.) This means you could even create an infinite sequence:

```
def natural_numbers():
    """returns 1, 2, 3, ..."""
    n = 1
    while True:
        yield n
        n += 1
```

although you probably shouldn't iterate over it without using some kind of `break` logic.

 The flip side of laziness is that you can only iterate through a generator once. If you need to iterate through something multiple times, you'll need to either recreate the generator each time or use a list.

A second way to create generators is by using `for` comprehensions wrapped in parentheses:

```
lazy_evens_below_20 = (i for i in lazy_range(20) if i % 2 == 0)
```

Recall also that every dict has an items() method that returns a list of its key-value pairs. More frequently we'll use the iteritems() method, which lazily yields the key-value pairs one at a time as we iterate over it.

Randomness

As we learn data science, we will frequently need to generate random numbers, which we can do with the random module:

```
import random

four_uniform_randoms = [random.random() for _ in range(4)]

#  [0.8444218515250481,     # random.random() produces numbers
#   0.7579544029403025,     # uniformly between 0 and 1
#   0.420571580830845,      # it's the random function we'll use
#   0.25891675029296335]    # most often
```

The random module actually produces pseudorandom (that is, deterministic) numbers based on an internal state that you can set with random.seed if you want to get reproducible results:

```
random.seed(10)          # set the seed to 10
print random.random()    # 0.57140259469
random.seed(10)          # reset the seed to 10
print random.random()    # 0.57140259469 again
```

We'll sometimes use random.randrange, which takes either 1 or 2 arguments and returns an element chosen randomly from the corresponding range():

```
random.randrange(10)     # choose randomly from range(10) = [0, 1, ..., 9]
random.randrange(3, 6)   # choose randomly from range(3, 6) = [3, 4, 5]
```

There are a few more methods that we'll sometimes find convenient. random.shuffle randomly reorders the elements of a list:

```
up_to_ten = range(10)
random.shuffle(up_to_ten)
print up_to_ten
# [2, 5, 1, 9, 7, 3, 8, 6, 4, 0]   (your results will probably be different)
```

If you need to randomly pick one element from a list you can use random.choice:

```
my_best_friend = random.choice(["Alice", "Bob", "Charlie"])     # "Bob" for me
```

And if you need to randomly choose a sample of elements without replacement (i.e., with no duplicates), you can use random.sample:

```
lottery_numbers = range(60)
winning_numbers = random.sample(lottery_numbers, 6)  # [16, 36, 10, 6, 25, 9]
```

To choose a sample of elements *with* replacement (i.e., allowing duplicates), you can just make multiple calls to `random.choice`:

```
four_with_replacement = [random.choice(range(10))
                         for _ in range(4)]
# [9, 4, 4, 2]
```

Regular Expressions

Regular expressions provide a way of searching text. They are incredibly useful but also fairly complicated, so much so that there are entire books written about them. We will explain their details the few times we encounter them; here are a few examples of how to use them in Python:

```
import re

print all([                             # all of these are true, because
    not re.match("a", "cat"),           # * 'cat' doesn't start with 'a'
    re.search("a", "cat"),              # * 'cat' has an 'a' in it
    not re.search("c", "dog"),          # * 'dog' doesn't have a 'c' in it
    3 == len(re.split("[ab]", "carbs")),  # * split on a or b to ['c','r','s']
    "R-D-" == re.sub("[0-9]", "-", "R2D2") # * replace digits with dashes
    ])  # prints True
```

Object-Oriented Programming

Like many languages, Python allows you to define *classes* that encapsulate data and the functions that operate on them. We'll use them sometimes to make our code cleaner and simpler. It's probably simplest to explain them by constructing a heavily annotated example.

Imagine we didn't have the built-in Python `set`. Then we might want to create our own `Set` class.

What behavior should our class have? Given an instance of `Set`, we'll need to be able to `add` items to it, `remove` items from it, and check whether it `contains` a certain value. We'll create all of these as *member* functions, which means we'll access them with a dot after a `Set` object:

```
# by convention, we give classes PascalCase names
class Set:

    # these are the member functions
    # every one takes a first parameter "self" (another convention)
    # that refers to the particular Set object being used

    def __init__(self, values=None):
        """This is the constructor.
        It gets called when you create a new Set.
        You would use it like
```

```
        s1 = Set()        # empty set
        s2 = Set([1,2,2,3]) # initialize with values"""

        self.dict = {} # each instance of Set has its own dict property
                     # which is what we'll use to track memberships
        if values is not None:
            for value in values:
                self.add(value)

    def __repr__(self):
        """this is the string representation of a Set object
        if you type it at the Python prompt or pass it to str()"""
        return "Set: " + str(self.dict.keys())

    # we'll represent membership by being a key in self.dict with value True
    def add(self, value):
        self.dict[value] = True

    # value is in the Set if it's a key in the dictionary
    def contains(self, value):
        return value in self.dict

    def remove(self, value):
        del self.dict[value]
```

Which we could then use like:

```
s = Set([1,2,3])
s.add(4)
print s.contains(4)     # True
s.remove(3)
print s.contains(3)     # False
```

Functional Tools

When passing functions around, sometimes we'll want to partially apply (or *curry*) functions to create new functions. As a simple example, imagine that we have a function of two variables:

```
def exp(base, power):
    return base ** power
```

and we want to use it to create a function of one variable two_to_the whose input is a power and whose output is the result of exp(2, power).

We can, of course, do this with def, but this can sometimes get unwieldy:

```
def two_to_the(power):
    return exp(2, power)
```

A different approach is to use functools.partial:

```
from functools import partial
two_to_the = partial(exp, 2)      # is now a function of one variable
print two_to_the(3)               # 8
```

You can also use `partial` to fill in later arguments if you specify their names:

```
square_of = partial(exp, power=2)
print square_of(3)                # 9
```

It starts to get messy if you curry arguments in the middle of the function, so we'll try to avoid doing that.

We will also occasionally use `map`, `reduce`, and `filter`, which provide functional alternatives to list comprehensions:

```
def double(x):
    return 2 * x

xs = [1, 2, 3, 4]
twice_xs = [double(x) for x in xs]      # [2, 4, 6, 8]
twice_xs = map(double, xs)              # same as above
list_doubler = partial(map, double)     # *function* that doubles a list
twice_xs = list_doubler(xs)             # again [2, 4, 6, 8]
```

You can use `map` with multiple-argument functions if you provide multiple lists:

```
def multiply(x, y): return x * y

products = map(multiply, [1, 2], [4, 5]) # [1 * 4, 2 * 5] = [4, 10]
```

Similarly, `filter` does the work of a list-comprehension `if`:

```
def is_even(x):
    """True if x is even, False if x is odd"""
    return x % 2 == 0

x_evens = [x for x in xs if is_even(x)]   # [2, 4]
x_evens = filter(is_even, xs)             # same as above
list_evener = partial(filter, is_even)    # *function* that filters a list
x_evens = list_evener(xs)                 # again [2, 4]
```

And `reduce` combines the first two elements of a list, then that result with the third, that result with the fourth, and so on, producing a single result:

```
x_product = reduce(multiply, xs)          # = 1 * 2 * 3 * 4 = 24
list_product = partial(reduce, multiply)  # *function* that reduces a list
x_product = list_product(xs)              # again = 24
```

enumerate

Not infrequently, you'll want to iterate over a list and use both its elements and their indexes:

```
# not Pythonic
for i in range(len(documents)):
    document = documents[i]
    do_something(i, document)

# also not Pythonic
i = 0
for document in documents:
    do_something(i, document)
    i += 1
```

The Pythonic solution is enumerate, which produces tuples (index, element):

```
for i, document in enumerate(documents):
    do_something(i, document)
```

Similarly, if we just want the indexes:

```
for i in range(len(documents)): do_something(i)      # not Pythonic
for i, _ in enumerate(documents): do_something(i)    # Pythonic
```

We'll use this a lot.

zip and Argument Unpacking

Often we will need to zip two or more lists together. zip transforms multiple lists into a single list of tuples of corresponding elements:

```
list1 = ['a', 'b', 'c']
list2 = [1, 2, 3]
zip(list1, list2)          # is [('a', 1), ('b', 2), ('c', 3)]
```

If the lists are different lengths, zip stops as soon as the first list ends.

You can also "unzip" a list using a strange trick:

```
pairs = [('a', 1), ('b', 2), ('c', 3)]
letters, numbers = zip(*pairs)
```

The asterisk performs *argument unpacking*, which uses the elements of pairs as individual arguments to zip. It ends up the same as if you'd called:

```
zip(('a', 1), ('b', 2), ('c', 3))
```

which returns [('a','b','c'), ('1','2','3')].

You can use argument unpacking with any function:

```
def add(a, b): return a + b

add(1, 2)       # returns 3
add([1, 2])     # TypeError!
add(*[1, 2])    # returns 3
```

It is rare that we'll find this useful, but when we do it's a neat trick.

args and kwargs

Let's say we want to create a higher-order function that takes as input some function f and returns a new function that for any input returns twice the value of f:

```python
def doubler(f):
    def g(x):
        return 2 * f(x)
    return g
```

This works in some cases:

```python
def f1(x):
    return x + 1

g = doubler(f1)
print g(3)          # 8 (== ( 3 + 1) * 2)
print g(-1)         # 0 (== (-1 + 1) * 2)
```

However, it breaks down with functions that take more than a single argument:

```python
def f2(x, y):
    return x + y

g = doubler(f2)
print g(1, 2)    # TypeError: g() takes exactly 1 argument (2 given)
```

What we need is a way to specify a function that takes arbitrary arguments. We can do this with argument unpacking and a little bit of magic:

```python
def magic(*args, **kwargs):
    print "unnamed args:", args
    print "keyword args:", kwargs

magic(1, 2, key="word", key2="word2")

# prints
#  unnamed args: (1, 2)
#  keyword args: {'key2': 'word2', 'key': 'word'}
```

That is, when we define a function like this, args is a tuple of its unnamed arguments and kwargs is a dict of its named arguments. It works the other way too, if you want to use a list (or tuple) and dict to *supply* arguments to a function:

```python
def other_way_magic(x, y, z):
    return x + y + z

x_y_list = [1, 2]
z_dict = { "z" : 3 }
print other_way_magic(*x_y_list, **z_dict)    # 6
```

You could do all sorts of strange tricks with this; we will only use it to produce higher-order functions whose inputs can accept arbitrary arguments:

```
def doubler_correct(f):
    """works no matter what kind of inputs f expects"""
    def g(*args, **kwargs):
        """whatever arguments g is supplied, pass them through to f"""
        return 2 * f(*args, **kwargs)
    return g

g = doubler_correct(f2)
print g(1, 2) # 6
```

Welcome to DataSciencester!

This concludes new-employee orientation. Oh, and also, try not to embezzle anything.

For Further Exploration

- There is no shortage of Python tutorials in the world. The official one (*https://docs.python.org/2/tutorial/*) is not a bad place to start.

- The official IPython tutorial (*http://ipython.org/ipython-doc/2/interactive/tutorial.html*) is not quite as good. You might be better off with their videos and presentations (*http://ipython.org/videos.html*). Alternatively, Wes McKinney's *Python for Data Analysis* (O'Reilly) has a really good IPython chapter.

## CHAPTER 3

Visualizing Data

I believe that visualization is one of the most powerful means of achieving personal goals.
—Harvey Mackay

A fundamental part of the data scientist's toolkit is data visualization. Although it is very easy to create visualizations, it's much harder to produce *good* ones.

There are two primary uses for data visualization:

- To *explore* data
- To *communicate* data

In this chapter, we will concentrate on building the skills that you'll need to start exploring your own data and to produce the visualizations we'll be using throughout the rest of the book. Like most of our chapter topics, data visualization is a rich field of study that deserves its own book. Nonetheless, we'll try to give you a sense of what makes for a good visualization and what doesn't.

matplotlib

A wide variety of tools exists for visualizing data. We will be using the `matplotlib` library (*http://matplotlib.org/*), which is widely used (although sort of showing its age). If you are interested in producing elaborate interactive visualizations for the Web, it is likely not the right choice, but for simple bar charts, line charts, and scatterplots, it works pretty well.

In particular, we will be using the `matplotlib.pyplot` module. In its simplest use, `pyplot` maintains an internal state in which you build up a visualization step by step. Once you're done, you can save it (with `savefig()`) or display it (with `show()`).

For example, making simple plots (like Figure 3-1) is pretty simple:

```
from matplotlib import pyplot as plt

years = [1950, 1960, 1970, 1980, 1990, 2000, 2010]
gdp = [300.2, 543.3, 1075.9, 2862.5, 5979.6, 10289.7, 14958.3]

# create a line chart, years on x-axis, gdp on y-axis
plt.plot(years, gdp, color='green', marker='o', linestyle='solid')

# add a title
plt.title("Nominal GDP")

# add a label to the y-axis
plt.ylabel("Billions of $")
plt.show()
```

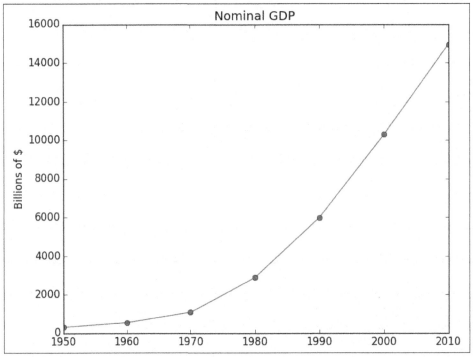

Figure 3-1. A simple line chart

Making plots that look publication-quality good is more complicated and beyond the scope of this chapter. There are many ways you can customize your charts with (for example) axis labels, line styles, and point markers. Rather than attempt a comprehensive treatment of these options, we'll just use (and call attention to) some of them in our examples.

Although we won't be using much of this functionality, `matplotlib` is capable of producing complicated plots within plots, sophisticated formatting, and interactive visualizations. Check out its documentation if you want to go deeper than we do in this book.

Bar Charts

A bar chart is a good choice when you want to show how some quantity varies among some *discrete* set of items. For instance, Figure 3-2 shows how many Academy Awards were won by each of a variety of movies:

```
movies = ["Annie Hall", "Ben-Hur", "Casablanca", "Gandhi", "West Side Story"]
num_oscars = [5, 11, 3, 8, 10]

# bars are by default width 0.8, so we'll add 0.1 to the left coordinates
# so that each bar is centered
xs = [i + 0.1 for i, _ in enumerate(movies)]

# plot bars with left x-coordinates [xs], heights [num_oscars]
plt.bar(xs, num_oscars)

plt.ylabel("# of Academy Awards")
plt.title("My Favorite Movies")

# label x-axis with movie names at bar centers
plt.xticks([i + 0.5 for i, _ in enumerate(movies)], movies)

plt.show()
```

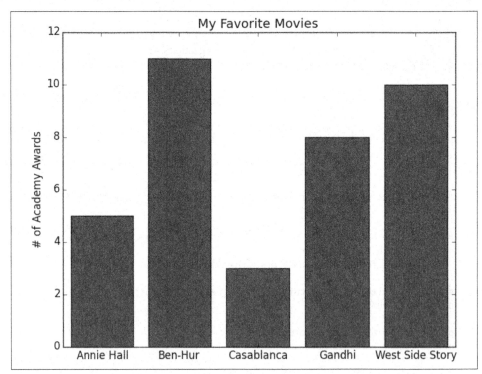

Figure 3-2. A simple bar chart

A bar chart can also be a good choice for plotting histograms of bucketed numeric values, in order to visually explore how the values are *distributed*, as in Figure 3-3:

```
grades = [83,95,91,87,70,0,85,82,100,67,73,77,0]
decile = lambda grade: grade // 10 * 10
histogram = Counter(decile(grade) for grade in grades)

plt.bar([x - 4 for x in histogram.keys()], # shift each bar to the left by 4
        histogram.values(),                # give each bar its correct height
        8)                                 # give each bar a width of 8

plt.axis([-5, 105, 0, 5])                  # x-axis from -5 to 105,
                                           # y-axis from 0 to 5

plt.xticks([10 * i for i in range(11)])    # x-axis labels at 0, 10, ..., 100
plt.xlabel("Decile")
plt.ylabel("# of Students")
plt.title("Distribution of Exam 1 Grades")
plt.show()
```

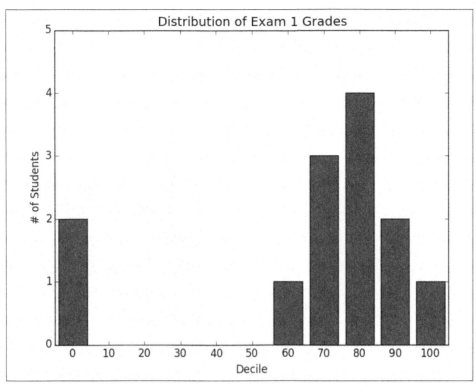

Figure 3-3. Using a bar chart for a histogram

The third argument to `plt.bar` specifies the bar width. Here we chose a width of 8 (which leaves a small gap between bars, since our buckets have width 10). And we shifted the bar left by 4, so that (for example) the "80" bar has its left and right sides at 76 and 84, and (hence) its center at 80.

The call to `plt.axis` indicates that we want the x-axis to range from -5 to 105 (so that the "0" and "100" bars are fully shown), and that the y-axis should range from 0 to 5. And the call to `plt.xticks` puts x-axis labels at 0, 10, 20, ..., 100.

Be judicious when using `plt.axis()`. When creating bar charts it is considered especially bad form for your y-axis not to start at 0, since this is an easy way to mislead people (Figure 3-4):

```
mentions = [500, 505]
years = [2013, 2014]

plt.bar([2012.6, 2013.6], mentions, 0.8)
plt.xticks(years)
plt.ylabel("# of times I heard someone say 'data science'")

# if you don't do this, matplotlib will label the x-axis 0, 1
```

```
# and then add a +2.013e3 off in the corner (bad matplotlib!)
plt.ticklabel_format(useOffset=False)

# misleading y-axis only shows the part above 500
plt.axis([2012.5,2014.5,499,506])
plt.title("Look at the 'Huge' Increase!")
plt.show()
```

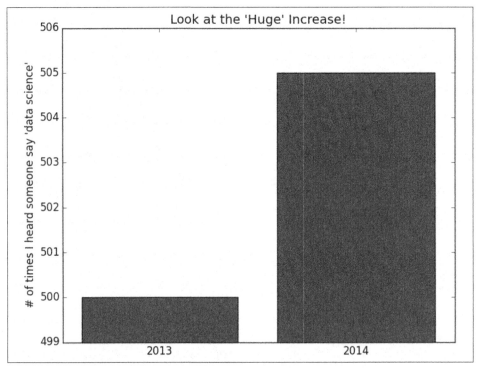

Figure 3-4. A chart with a misleading y-axis

In Figure 3-5, we use more-sensible axes, and it looks far less impressive:

```
plt.axis([2012.5,2014.5,0,550])
plt.title("Not So Huge Anymore")
plt.show()
```

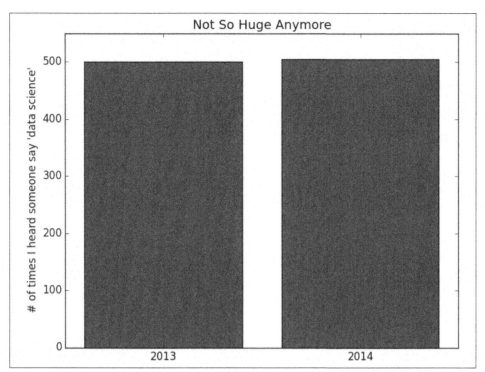

Figure 3-5. The same chart with a nonmisleading y-axis

Line Charts

As we saw already, we can make line charts using `plt.plot()`. These are a good choice for showing *trends*, as illustrated in Figure 3-6:

```
variance     = [1, 2, 4, 8, 16, 32, 64, 128, 256]
bias_squared = [256, 128, 64, 32, 16, 8, 4, 2, 1]
total_error  = [x + y for x, y in zip(variance, bias_squared)]
xs = [i for i, _ in enumerate(variance)]

# we can make multiple calls to plt.plot
# to show multiple series on the same chart
plt.plot(xs, variance,     'g-',  label='variance')    # green solid line
plt.plot(xs, bias_squared, 'r-.', label='bias^2')      # red dot-dashed line
plt.plot(xs, total_error,  'b:',  label='total error') # blue dotted line

# because we've assigned labels to each series
# we can get a legend for free
# loc=9 means "top center"
plt.legend(loc=9)
plt.xlabel("model complexity")
plt.title("The Bias-Variance Tradeoff")
plt.show()
```

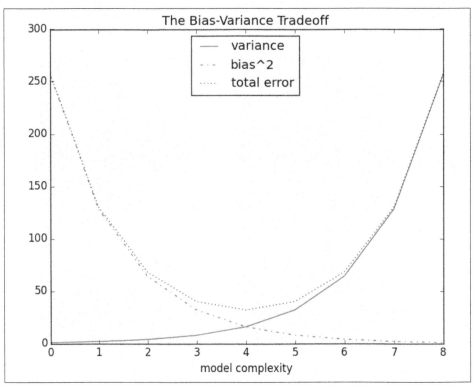

Figure 3-6. Several line charts with a legend

Scatterplots

A scatterplot is the right choice for visualizing the relationship between two paired sets of data. For example, Figure 3-7 illustrates the relationship between the number of friends your users have and the number of minutes they spend on the site every day:

```
friends = [ 70,  65,  72,  63,  71,  64,  60,  64,  67]
minutes = [175, 170, 205, 120, 220, 130, 105, 145, 190]
labels = ['a', 'b', 'c', 'd', 'e', 'f', 'g', 'h', 'i']

plt.scatter(friends, minutes)

# label each point
for label, friend_count, minute_count in zip(labels, friends, minutes):
    plt.annotate(label,
        xy=(friend_count, minute_count), # put the label with its point
        xytext=(5, -5),                  # but slightly offset
        textcoords='offset points')

plt.title("Daily Minutes vs. Number of Friends")
```

```
plt.xlabel("# of friends")
plt.ylabel("daily minutes spent on the site")
plt.show()
```

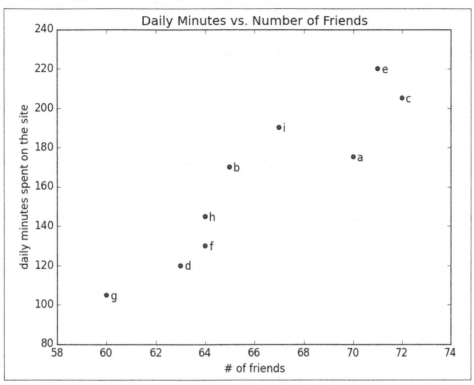

Figure 3-7. A scatterplot of friends and time on the site

If you're scattering comparable variables, you might get a misleading picture if you let
matplotlib choose the scale, as in Figure 3-8:

```
test_1_grades = [ 99, 90, 85, 97, 80]
test_2_grades = [100, 85, 60, 90, 70]

plt.scatter(test_1_grades, test_2_grades)
plt.title("Axes Aren't Comparable")
plt.xlabel("test 1 grade")
plt.ylabel("test 2 grade")
plt.show()
```

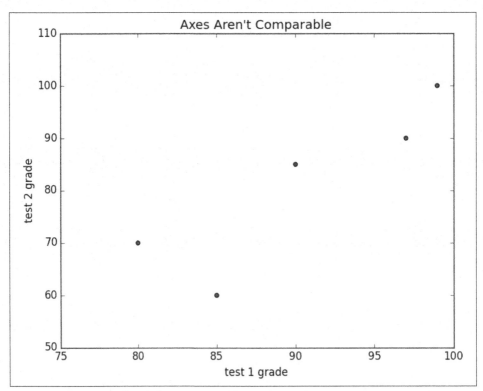

Figure 3-8. A scatterplot with uncomparable axes

If we include a call to `plt.axis("equal")`, the plot (Figure 3-9) more accurately shows that most of the variation occurs on test 2.

That's enough to get you started doing visualization. We'll learn much more about visualization throughout the book.

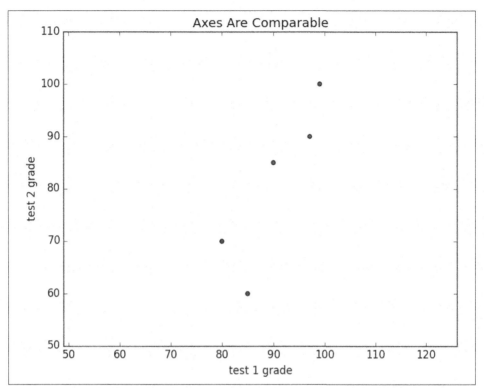

Figure 3-9. The same scatterplot with equal axes

For Further Exploration

- seaborn (*http://stanford.io/1ycOjdI*) is built on top of `matplotlib` and allows you to easily produce prettier (and more complex) visualizations.

- D3.js (*http://d3js.org*) is a JavaScript library for producing sophisticated interactive visualizations for the web. Although it is not in Python, it is both trendy and widely used, and it is well worth your while to be familiar with it.

- Bokeh (*http://bokeh.pydata.org*) is a newer library that brings D3-style visualizations into Python.

- ggplot (*http://bit.ly/1ycOk1u*) is a Python port of the popular R library `ggplot2`, which is widely used for creating "publication quality" charts and graphics. It's probably most interesting if you're already an avid `ggplot2` user, and possibly a little opaque if you're not.

## CHAPTER 4

Linear Algebra

Is there anything more useless or less useful than Algebra?
—Billy Connolly

Linear algebra is the branch of mathematics that deals with *vector spaces*. Although I can't hope to teach you linear algebra in a brief chapter, it underpins a large number of data science concepts and techniques, which means I owe it to you to at least try. What we learn in this chapter we'll use heavily throughout the rest of the book.

Vectors

Abstractly, *vectors* are objects that can be added together (to form new vectors) and that can be multiplied by *scalars* (i.e., numbers), also to form new vectors.

Concretely (for us), vectors are points in some finite-dimensional space. Although you might not think of your data as vectors, they are a good way to represent numeric data.

For example, if you have the heights, weights, and ages of a large number of people, you can treat your data as three-dimensional vectors (height, weight, age). If you're teaching a class with four exams, you can treat student grades as four-dimensional vectors (exam1, exam2, exam3, exam4).

The simplest from-scratch approach is to represent vectors as lists of numbers. A list of three numbers corresponds to a vector in three-dimensional space, and vice versa:

```
height_weight_age = [70,  # inches,
                     170, # pounds,
                     40 ] # years

grades = [95,    # exam1
          80,    # exam2
```

```
    75,    # exam3
    62 ]   # exam4
```

One problem with this approach is that we will want to perform *arithmetic* on vectors. Because Python lists aren't vectors (and hence provide no facilities for vector arithmetic), we'll need to build these arithmetic tools ourselves. So let's start with that.

To begin with, we'll frequently need to add two vectors. Vectors add *componentwise*. This means that if two vectors v and w are the same length, their sum is just the vector whose first element is v[0] + w[0], whose second element is v[1] + w[1], and so on. (If they're not the same length, then we're not allowed to add them.)

For example, adding the vectors [1, 2] and [2, 1] results in [1 + 2, 2 + 1] or [3, 3], as shown in Figure 4-1.

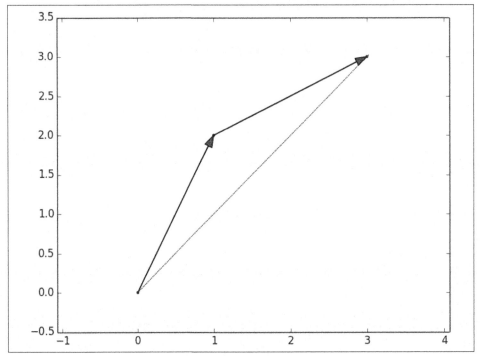

Figure 4-1. Adding two vectors

We can easily implement this by zip-ing the vectors together and using a list comprehension to add the corresponding elements:

```
def vector_add(v, w):
    """adds corresponding elements"""
    return [v_i + w_i
            for v_i, w_i in zip(v, w)]
```

Similarly, to subtract two vectors we just subtract corresponding elements:

```
def vector_subtract(v, w):
    """subtracts corresponding elements"""
    return [v_i - w_i
            for v_i, w_i in zip(v, w)]
```

We'll also sometimes want to componentwise sum a list of vectors. That is, create a new vector whose first element is the sum of all the first elements, whose second element is the sum of all the second elements, and so on. The easiest way to do this is by adding one vector at a time:

```
def vector_sum(vectors):
    """sums all corresponding elements"""
    result = vectors[0]               # start with the first vector
    for vector in vectors[1:]:        # then loop over the others
        result = vector_add(result, vector)   # and add them to the result
    return result
```

If you think about it, we are just reduce-ing the list of vectors using vector_add, which means we can rewrite this more briefly using higher-order functions:

```
def vector_sum(vectors):
    return reduce(vector_add, vectors)
```

or even:

```
vector_sum = partial(reduce, vector_add)
```

although this last one is probably more clever than helpful.

We'll also need to be able to multiply a vector by a scalar, which we do simply by multiplying each element of the vector by that number:

```
def scalar_multiply(c, v):
    """c is a number, v is a vector"""
    return [c * v_i for v_i in v]
```

This allows us to compute the componentwise means of a list of (same-sized) vectors:

```
def vector_mean(vectors):
    """compute the vector whose ith element is the mean of the
    ith elements of the input vectors"""
    n = len(vectors)
    return scalar_multiply(1/n, vector_sum(vectors))
```

A less obvious tool is the *dot product*. The dot product of two vectors is the sum of their componentwise products:

```
def dot(v, w):
    """v_1 * w_1 + ... + v_n * w_n"""
    return sum(v_i * w_i
               for v_i, w_i in zip(v, w))
```

The dot product measures how far the vector *v* extends in the *w* direction. For example, if w = [1, 0] then dot(v, w) is just the first component of v. Another way of saying this is that it's the length of the vector you'd get if you *projected v* onto *w* (Figure 4-2).

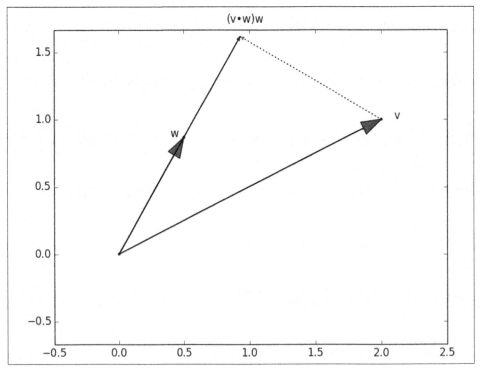

Figure 4-2. The dot product as vector projection

Using this, it's easy to compute a vector's *sum of squares*:

```
def sum_of_squares(v):
    """v_1 * v_1 + ... + v_n * v_n"""
    return dot(v, v)
```

Which we can use to compute its *magnitude* (or length):

```
import math

def magnitude(v):
    return math.sqrt(sum_of_squares(v))    # math.sqrt is square root function
```

We now have all the pieces we need to compute the distance between two vectors, defined as:

$$\sqrt{(v_1 - w_1)^2 + \ldots + (v_n - w_n)^2}$$

```
def squared_distance(v, w):
    """(v_1 - w_1) ** 2 + ... + (v_n - w_n) ** 2"""
    return sum_of_squares(vector_subtract(v, w))

def distance(v, w):
    return math.sqrt(squared_distance(v, w))
```

Which is possibly clearer if we write it as (the equivalent):

```
def distance(v, w):
    return magnitude(vector_subtract(v, w))
```

That should be plenty to get us started. We'll be using these functions heavily throughout the book.

Using lists as vectors is great for exposition but terrible for performance.

In production code, you would want to use the NumPy library, which includes a high-performance array class with all sorts of arithmetic operations included.

Matrices

A *matrix* is a two-dimensional collection of numbers. We will represent matrices as lists of lists, with each inner list having the same size and representing a *row* of the matrix. If A is a matrix, then A[i][j] is the element in the *i*th row and the *j*th column. Per mathematical convention, we will typically use capital letters to represent matrices. For example:

```
A = [[1, 2, 3],   # A has 2 rows and 3 columns
     [4, 5, 6]]

B = [[1, 2],      # B has 3 rows and 2 columns
     [3, 4],
     [5, 6]]
```

In mathematics, you would usually name the first row of the matrix "row 1" and the first column "column 1." Because we're representing matrices with Python lists, which are zero-indexed, we'll call the first row of a matrix "row 0" and the first column "column 0."

Given this list-of-lists representation, the matrix A has len(A) rows and len(A[0]) columns, which we consider its shape:

```
def shape(A):
    num_rows = len(A)
    num_cols = len(A[0]) if A else 0   # number of elements in first row
    return num_rows, num_cols
```

If a matrix has n rows and k columns, we will refer to it as a $n \times k$ matrix. We can (and sometimes will) think of each row of a $n \times k$ matrix as a vector of length k, and each column as a vector of length n:

```python
def get_row(A, i):
    return A[i]              # A[i] is already the ith row

def get_column(A, j):
    return [A_i[j]           # jth element of row A_i
            for A_i in A]    # for each row A_i
```

We'll also want to be able to create a matrix given its shape and a function for generating its elements. We can do this using a nested list comprehension:

```python
def make_matrix(num_rows, num_cols, entry_fn):
    """returns a num_rows x num_cols matrix
    whose (i,j)th entry is entry_fn(i, j)"""
    return [[entry_fn(i, j)                 # given i, create a list
             for j in range(num_cols)]      #   [entry_fn(i, 0), ... ]
            for i in range(num_rows)]       # create one list for each i
```

Given this function, you could make a 5×5 *identity matrix* (with 1s on the diagonal and 0s elsewhere) with:

```python
def is_diagonal(i, j):
    """1's on the 'diagonal', 0's everywhere else"""
    return 1 if i == j else 0

identity_matrix = make_matrix(5, 5, is_diagonal)

# [[1, 0, 0, 0, 0],
#  [0, 1, 0, 0, 0],
#  [0, 0, 1, 0, 0],
#  [0, 0, 0, 1, 0],
#  [0, 0, 0, 0, 1]]
```

Matrices will be important to us for several reasons.

First, we can use a matrix to represent a data set consisting of multiple vectors, simply by considering each vector as a row of the matrix. For example, if you had the heights, weights, and ages of 1,000 people you could put them in a $1,000 \times 3$ matrix:

```python
data = [[70, 170, 40],
        [65, 120, 26],
        [77, 250, 19],
        # ....
        ]
```

Second, as we'll see later, we can use an $n \times k$ matrix to represent a linear function that maps k-dimensional vectors to n-dimensional vectors. Several of our techniques and concepts will involve such functions.

Third, matrices can be used to represent binary relationships. In Chapter 1, we represented the edges of a network as a collection of pairs (i, j). An alternative representation would be to create a matrix A such that A[i][j] is 1 if nodes i and j are connected and 0 otherwise.

Recall that before we had:

```
friendships = [(0, 1), (0, 2), (1, 2), (1, 3), (2, 3), (3, 4),
               (4, 5), (5, 6), (5, 7), (6, 8), (7, 8), (8, 9)]
```

We could also represent this as:

```
        #      user 0 1 2 3 4 5 6 7 8 9
        #
friendships = [[0, 1, 1, 0, 0, 0, 0, 0, 0, 0], # user 0
               [1, 0, 1, 1, 0, 0, 0, 0, 0, 0], # user 1
               [1, 1, 0, 1, 0, 0, 0, 0, 0, 0], # user 2
               [0, 1, 1, 0, 1, 0, 0, 0, 0, 0], # user 3
               [0, 0, 0, 1, 0, 1, 0, 0, 0, 0], # user 4
               [0, 0, 0, 0, 1, 0, 1, 1, 0, 0], # user 5
               [0, 0, 0, 0, 0, 1, 0, 0, 1, 0], # user 6
               [0, 0, 0, 0, 0, 1, 0, 0, 1, 0], # user 7
               [0, 0, 0, 0, 0, 0, 1, 1, 0, 1], # user 8
               [0, 0, 0, 0, 0, 0, 0, 0, 1, 0]] # user 9
```

If there are very few connections, this is a much more inefficient representation, since you end up having to store a lot of zeroes. However, with the matrix representation it is much quicker to check whether two nodes are connected—you just have to do a matrix lookup instead of (potentially) inspecting every edge:

```
friendships[0][2] == 1   # True, 0 and 2 are friends
friendships[0][8] == 1   # False, 0 and 8 are not friends
```

Similarly, to find the connections a node has, you only need to inspect the column (or the row) corresponding to that node:

```
friends_of_five = [i                                      # only need
                   for i, is_friend in enumerate(friendships[5])  # to look at
                   if is_friend]                          # one row
```

Previously we added a list of connections to each node object to speed up this process, but for a large, evolving graph that would probably be too expensive and difficult to maintain.

We'll revisit matrices throughout the book.

For Further Exploration

- Linear algebra is widely used by data scientists (frequently implicitly, and not infrequently by people who don't understand it). It wouldn't be a bad idea to read a textbook. You can find several freely available online:

— Linear Algebra, from UC Davis (*http://bit.ly/1ycOq96*)

— Linear Algebra, from Saint Michael's College (*http://bit.ly/1ycOpSF*)

— If you are feeling adventurous, Linear Algebra Done Wrong (*http://bit.ly/ 1ycOt4W*) is a more advanced introduction

- All of the machinery we built here you get for free if you use NumPy (*http:// www.numpy.org*). (You get a lot more too.)

## CHAPTER 5

Statistics

Facts are stubborn, but statistics are more pliable.
—Mark Twain

Statistics refers to the mathematics and techniques with which we understand data. It is a rich, enormous field, more suited to a shelf (or room) in a library rather than a chapter in a book, and so our discussion will necessarily not be a deep one. Instead, I'll try to teach you just enough to be dangerous, and pique your interest just enough that you'll go off and learn more.

Describing a Single Set of Data

Through a combination of word-of-mouth and luck, DataSciencester has grown to dozens of members, and the VP of Fundraising asks you for some sort of description of how many friends your members have that he can include in his elevator pitches.

Using techniques from Chapter 1, you are easily able to produce this data. But now you are faced with the problem of how to *describe* it.

One obvious description of any data set is simply the data itself:

```
num_friends = [100, 49, 41, 40, 25,
               # ... and lots more
               ]
```

For a small enough data set this might even be the best description. But for a larger data set, this is unwieldy and probably opaque. (Imagine staring at a list of 1 million numbers.) For that reason we use statistics to distill and communicate relevant features of our data.

As a first approach you put the friend counts into a histogram using `Counter` and `plt.bar()` (Figure 5-1):

```
friend_counts = Counter(num_friends)
xs = range(101)                          # largest value is 100
ys = [friend_counts[x] for x in xs]      # height is just # of friends
plt.bar(xs, ys)
plt.axis([0, 101, 0, 25])
plt.title("Histogram of Friend Counts")
plt.xlabel("# of friends")
plt.ylabel("# of people")
plt.show()
```

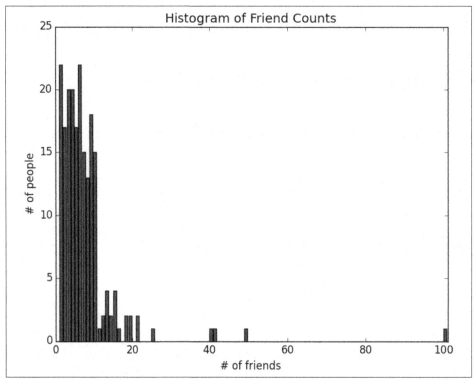

Figure 5-1. A histogram of friend counts

Unfortunately, this chart is still too difficult to slip into conversations. So you start generating some statistics. Probably the simplest statistic is simply the number of data points:

```
num_points = len(num_friends)           # 204
```

You're probably also interested in the largest and smallest values:

```
largest_value = max(num_friends)        # 100
smallest_value = min(num_friends)        # 1
```

which are just special cases of wanting to know the values in specific positions:

```
sorted_values = sorted(num_friends)
smallest_value = sorted_values[0]          # 1
second_smallest_value = sorted_values[1]   # 1
second_largest_value = sorted_values[-2]   # 49
```

But we're only getting started.

Central Tendencies

Usually, we'll want some notion of where our data is centered. Most commonly we'll use the *mean* (or average), which is just the sum of the data divided by its count:

```
# this isn't right if you don't from __future__ import division
def mean(x):
    return sum(x) / len(x)

mean(num_friends)   # 7.333333
```

If you have two data points, the mean is simply the point halfway between them. As you add more points, the mean shifts around, but it always depends on the value of every point.

We'll also sometimes be interested in the *median*, which is the middle-most value (if the number of data points is odd) or the average of the two middle-most values (if the number of data points is even).

For instance, if we have five data points in a sorted vector x, the median is x[5 // 2] or x[2]. If we have six data points, we want the average of x[2] (the third point) and x[3] (the fourth point).

Notice that—unlike the mean—the median doesn't depend on every value in your data. For example, if you make the largest point larger (or the smallest point smaller), the middle points remain unchanged, which means so does the median.

The median function is slightly more complicated than you might expect, mostly because of the "even" case:

```
def median(v):
    """finds the 'middle-most' value of v"""
    n = len(v)
    sorted_v = sorted(v)
    midpoint = n // 2

    if n % 2 == 1:
        # if odd, return the middle value
        return sorted_v[midpoint]
    else:
        # if even, return the average of the middle values
        lo = midpoint - 1
        hi = midpoint
        return (sorted_v[lo] + sorted_v[hi]) / 2
```

```
median(num_friends) # 6.0
```

Clearly, the mean is simpler to compute, and it varies smoothly as our data changes. If we have *n* data points and one of them increases by some small amount *e*, then necessarily the mean will increase by *e* / *n*. (This makes the mean amenable to all sorts of calculus tricks.) Whereas in order to find the median, we have to sort our data. And changing one of our data points by a small amount *e* might increase the median by *e*, by some number less than *e*, or not at all (depending on the rest of the data).

 There are, in fact, nonobvious tricks to efficiently compute medians (*http://en.wikipedia.org/wiki/Quickselect*) without sorting the data. However, they are beyond the scope of this book, so *we have to sort the data.*

At the same time, the mean is very sensitive to outliers in our data. If our friendliest user had 200 friends (instead of 100), then the mean would rise to 7.82, while the median would stay the same. If outliers are likely to be bad data (or otherwise unrepresentative of whatever phenomenon we're trying to understand), then the mean can sometimes give us a misleading picture. For example, the story is often told that in the mid-1980s, the major at the University of North Carolina with the highest average starting salary was geography, mostly on account of NBA star (and outlier) Michael Jordan.

A generalization of the median is the *quantile*, which represents the value less than which a certain percentile of the data lies. (The median represents the value less than which 50% of the data lies.)

```
def quantile(x, p):
    """returns the pth-percentile value in x"""
    p_index = int(p * len(x))
    return sorted(x)[p_index]

quantile(num_friends, 0.10) # 1
quantile(num_friends, 0.25) # 3
quantile(num_friends, 0.75) # 9
quantile(num_friends, 0.90) # 13
```

Less commonly you might want to look at the *mode*, or most-common value[s]:

```
def mode(x):
    """returns a list, might be more than one mode"""
    counts = Counter(x)
    max_count = max(counts.values())
    return [x_i for x_i, count in counts.iteritems()
            if count == max_count]

mode(num_friends)       # 1 and 6
```

But most frequently we'll just use the mean.

Dispersion

Dispersion refers to measures of how spread out our data is. Typically they're statistics for which values near zero signify *not spread out at all* and for which large values (whatever that means) signify *very spread out*. For instance, a very simple measure is the *range*, which is just the difference between the largest and smallest elements:

```python
# "range" already means something in Python, so we'll use a different name
def data_range(x):
    return max(x) - min(x)

data_range(num_friends) # 99
```

The range is zero precisely when the max and min are equal, which can only happen if the elements of x are all the same, which means the data is as undispersed as possible. Conversely, if the range is large, then the max is much larger than the min and the data is more spread out.

Like the median, the range doesn't really depend on the whole data set. A data set whose points are all either 0 or 100 has the same range as a data set whose values are 0, 100, and lots of 50s. But it seems like the first data set "should" be more spread out.

A more complex measure of dispersion is the *variance*, which is computed as:

```python
def de_mean(x):
    """translate x by subtracting its mean (so the result has mean 0)"""
    x_bar = mean(x)
    return [x_i - x_bar for x_i in x]

def variance(x):
    """assumes x has at least two elements"""
    n = len(x)
    deviations = de_mean(x)
    return sum_of_squares(deviations) / (n - 1)

variance(num_friends) # 81.54
```

This looks like it is almost the average squared deviation from the mean, except that we're dividing by n-1 instead of n. In fact, when we're dealing with a sample from a larger population, x_bar is only an *estimate* of the actual mean, which means that on average (x_i - x_bar) ** 2 is an underestimate of x_i's squared deviation from the mean, which is why we divide by n-1 instead of n. See Wikipedia (*http://bit.ly/1L2EapI*).

Now, whatever units our data is in (e.g., "friends"), all of our measures of central tendency are in that same unit. The range will similarly be in that same unit. The variance, on the other hand, has units that are the *square* of the original units (e.g., "friends squared"). As it can be hard to make sense of these, we often look instead at the *standard deviation*:

```
def standard_deviation(x):
    return math.sqrt(variance(x))

standard_deviation(num_friends) # 9.03
```

Both the range and the standard deviation have the same outlier problem that we saw earlier for the mean. Using the same example, if our friendliest user had instead 200 friends, the standard deviation would be 14.89, more than 60% higher!

A more robust alternative computes the difference between the 75th percentile value and the 25th percentile value:

```
def interquartile_range(x):
    return quantile(x, 0.75) - quantile(x, 0.25)

interquartile_range(num_friends) # 6
```

which is quite plainly unaffected by a small number of outliers.

Correlation

DataSciencester's VP of Growth has a theory that the amount of time people spend on the site is related to the number of friends they have on the site (she's not a VP for nothing), and she's asked you to verify this.

After digging through traffic logs, you've come up with a list `daily_minutes` that shows how many minutes per day each user spends on DataSciencester, and you've ordered it so that its elements correspond to the elements of our previous `num_friends` list. We'd like to investigate the relationship between these two metrics.

We'll first look at *covariance*, the paired analogue of variance. Whereas variance measures how a single variable deviates from its mean, covariance measures how two variables vary in tandem from their means:

```
def covariance(x, y):
    n = len(x)
    return dot(de_mean(x), de_mean(y)) / (n - 1)

covariance(num_friends, daily_minutes) # 22.43
```

Recall that dot sums up the products of corresponding pairs of elements. When corresponding elements of x and y are either both above their means or both below their means, a positive number enters the sum. When one is above its mean and the other below, a negative number enters the sum. Accordingly, a "large" positive covariance means that x tends to be large when y is large and small when y is small. A "large" negative covariance means the opposite—that x tends to be small when y is large and vice versa. A covariance close to zero means that no such relationship exists.

Nonetheless, this number can be hard to interpret, for a couple of reasons:

- Its units are the product of the inputs' units (e.g., friend-minutes-per-day), which can be hard to make sense of. (What's a "friend-minute-per-day"?)
- If each user had twice as many friends (but the same number of minutes), the covariance would be twice as large. But in a sense the variables would be just as interrelated. Said differently, it's hard to say what counts as a "large" covariance.

For this reason, it's more common to look at the *correlation*, which divides out the standard deviations of both variables:

```
def correlation(x, y):
    stdev_x = standard_deviation(x)
    stdev_y = standard_deviation(y)
    if stdev_x > 0 and stdev_y > 0:
        return covariance(x, y) / stdev_x / stdev_y
    else:
        return 0     # if no variation, correlation is zero

correlation(num_friends, daily_minutes) # 0.25
```

The correlation is unitless and always lies between -1 (perfect anti-correlation) and 1 (perfect correlation). A number like 0.25 represents a relatively weak positive correlation.

However, one thing we neglected to do was examine our data. Check out Figure 5-2.

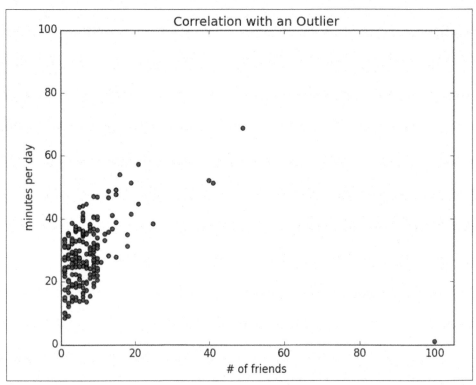

Figure 5-2. Correlation with an outlier

The person with 100 friends (who spends only one minute per day on the site) is a huge outlier, and correlation can be very sensitive to outliers. What happens if we ignore him?

```
outlier = num_friends.index(100)    # index of outlier

num_friends_good = [x
                    for i, x in enumerate(num_friends)
                    if i != outlier]

daily_minutes_good = [x
                      for i, x in enumerate(daily_minutes)
                      if i != outlier]

correlation(num_friends_good, daily_minutes_good) # 0.57
```

Without the outlier, there is a much stronger correlation (Figure 5-3).

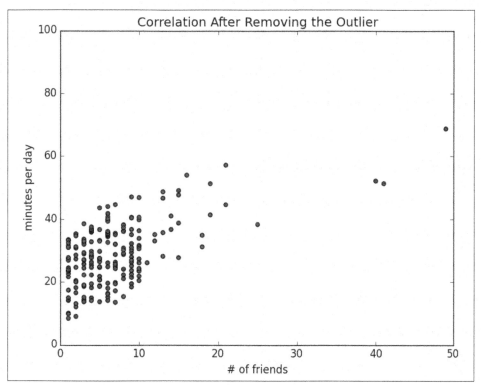

Figure 5-3. Correlation after removing the outlier

You investigate further and discover that the outlier was actually an internal *test* account that no one ever bothered to remove. So you feel pretty justified in excluding it.

Simpson's Paradox

One not uncommon surprise when analyzing data is Simpson's Paradox, in which correlations can be misleading when *confounding* variables are ignored.

For example, imagine that you can identify all of your members as either East Coast data scientists or West Coast data scientists. You decide to examine which coast's data scientists are friendlier:

coast	# of members	avg. # of friends
West Coast	101	8.2
East Coast	103	6.5

It certainly looks like the West Coast data scientists are friendlier than the East Coast data scientists. Your coworkers advance all sorts of theories as to why this might be: maybe it's the sun, or the coffee, or the organic produce, or the laid-back Pacific vibe?

When playing with the data you discover something very strange. If you only look at people with PhDs, the East Coast data scientists have more friends on average. And if you only look at people without PhDs, the East Coast data scientists also have more friends on average!

coast	degree	# of members	avg. # of friends
West Coast	PhD	35	3.1
East Coast	PhD	70	3.2
West Coast	no PhD	66	10.9
East Coast	no PhD	33	13.4

Once you account for the users' degrees, the correlation goes in the opposite direction! Bucketing the data as East Coast/West Coast disguised the fact that the East Coast data scientists skew much more heavily toward PhD types.

This phenomenon crops up in the real world with some regularity. The key issue is that correlation is measuring the relationship between your two variables *all else being equal*. If your data classes are assigned at random, as they might be in a well-designed experiment, "all else being equal" might not be a terrible assumption. But when there is a deeper pattern to class assignments, "all else being equal" can be an awful assumption.

The only real way to avoid this is by *knowing your data* and by doing what you can to make sure you've checked for possible confounding factors. Obviously, this is not always possible. If you didn't have the educational attainment of these 200 data scientists, you might simply conclude that there was something inherently more sociable about the West Coast.

Some Other Correlational Caveats

A correlation of zero indicates that there is no linear relationship between the two variables. However, there may be other sorts of relationships. For example, if:

```
x = [-2, -1, 0, 1, 2]
y = [ 2,  1, 0, 1, 2]
```

then x and y have zero correlation. But they certainly have a relationship—each element of y equals the absolute value of the corresponding element of x. What they don't have is a relationship in which knowing how x_i compares to mean(x) gives us information about how y_i compares to mean(y). That is the sort of relationship that correlation looks for.

In addition, correlation tells you nothing about how large the relationship is. The variables:

```
x = [-2, 1, 0, 1, 2]
y = [99.98, 99.99, 100, 100.01, 100.02]
```

are perfectly correlated, but (depending on what you're measuring) it's quite possible that this relationship isn't all that interesting.

Correlation and Causation

You have probably heard at some point that "correlation is not causation," most likely by someone looking at data that posed a challenge to parts of his worldview that he was reluctant to question. Nonetheless, this is an important point—if x and y are strongly correlated, that might mean that x causes y, that y causes x, that each causes the other, that some third factor causes both, or it might mean nothing.

Consider the relationship between num_friends and daily_minutes. It's possible that having more friends on the site *causes* DataSciencester users to spend more time on the site. This might be the case if each friend posts a certain amount of content each day, which means that the more friends you have, the more time it takes to stay current with their updates.

However, it's also possible that the more time you spend arguing in the DataSciencester forums, the more you encounter and befriend like-minded people. That is, spending more time on the site *causes* users to have more friends.

A third possibility is that the users who are most passionate about data science spend more time on the site (because they find it more interesting) and more actively collect data science friends (because they don't want to associate with anyone else).

One way to feel more confident about causality is by conducting randomized trials. If you can randomly split your users into two groups with similar demographics and give one of the groups a slightly different experience, then you can often feel pretty good that the different experiences are causing the different outcomes.

For instance, if you don't mind being angrily accused of experimenting on your users (*http://nyti.ms/1L2DzEg*), you could randomly choose a subset of your users and show them content from only a fraction of their friends. If this subset subsequently spent less time on the site, this would give you some confidence that having more friends *causes* more time on the site.

For Further Exploration

- SciPy (*http://bit.ly/1L2H0Lj*), pandas (*http://pandas.pydata.org*), and StatsModels (*http://bit.ly/1L2GQnc*) all come with a wide variety of statistical functions.

- Statistics is *important*. (Or maybe statistics *are* important?) If you want to be a good data scientist it would be a good idea to read a statistics textbook. Many are freely available online. A couple that I like are:

  — *OpenIntro Statistics* (*http://bit.ly/1L2GKvG*)

  — *OpenStax Introductory Statistics* (*http://bit.ly/1L2GJrM*)

## CHAPTER 6

Probability

The laws of probability, so true in general, so fallacious in particular.
—Edward Gibbon

It is hard to do data science without some sort of understanding of *probability* and its mathematics. As with our treatment of statistics in Chapter 5, we'll wave our hands a lot and elide many of the technicalities.

For our purposes you should think of probability as a way of quantifying the uncertainty associated with *events* chosen from a some *universe* of events. Rather than getting technical about what these terms mean, think of rolling a die. The universe consists of all possible outcomes. And any subset of these outcomes is an event; for example, "the die rolls a one" or "the die rolls an even number."

Notationally, we write $P(E)$ to mean "the probability of the event E."

We'll use probability theory to build models. We'll use probability theory to evaluate models. We'll use probability theory all over the place.

One could, were one so inclined, get really deep into the philosophy of what probability theory *means*. (This is best done over beers.) We won't be doing that.

Dependence and Independence

Roughly speaking, we say that two events E and F are *dependent* if knowing something about whether E happens gives us information about whether F happens (and vice versa). Otherwise they are *independent*.

For instance, if we flip a fair coin twice, knowing whether the first flip is Heads gives us no information about whether the second flip is Heads. These events are independent. On the other hand, knowing whether the first flip is Heads certainly gives us information about whether both flips are Tails. (If the first flip is Heads, then definitely it's not the case that both flips are Tails.) These two events are dependent.

Mathematically, we say that two events E and F are independent if the probability that they both happen is the product of the probabilities that each one happens:

$$P(E, F) = P(E)P(F)$$

In the example above, the probability of "first flip Heads" is 1/2, and the probability of "both flips Tails" is 1/4, but the probability of "first flip Heads *and* both flips Tails" is 0.

Conditional Probability

When two events E and F are independent, then by definition we have:

$$P(E, F) = P(E)P(F)$$

If they are not necessarily independent (and if the probability of F is not zero), then we define the probability of E "conditional on F" as:

$$P(E|F) = P(E, F)/P(F)$$

You should think of this as the probability that E happens, given that we know that F happens.

We often rewrite this as:

$$P(E, F) = P(E|F)P(F)$$

When E and F are independent, you can check that this gives:

$$P(E|F) = P(E)$$

which is the mathematical way of expressing that knowing F occurred gives us no additional information about whether E occurred.

One common tricky example involves a family with two (unknown) children.

If we assume that:

1. Each child is equally likely to be a boy or a girl
2. The gender of the second child is independent of the gender of the first child

then the event "no girls" has probability 1/4, the event "one girl, one boy" has probability 1/2, and the event "two girls" has probability 1/4.

Now we can ask what is the probability of the event "both children are girls" (B) conditional on the event "the older child is a girl" (G)? Using the definition of conditional probability:

$$P(B\,|\,G) = P(B, G)/P(G) = P(B)/P(G) = 1/2$$

since the event B and G ("both children are girls *and* the older child is a girl") is just the event B. (Once you know that both children are girls, it's necessarily true that the older child is a girl.)

Most likely this result accords with your intuition.

We could also ask about the probability of the event "both children are girls" conditional on the event "at least one of the children is a girl" (L). Surprisingly, the answer is different from before!

As before, the event B and L ("both children are girls *and* at least one of the children is a girl") is just the event B. This means we have:

$$P(B\,|\,L) = P(B, L)/P(L) = P(B)/P(L) = 1/3$$

How can this be the case? Well, if all you know is that at least one of the children is a girl, then it is twice as likely that the family has one boy and one girl than that it has both girls.

We can check this by "generating" a lot of families:

```python
def random_kid():
    return random.choice(["boy", "girl"])

both_girls = 0
older_girl = 0
either_girl = 0

random.seed(0)
for _ in range(10000):
    younger = random_kid()
    older = random_kid()
    if older == "girl":
        older_girl += 1
    if older == "girl" and younger == "girl":
        both_girls += 1
    if older == "girl" or younger == "girl":
        either_girl += 1
```

```
print "P(both | older):", both_girls / older_girl      # 0.514 ~ 1/2
print "P(both | either): ", both_girls / either_girl   # 0.342 ~ 1/3
```

Bayes's Theorem

One of the data scientist's best friends is Bayes's Theorem, which is a way of "reversing" conditional probabilities. Let's say we need to know the probability of some event E conditional on some other event F occurring. But we only have information about the probability of F conditional on E occurring. Using the definition of conditional probability twice tells us that:

$$P(E|F) = P(E, F)/P(F) = P(F|E)P(E)/P(F)$$

The event F can be split into the two mutually exclusive events "F and E" and "F and not E." If we write $\neg E$ for "not E" (i.e., "E doesn't happen"), then:

$$P(F) = P(F, E) + P(F, \neg E)$$

so that:

$$P(E|F) = P(F|E)P(E)/[P(F|E)P(E) + P(F|\neg E)P(\neg E)]$$

which is how Bayes's Theorem is often stated.

This theorem often gets used to demonstrate why data scientists are smarter than doctors. Imagine a certain disease that affects 1 in every 10,000 people. And imagine that there is a test for this disease that gives the correct result ("diseased" if you have the disease, "nondiseased" if you don't) 99% of the time.

What does a positive test mean? Let's use T for the event "your test is positive" and D for the event "you have the disease." Then Bayes's Theorem says that the probability that you have the disease, conditional on testing positive, is:

$$P(D|T) = P(T|D)P(D)/[P(T|D)P(D) + P(T|\neg D)P(\neg D)]$$

Here we know that $P(T|D)$, the probability that someone with the disease tests positive, is 0.99. $P(D)$, the probability that any given person has the disease, is 1/10,000 = 0.0001. $P(T|\neg D)$, the probability that someone without the disease tests positive, is 0.01. And $P(\neg D)$, the probability that any given person doesn't have the disease, is 0.9999. If you substitute these numbers into Bayes's Theorem you find

$$P(D|T) = 0.98\,\%$$

That is, less than 1% of the people who test positive actually have the disease.

 This assumes that people take the test more or less at random. If only people with certain symptoms take the test we would instead have to condition on the event "positive test *and* symptoms" and the number would likely be a lot higher.

While this is a simple calculation for a data scientist, most doctors will guess that $P(D \mid T)$ is approximately 2.

A more intuitive way to see this is to imagine a population of 1 million people. You'd expect 100 of them to have the disease, and 99 of those 100 to test positive. On the other hand, you'd expect 999,900 of them not to have the disease, and 9,999 of those to test positive. Which means that you'd expect only 99 out of (99 + 9999) positive testers to actually have the disease.

Random Variables

A *random variable* is a variable whose possible values have an associated probability distribution. A very simple random variable equals 1 if a coin flip turns up heads and 0 if the flip turns up tails. A more complicated one might measure the number of heads observed when flipping a coin 10 times or a value picked from `range(10)` where each number is equally likely.

The associated distribution gives the probabilities that the variable realizes each of its possible values. The coin flip variable equals 0 with probability 0.5 and 1 with probability 0.5. The `range(10)` variable has a distribution that assigns probability 0.1 to each of the numbers from 0 to 9.

We will sometimes talk about the *expected value* of a random variable, which is the average of its values weighted by their probabilities. The coin flip variable has an expected value of 1/2 (= 0 * 1/2 + 1 * 1/2), and the `range(10)` variable has an expected value of 4.5.

Random variables can be *conditioned* on events just as other events can. Going back to the two-child example from "Conditional Probability" on page 70, if X is the random variable representing the number of girls, X equals 0 with probability 1/4, 1 with probability 1/2, and 2 with probability 1/4.

We can define a new random variable Y that gives the number of girls conditional on at least one of the children being a girl. Then Y equals 1 with probability 2/3 and 2 with probability 1/3. And a variable Z that's the number of girls conditional on the older child being a girl equals 1 with probability 1/2 and 2 with probability 1/2.

For the most part, we will be using random variables *implicitly* in what we do without calling special attention to them. But if you look deeply you'll see them.

Continuous Distributions

A coin flip corresponds to a *discrete distribution*—one that associates positive probability with discrete outcomes. Often we'll want to model distributions across a continuum of outcomes. (For our purposes, these outcomes will always be real numbers, although that's not always the case in real life.) For example, the *uniform distribution* puts *equal weight* on all the numbers between 0 and 1.

Because there are infinitely many numbers between 0 and 1, this means that the weight it assigns to individual points must necessarily be zero. For this reason, we represent a continuous distribution with a *probability density function* (pdf) such that the probability of seeing a value in a certain interval equals the integral of the density function over the interval.

 If your integral calculus is rusty, a simpler way of understanding this is that if a distribution has density function f, then the probability of seeing a value between x and $x + h$ is approximately $h * f(x)$ if h is small.

The density function for the uniform distribution is just:

```
def uniform_pdf(x):
    return 1 if x >= 0 and x < 1 else 0
```

The probability that a random variable following that distribution is between 0.2 and 0.3 is 1/10, as you'd expect. Python's `random.random()` is a [pseudo]random variable with a uniform density.

We will often be more interested in the *cumulative distribution function* (cdf), which gives the probability that a random variable is less than or equal to a certain value. It's not hard to create the cumulative distribution function for the uniform distribution (Figure 6-1):

```
def uniform_cdf(x):
    "returns the probability that a uniform random variable is <= x"
    if x < 0:   return 0    # uniform random is never less than 0
    elif x < 1: return x    # e.g. P(X <= 0.4) = 0.4
    else:       return 1    # uniform random is always less than 1
```

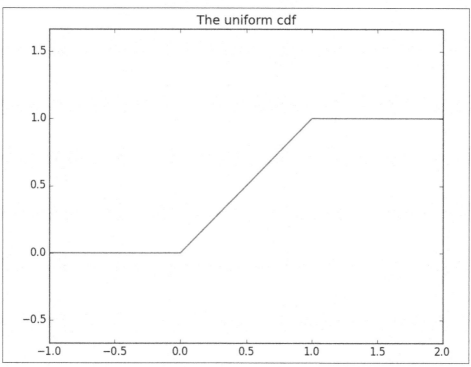

Figure 6-1. The uniform cdf

The Normal Distribution

The normal distribution is the king of distributions. It is the classic bell curve–shaped distribution and is completely determined by two parameters: its mean μ (mu) and its standard deviation σ (sigma). The mean indicates where the bell is centered, and the standard deviation how "wide" it is.

It has the distribution function:

$$f(x|\mu, \sigma) = \frac{1}{\sqrt{2\pi}\sigma} \exp\left(-\frac{(x-\mu)^2}{2\sigma^2}\right)$$

which we can implement as:

```
def normal_pdf(x, mu=0, sigma=1):
    sqrt_two_pi = math.sqrt(2 * math.pi)
    return (math.exp(-(x-mu) ** 2 / 2 / sigma ** 2) / (sqrt_two_pi * sigma))
```

In Figure 6-2, we plot some of these pdfs to see what they look like:

```
xs = [x / 10.0 for x in range(-50, 50)]
plt.plot(xs,[normal_pdf(x,sigma=1) for x in xs],'-',label='mu=0,sigma=1')
plt.plot(xs,[normal_pdf(x,sigma=2) for x in xs],'--',label='mu=0,sigma=2')
plt.plot(xs,[normal_pdf(x,sigma=0.5) for x in xs],':',label='mu=0,sigma=0.5')
plt.plot(xs,[normal_pdf(x,mu=-1)   for x in xs],'-.',label='mu=-1,sigma=1')
plt.legend()
plt.title("Various Normal pdfs")
plt.show()
```

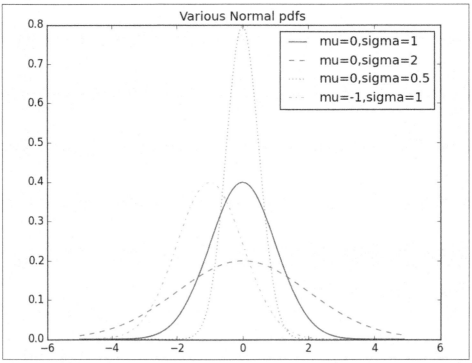

Figure 6-2. Various normal pdfs

When $\mu = 0$ and $\sigma = 1$, it's called the *standard normal distribution*. If Z is a standard normal random variable, then it turns out that:

$$X = \sigma Z + \mu$$

is also normal but with mean μ and standard deviation σ. Conversely, if X is a normal random variable with mean μ and standard deviation σ,

$$Z = (X - \mu)/\sigma$$

is a standard normal variable.

The cumulative distribution function for the normal distribution cannot be written in an "elementary" manner, but we can write it using Python's math.erf (*http://en.wiki pedia.org/wiki/Error_function*):

```
def normal_cdf(x, mu=0,sigma=1):
    return (1 + math.erf((x - mu) / math.sqrt(2) / sigma)) / 2
```

Again, in Figure 6-3, we plot a few:

```
xs = [x / 10.0 for x in range(-50, 50)]
plt.plot(xs,[normal_cdf(x,sigma=1) for x in xs],'-',label='mu=0,sigma=1')
plt.plot(xs,[normal_cdf(x,sigma=2) for x in xs],'--',label='mu=0,sigma=2')
plt.plot(xs,[normal_cdf(x,sigma=0.5) for x in xs],':',label='mu=0,sigma=0.5')
plt.plot(xs,[normal_cdf(x,mu=-1) for x in xs],'-.',label='mu=-1,sigma=1')
plt.legend(loc=4) # bottom right
plt.title("Various Normal cdfs")
plt.show()
```

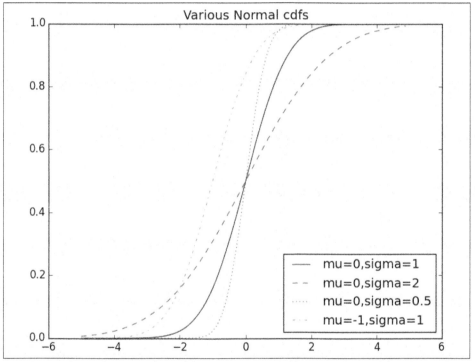

Figure 6-3. Various normal cdfs

Sometimes we'll need to invert normal_cdf to find the value corresponding to a specified probability. There's no simple way to compute its inverse, but normal_cdf is continuous and strictly increasing, so we can use a binary search (*http://en.wikipe dia.org/wiki/Binary_search_algorithm*):

```
def inverse_normal_cdf(p, mu=0, sigma=1, tolerance=0.00001):
    """find approximate inverse using binary search"""

    # if not standard, compute standard and rescale
    if mu != 0 or sigma != 1:
        return mu + sigma * inverse_normal_cdf(p, tolerance=tolerance)

    low_z, low_p = -10.0, 0          # normal_cdf(-10) is (very close to) 0
    hi_z,  hi_p  =  10.0, 1          # normal_cdf(10)  is (very close to) 1
    while hi_z - low_z > tolerance:
        mid_z = (low_z + hi_z) / 2   # consider the midpoint
        mid_p = normal_cdf(mid_z)    # and the cdf's value there
        if mid_p < p:
            # midpoint is still too low, search above it
            low_z, low_p = mid_z, mid_p
        elif mid_p > p:
            # midpoint is still too high, search below it
            hi_z, hi_p = mid_z, mid_p
        else:
            break

    return mid_z
```

The function repeatedly bisects intervals until it narrows in on a Z that's close enough to the desired probability.

The Central Limit Theorem

One reason the normal distribution is so useful is the *central limit theorem*, which says (in essence) that a random variable defined as the average of a large number of independent and identically distributed random variables is itself approximately normally distributed.

In particular, if $x_1, ..., x_n$ are random variables with mean μ and standard deviation σ, and if n is large, then:

$$\frac{1}{n}(x_1 + ... + x_n)$$

is approximately normally distributed with mean μ and standard deviation $\sigma/\sqrt{n}$. Equivalently (but often more usefully),

$$\frac{(x_1 + ... + x_n) - \mu n}{\sigma \sqrt{n}}$$

is approximately normally distributed with mean 0 and standard deviation 1.

An easy way to illustrate this is by looking at *binomial* random variables, which have two parameters n and p. A Binomial(n,p) random variable is simply the sum of n independent Bernoulli(p) random variables, each of which equals 1 with probability p and 0 with probability $1 - p$:

```
def bernoulli_trial(p):
    return 1 if random.random() < p else 0

def binomial(n, p):
    return sum(bernoulli_trial(p) for _ in range(n))
```

The mean of a Bernoulli(p) variable is p, and its standard deviation is $\sqrt{p(1 - p)}$. The central limit theorem says that as n gets large, a Binomial(n,p) variable is approximately a normal random variable with mean $\mu = np$ and standard deviation $\sigma = \sqrt{np(1 - p)}$. If we plot both, you can easily see the resemblance:

```
def make_hist(p, n, num_points):

    data = [binomial(n, p) for _ in range(num_points)]

    # use a bar chart to show the actual binomial samples
    histogram = Counter(data)
    plt.bar([x - 0.4 for x in histogram.keys()],
            [v / num_points for v in histogram.values()],
            0.8,
            color='0.75')

    mu = p * n
    sigma = math.sqrt(n * p * (1 - p))

    # use a line chart to show the normal approximation
    xs = range(min(data), max(data) + 1)
    ys = [normal_cdf(i + 0.5, mu, sigma) - normal_cdf(i - 0.5, mu, sigma)
          for i in xs]
    plt.plot(xs,ys)
    plt.title("Binomial Distribution vs. Normal Approximation")
    plt.show()
```

For example, when you call make_hist(0.75, 100, 10000), you get the graph in Figure 6-4.

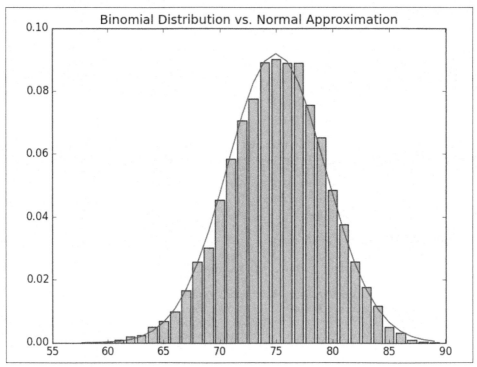

Figure 6-4. The output from `make_hist`

The moral of this approximation is that if you want to know the probability that (say) a fair coin turns up more than 60 heads in 100 flips, you can estimate it as the probability that a Normal(50,5) is greater than 60, which is easier than computing the Binomial(100,0.5) cdf. (Although in most applications you'd probably be using statistical software that would gladly compute whatever probabilities you want.)

For Further Exploration

- scipy.stats (*http://bit.ly/1L2H0Lj*) contains pdf and cdf functions for most of the popular probability distributions.

- Remember how, at the end of Chapter 5, I said that it would be a good idea to study a statistics textbook? It would also be a good idea to study a probability textbook. The best one I know that's available online is *Introduction to Probability* (*http://bit.ly/1L2MTYI*).

## CHAPTER 7

Hypothesis and Inference

It is the mark of a truly intelligent person to be moved by statistics.
—George Bernard Shaw

What will we do with all this statistics and probability theory? The *science* part of data science frequently involves forming and testing *hypotheses* about our data and the processes that generate it.

Statistical Hypothesis Testing

Often, as data scientists, we'll want to test whether a certain hypothesis is likely to be true. For our purposes, hypotheses are assertions like "this coin is fair" or "data scientists prefer Python to R" or "people are more likely to navigate away from the page without ever reading the content if we pop up an irritating interstitial advertisement with a tiny, hard-to-find close button" that can be translated into statistics about data. Under various assumptions, those statistics can be thought of as observations of random variables from known distributions, which allows us to make statements about how likely those assumptions are to hold.

In the classical setup, we have a *null hypothesis* H_0 that represents some default position, and some alternative hypothesis H_1 that we'd like to compare it with. We use statistics to decide whether we can reject H_0 as false or not. This will probably make more sense with an example.

Example: Flipping a Coin

Imagine we have a coin and we want to test whether it's fair. We'll make the assumption that the coin has some probability p of landing heads, and so our null hypothesis is that the coin is fair—that is, that $p = 0.5$. We'll test this against the alternative hypothesis $p \neq 0.5$.

In particular, our test will involve flipping the coin some number n times and counting the number of heads X. Each coin flip is a Bernoulli trial, which means that X is a Binomial(n,p) random variable, which (as we saw in Chapter 6) we can approximate using the normal distribution:

```python
def normal_approximation_to_binomial(n, p):
    """finds mu and sigma corresponding to a Binomial(n, p)"""
    mu = p * n
    sigma = math.sqrt(p * (1 - p) * n)
    return mu, sigma
```

Whenever a random variable follows a normal distribution, we can use `normal_cdf` to figure out the probability that its realized value lies within (or outside) a particular interval:

```python
# the normal cdf _is_ the probability the variable is below a threshold
normal_probability_below = normal_cdf

# it's above the threshold if it's not below the threshold
def normal_probability_above(lo, mu=0, sigma=1):
    return 1 - normal_cdf(lo, mu, sigma)

# it's between if it's less than hi, but not less than lo
def normal_probability_between(lo, hi, mu=0, sigma=1):
    return normal_cdf(hi, mu, sigma) - normal_cdf(lo, mu, sigma)

# it's outside if it's not between
def normal_probability_outside(lo, hi, mu=0, sigma=1):
    return 1 - normal_probability_between(lo, hi, mu, sigma)
```

We can also do the reverse—find either the nontail region or the (symmetric) interval around the mean that accounts for a certain level of likelihood. For example, if we want to find an interval centered at the mean and containing 60% probability, then we find the cutoffs where the upper and lower tails each contain 20% of the probability (leaving 60%):

```python
def normal_upper_bound(probability, mu=0, sigma=1):
    """returns the z for which P(Z <= z) = probability"""
    return inverse_normal_cdf(probability, mu, sigma)

def normal_lower_bound(probability, mu=0, sigma=1):
    """returns the z for which P(Z >= z) = probability"""
    return inverse_normal_cdf(1 - probability, mu, sigma)

def normal_two_sided_bounds(probability, mu=0, sigma=1):
    """returns the symmetric (about the mean) bounds
    that contain the specified probability"""
    tail_probability = (1 - probability) / 2
```

```
# upper bound should have tail_probability above it
upper_bound = normal_lower_bound(tail_probability, mu, sigma)

# lower bound should have tail_probability below it
lower_bound = normal_upper_bound(tail_probability, mu, sigma)

return lower_bound, upper_bound
```

In particular, let's say that we choose to flip the coin $n = 1000$ times. If our hypothesis of fairness is true, X should be distributed approximately normally with mean 50 and standard deviation 15.8:

```
mu_0, sigma_0 = normal_approximation_to_binomial(1000, 0.5)
```

We need to make a decision about *significance*—how willing we are to make a *type 1 error* ("false positive"), in which we reject H_0 even though it's true. For reasons lost to the annals of history, this willingness is often set at 5% or 1%. Let's choose 5%.

Consider the test that rejects H_0 if X falls outside the bounds given by:

```
normal_two_sided_bounds(0.95, mu_0, sigma_0)   # (469, 531)
```

Assuming p really equals 0.5 (i.e., H_0 is true), there is just a 5% chance we observe an X that lies outside this interval, which is the exact significance we wanted. Said differently, if H_0 is true, then, approximately 19 times out of 20, this test will give the correct result.

We are also often interested in the *power* of a test, which is the probability of not making a *type 2 error*, in which we fail to reject H_0 even though it's false. In order to measure this, we have to specify what exactly H_0 being false *means*. (Knowing merely that p is *not* 0.5 doesn't give you a ton of information about the distribution of X.) In particular, let's check what happens if p is really 0.55, so that the coin is slightly biased toward heads.

In that case, we can calculate the power of the test with:

```
# 95% bounds based on assumption p is 0.5
lo, hi = normal_two_sided_bounds(0.95, mu_0, sigma_0)

# actual mu and sigma based on p = 0.55
mu_1, sigma_1 = normal_approximation_to_binomial(1000, 0.55)

# a type 2 error means we fail to reject the null hypothesis
# which will happen when X is still in our original interval
type_2_probability = normal_probability_between(lo, hi, mu_1, sigma_1)
power = 1 - type_2_probability        # 0.887
```

Imagine instead that our null hypothesis was that the coin is not biased toward heads, or that $p \leq 0.5$. In that case we want a *one-sided test* that rejects the null hypothesis when X is much larger than 50 but not when X is smaller than 50. So a 5%-

significance test involves using `normal_probability_below` to find the cutoff below which 95% of the probability lies:

```
hi = normal_upper_bound(0.95, mu_0, sigma_0)
# is 526 (< 531, since we need more probability in the upper tail)

type_2_probability = normal_probability_below(hi, mu_1, sigma_1)
power = 1 - type_2_probability      # 0.936
```

This is a more powerful test, since it no longer rejects H_0 when X is below 469 (which is very unlikely to happen if H_1 is true) and instead rejects H_0 when X is between 526 and 531 (which is somewhat likely to happen if H_1 is true). === p-values

An alternative way of thinking about the preceding test involves *p-values*. Instead of choosing bounds based on some probability cutoff, we compute the probability—assuming H_0 is true—that we would see a value at least as extreme as the one we actually observed.

For our two-sided test of whether the coin is fair, we compute:

```
def two_sided_p_value(x, mu=0, sigma=1):
    if x >= mu:
        # if x is greater than the mean, the tail is what's greater than x
        return 2 * normal_probability_above(x, mu, sigma)
    else:
        # if x is less than the mean, the tail is what's less than x
        return 2 * normal_probability_below(x, mu, sigma)
```

If we were to see 530 heads, we would compute:

```
two_sided_p_value(529.5, mu_0, sigma_0)    # 0.062
```

Why did we use 529.5 instead of 530? This is what's called a *continuity correction* (*http://en.wikipedia.org/wiki/Continuity_correction*). It reflects the fact that `normal_probability_between(529.5, 530.5, mu_0, sigma_0)` is a better estimate of the probability of seeing 530 heads than `normal_probability_between(530, 531, mu_0, sigma_0)` is.

Correspondingly, `normal_probability_above(529.5, mu_0, sigma_0)` is a better estimate of the probability of seeing at least 530 heads. You may have noticed that we also used this in the code that produced Figure 6-4.

One way to convince yourself that this is a sensible estimate is with a simulation:

```
extreme_value_count = 0
for _ in range(100000):
    num_heads = sum(1 if random.random() < 0.5 else 0    # count # of heads
                    for _ in range(1000))                # in 1000 flips
```

```
    if num_heads >= 530 or num_heads <= 470:        # and count how often
        extreme_value_count += 1                     # the # is 'extreme'

    print extreme_value_count / 100000   # 0.062
```

Since the *p*-value is greater than our 5% significance, we don't reject the null. If we instead saw 532 heads, the *p*-value would be:

```
    two_sided_p_value(531.5, mu_0, sigma_0)    # 0.0463
```

which is smaller than the 5% significance, which means we would reject the null. It's the exact same test as before. It's just a different way of approaching the statistics.

Similarly, we would have:

```
    upper_p_value = normal_probability_above
    lower_p_value = normal_probability_below
```

For our one-sided test, if we saw 525 heads we would compute:

```
    upper_p_value(524.5, mu_0, sigma_0) # 0.061
```

which means we wouldn't reject the null. If we saw 527 heads, the computation would be:

```
    upper_p_value(526.5, mu_0, sigma_0) # 0.047
```

and we would reject the null.

 Make sure your data is roughly normally distributed before using normal_probability_above to compute p-values. The annals of bad data science are filled with examples of people opining that the chance of some observed event occurring at random is one in a million, when what they really mean is "the chance, assuming the data is distributed normally," which is pretty meaningless if the data isn't.

There are various statistical tests for normality, but even plotting the data is a good start.

Confidence Intervals

We've been testing hypotheses about the value of the heads probability p, which is a *parameter* of the unknown "heads" distribution. When this is the case, a third approach is to construct a *confidence interval* around the observed value of the parameter.

For example, we can estimate the probability of the unfair coin by looking at the average value of the Bernoulli variables corresponding to each flip—1 if heads, 0 if tails. If we observe 525 heads out of 1,000 flips, then we estimate p equals 0.525.

How *confident* can we be about this estimate? Well, if we knew the exact value of *p*, the central limit theorem (recall "The Central Limit Theorem" on page 78) tells us that the average of those Bernoulli variables should be approximately normal, with mean *p* and standard deviation:

```
math.sqrt(p * (1 - p) / 1000)
```

Here we don't know *p*, so instead we use our estimate:

```
p_hat = 525 / 1000
mu = p_hat
sigma = math.sqrt(p_hat * (1 - p_hat) / 1000)   # 0.0158
```

This is not entirely justified, but people seem to do it anyway. Using the normal approximation, we conclude that we are "95% confident" that the following interval contains the true parameter *p*:

```
normal_two_sided_bounds(0.95, mu, sigma)        # [0.4940, 0.5560]
```

 This is a statement about the *interval*, not about *p*. You should understand it as the assertion that if you were to repeat the experiment many times, 95% of the time the "true" parameter (which is the same every time) would lie within the observed confidence interval (which might be different every time).

In particular, we do not conclude that the coin is unfair, since 0.5 falls within our confidence interval.

If instead we'd seen 540 heads, then we'd have:

```
p_hat = 540 / 1000
mu = p_hat
sigma = math.sqrt(p_hat * (1 - p_hat) / 1000) # 0.0158
normal_two_sided_bounds(0.95, mu, sigma) # [0.5091, 0.5709]
```

Here, "fair coin" doesn't lie in the confidence interval. (The "fair coin" hypothesis doesn't pass a test that you'd expect it to pass 95% of the time if it were true.)

P-hacking

A procedure that erroneously rejects the null hypothesis only 5% of the time will—by definition—5% of the time erroneously reject the null hypothesis:

```
def run_experiment():
    """flip a fair coin 1000 times, True = heads, False = tails"""
    return [random.random() < 0.5 for _ in range(1000)]

def reject_fairness(experiment):
    """using the 5% significance levels"""
    num_heads = len([flip for flip in experiment if flip])
```

```
        return num_heads < 469 or num_heads > 531

random.seed(0)
experiments = [run_experiment() for _ in range(1000)]
num_rejections = len([experiment
                      for experiment in experiments
                      if reject_fairness(experiment)])

print num_rejections    # 46
```

What this means is that if you're setting out to find "significant" results, you usually can. Test enough hypotheses against your data set, and one of them will almost certainly appear significant. Remove the right outliers, and you can probably get your p value below 0.05. (We did something vaguely similar in "Correlation" on page 62; did you notice?)

This is sometimes called P-hacking (*http://bit.ly/1L2QtCr*) and is in some ways a consequence of the "inference from *p*-values framework." A good article criticizing this approach is "The Earth Is Round." (*http://bit.ly/1L2QJ4a*)

If you want to do good *science*, you should determine your hypotheses before looking at the data, you should clean your data without the hypotheses in mind, and you should keep in mind that *p*-values are not substitutes for common sense. (An alternative approach is "Bayesian Inference" on page 88.)

Example: Running an A/B Test

One of your primary responsibilities at DataSciencester is experience optimization, which is a euphemism for trying to get people to click on advertisements. One of your advertisers has developed a new energy drink targeted at data scientists, and the VP of Advertisements wants your help choosing between advertisement A ("tastes great!") and advertisement B ("less bias!").

Being a *scientist*, you decide to run an *experiment* by randomly showing site visitors one of the two advertisements and tracking how many people click on each one.

If 990 out of 1,000 A-viewers click their ad while only 10 out of 1,000 B-viewers click their ad, you can be pretty confident that A is the better ad. But what if the differences are not so stark? Here's where you'd use statistical inference.

Let's say that N_A people see ad A, and that n_A of them click it. We can think of each ad view as a Bernoulli trial where p_A is the probability that someone clicks ad A. Then (if N_A is large, which it is here) we know that n_A/N_A is approximately a normal random variable with mean p_A and standard deviation $\sigma_A = \sqrt{p_A(1 - p_A)/N_A}$.

Similarly, n_B/N_B is approximately a normal random variable with mean p_B and standard deviation $\sigma_B = \sqrt{p_B(1 - p_B)/N_B}$:

```
def estimated_parameters(N, n):
    p = n / N
    sigma = math.sqrt(p * (1 - p) / N)
    return p, sigma
```

If we assume those two normals are independent (which seems reasonable, since the individual Bernoulli trials ought to be), then their difference should also be normal with mean $p_B - p_A$ and standard deviation $\sqrt{\sigma_A^2 + \sigma_B^2}$.

 This is sort of cheating. The math only works out exactly like this if you *know* the standard deviations. Here we're estimating them from the data, which means that we really should be using a *t*-distribution. But for large enough data sets, it's close enough that it doesn't make much of a difference.

This means we can test the *null hypothesis* that p_A and p_B are the same (that is, that $p_A - p_B$ is zero), using the statistic:

```
def a_b_test_statistic(N_A, n_A, N_B, n_B):
    p_A, sigma_A = estimated_parameters(N_A, n_A)
    p_B, sigma_B = estimated_parameters(N_B, n_B)
    return (p_B - p_A) / math.sqrt(sigma_A ** 2 + sigma_B ** 2)
```

which should approximately be a standard normal.

For example, if "tastes great" gets 200 clicks out of 1,000 views and "less bias" gets 180 clicks out of 1,000 views, the statistic equals:

```
z = a_b_test_statistic(1000, 200, 1000, 180)    # -1.14
```

The probability of seeing such a large difference if the means were actually equal would be:

```
two_sided_p_value(z)                            # 0.254
```

which is large enough that you can't conclude there's much of a difference. On the other hand, if "less bias" only got 150 clicks, we'd have:

```
z = a_b_test_statistic(1000, 200, 1000, 150)    # -2.94
two_sided_p_value(z)                            # 0.003
```

which means there's only a 0.003 probability you'd see such a large difference if the ads were equally effective.

Bayesian Inference

The procedures we've looked at have involved making probability statements about our *tests*: "there's only a 3% chance you'd observe such an extreme statistic if our null hypothesis were true."

An alternative approach to inference involves treating the unknown parameters themselves as random variables. The analyst (that's you) starts with a *prior distribution* for the parameters and then uses the observed data and Bayes's Theorem to get an updated *posterior distribution* for the parameters. Rather than making probability judgments about the tests, you make probability judgments about the parameters themselves.

For example, when the unknown parameter is a probability (as in our coin-flipping example), we often use a prior from the *Beta distribution*, which puts all its probability between 0 and 1:

```
def B(alpha, beta):
    """a normalizing constant so that the total probability is 1"""
    return math.gamma(alpha) * math.gamma(beta) / math.gamma(alpha + beta)

def beta_pdf(x, alpha, beta):
    if x < 0 or x > 1:          # no weight outside of [0, 1]
        return 0
    return x ** (alpha - 1) * (1 - x) ** (beta - 1) / B(alpha, beta)
```

Generally speaking, this distribution centers its weight at:

```
alpha / (alpha + beta)
```

and the larger `alpha` and `beta` are, the "tighter" the distribution is.

For example, if `alpha` and `beta` are both 1, it's just the uniform distribution (centered at 0.5, very dispersed). If `alpha` is much larger than `beta`, most of the weight is near 1. And if `alpha` is much smaller than `beta`, most of the weight is near zero. Figure 7-1 shows several different Beta distributions.

So let's say we assume a prior distribution on p. Maybe we don't want to take a stand on whether the coin is fair, and we choose `alpha` and `beta` to both equal 1. Or maybe we have a strong belief that it lands heads 55% of the time, and we choose `alpha` equals 55, `beta` equals 45.

Then we flip our coin a bunch of times and see h heads and t tails. Bayes's Theorem (and some mathematics that's too tedious for us to go through here) tells us that the posterior distribution for p is again a Beta distribution but with parameters `alpha + h` and `beta + t`.

It is no coincidence that the posterior distribution was again a Beta distribution. The number of heads is given by a Binomial distribution, and the Beta is the *conjugate prior* (*http://www.johndcook.com/blog/conjugate_prior_diagram/*) to the Binomial distribution. This means that whenever you update a Beta prior using observations from the corresponding binomial, you will get back a Beta posterior.

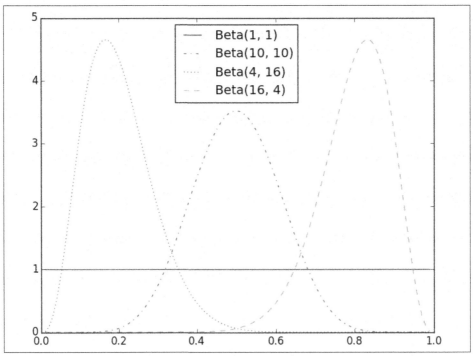

Figure 7-1. Example Beta distributions

Let's say you flip the coin 10 times and see only 3 heads.

If you started with the uniform prior (in some sense refusing to take a stand about the coin's fairness), your posterior distribution would be a Beta(4, 8), centered around 0.33. Since you considered all probabilities equally likely, your best guess is something pretty close to the observed probability.

If you started with a Beta(20, 20) (expressing the belief that the coin was roughly fair), your posterior distribution would be a Beta(23, 27), centered around 0.46, indicating a revised belief that maybe the coin is slightly biased toward tails.

And if you started with a Beta(30, 10) (expressing a belief that the coin was biased to flip 75% heads), your posterior distribution would be a Beta(33, 17), centered around 0.66. In that case you'd still believe in a heads bias, but less strongly than you did initially. These three different posteriors are plotted in Figure 7-2.

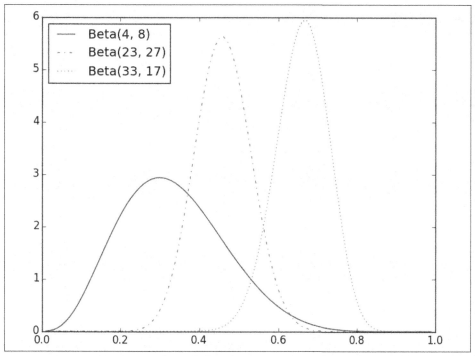

Figure 7-2. Posteriors arising from different priors

If you flipped the coin more and more times, the prior would matter less and less until eventually you'd have (nearly) the same posterior distribution no matter which prior you started with.

For example, no matter how biased you initially thought the coin was, it would be hard to maintain that belief after seeing 1,000 heads out of 2,000 flips (unless you are a lunatic who picks something like a Beta(1000000,1) prior).

What's interesting is that this allows us to make probability statements about hypotheses: "Based on the prior and the observed data, there is only a 5% likelihood the coin's heads probability is between 49% and 51%." This is philosophically very different from a statement like "if the coin were fair we would expect to observe data so extreme only 5% of the time."

Using Bayesian inference to test hypotheses is considered somewhat controversial—in part because its mathematics can get somewhat complicated, and in part because of the subjective nature of choosing a prior. We won't use it any further in this book, but it's good to know about.

For Further Exploration

- We've barely scratched the surface of what you should know about statistical inference. The books recommended at the end of Chapter 5 go into a lot more detail.

- Coursera offers a Data Analysis and Statistical Inference (*https://www.coursera.org/course/statistics*) course that covers many of these topics.

## CHAPTER 8

Gradient Descent

Those who boast of their descent, brag on what they owe to others.

—Seneca

Frequently when doing data science, we'll be trying to the find the best model for a certain situation. And usually "best" will mean something like "minimizes the error of the model" or "maximizes the likelihood of the data." In other words, it will represent the solution to some sort of optimization problem.

This means we'll need to solve a number of optimization problems. And in particular, we'll need to solve them from scratch. Our approach will be a technique called *gradient descent*, which lends itself pretty well to a from-scratch treatment. You might not find it super exciting in and of itself, but it will enable us to do exciting things throughout the book, so bear with me.

The Idea Behind Gradient Descent

Suppose we have some function f that takes as input a vector of real numbers and outputs a single real number. One simple such function is:

```python
def sum_of_squares(v):
    """computes the sum of squared elements in v"""
    return sum(v_i ** 2 for v_i in v)
```

We'll frequently need to maximize (or minimize) such functions. That is, we need to find the input v that produces the largest (or smallest) possible value.

For functions like ours, the *gradient* (if you remember your calculus, this is the vector of partial derivatives) gives the input direction in which the function most quickly increases. (If you don't remember your calculus, take my word for it or look it up on the Internet.)

Accordingly, one approach to maximizing a function is to pick a random starting point, compute the gradient, take a small step in the direction of the gradient (i.e., the direction that causes the function to increase the most), and repeat with the new starting point. Similarly, you can try to minimize a function by taking small steps in the *opposite* direction, as shown in Figure 8-1.

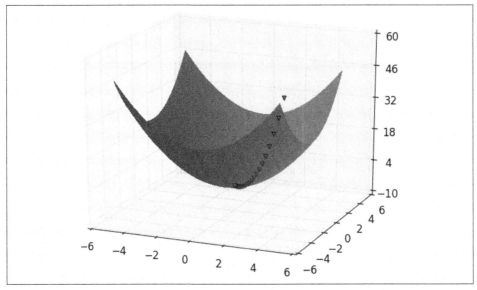

Figure 8-1. Finding a minimum using gradient descent

 If a function has a unique global minimum, this procedure is likely to find it. If a function has multiple (local) minima, this procedure might "find" the wrong one of them, in which case you might rerun the procedure from a variety of starting points. If a function has no minimum, then it's possible the procedure might go on forever.

Estimating the Gradient

If f is a function of one variable, its derivative at a point x measures how f(x) changes when we make a very small change to x. It is defined as the limit of the difference quotients:

```
def difference_quotient(f, x, h):
    return (f(x + h) - f(x)) / h
```

as h approaches zero.

(Many a would-be calculus student has been stymied by the mathematical definition of limit. Here we'll cheat and simply say that it means what you think it means.)

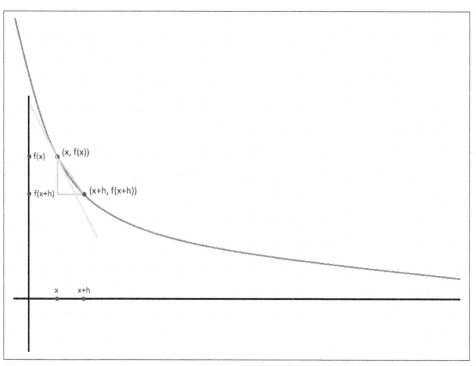

Figure 8-2. Approximating a derivative with a difference quotient

The derivative is the slope of the tangent line at $(x, f(x))$, while the difference quotient is the slope of the not-quite-tangent line that runs through $(x + h, f(x + h))$. As h gets smaller and smaller, the not-quite-tangent line gets closer and closer to the tangent line (Figure 8-2).

For many functions it's easy to exactly calculate derivatives. For example, the `square` function:

```
def square(x):
    return x * x
```

has the derivative:

```
def derivative(x):
    return 2 * x
```

which you can check—if you are so inclined—by explicitly computing the difference quotient and taking the limit.

What if you couldn't (or didn't want to) find the gradient? Although we can't take limits in Python, we can estimate derivatives by evaluating the difference quotient for a very small **e**. Figure 8-3 shows the results of one such estimation:

```
derivative_estimate = partial(difference_quotient, square, h=0.00001)

# plot to show they're basically the same
import matplotlib.pyplot as plt
x = range(-10,10)
plt.title("Actual Derivatives vs. Estimates")
plt.plot(x, map(derivative, x), 'rx', label='Actual')        # red   x
plt.plot(x, map(derivative_estimate, x), 'b+', label='Estimate')  # blue  +
plt.legend(loc=9)
plt.show()
```

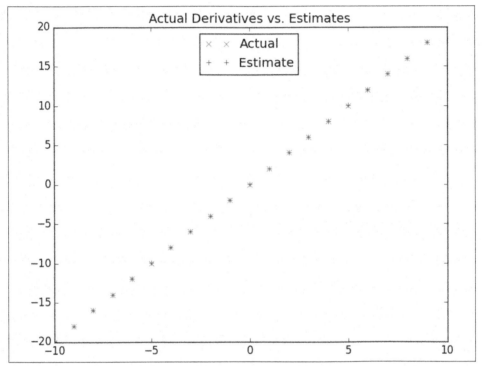

Figure 8-3. Goodness of difference quotient approximation

When f is a function of many variables, it has multiple *partial derivatives*, each indicating how f changes when we make small changes in just one of the input variables.

We calculate its *i*th partial derivative by treating it as a function of just its *i*th variable, holding the other variables fixed:

```
def partial_difference_quotient(f, v, i, h):
    """compute the ith partial difference quotient of f at v"""
    w = [v_j + (h if j == i else 0)    # add h to just the ith element of v
         for j, v_j in enumerate(v)]

    return (f(w) - f(v)) / h
```

after which we can estimate the gradient the same way:

```
def estimate_gradient(f, v, h=0.00001):
    return [partial_difference_quotient(f, v, i, h)
            for i, _ in enumerate(v)]
```

 A major drawback to this "estimate using difference quotients" approach is that it's computationally expensive. If v has length *n*, estimate_gradient has to evaluate f on *2n* different inputs. If you're repeatedly estimating gradients, you're doing a whole lot of extra work.

Using the Gradient

It's easy to see that the sum_of_squares function is smallest when its input v is a vector of zeroes. But imagine we didn't know that. Let's use gradients to find the minimum among all three-dimensional vectors. We'll just pick a random starting point and then take tiny steps in the opposite direction of the gradient until we reach a point where the gradient is very small:

```
def step(v, direction, step_size):
    """move step_size in the direction from v"""
    return [v_i + step_size * direction_i
            for v_i, direction_i in zip(v, direction)]

def sum_of_squares_gradient(v):
    return [2 * v_i for v_i in v]

# pick a random starting point
v = [random.randint(-10,10) for i in range(3)]

tolerance = 0.0000001

while True:
    gradient = sum_of_squares_gradient(v)    # compute the gradient at v
    next_v = step(v, gradient, -0.01)        # take a negative gradient step
    if distance(next_v, v) < tolerance:      # stop if we're converging
        break
    v = next_v                               # continue if we're not
```

If you run this, you'll find that it always ends up with a v that's very close to [0,0,0]. The smaller you make the tolerance, the closer it will get.

Choosing the Right Step Size

Although the rationale for moving against the gradient is clear, how far to move is not. Indeed, choosing the right step size is more of an art than a science. Popular options include:

- Using a fixed step size
- Gradually shrinking the step size over time
- At each step, choosing the step size that minimizes the value of the objective function

The last sounds optimal but is, in practice, a costly computation. We can approximate it by trying a variety of step sizes and choosing the one that results in the smallest value of the objective function:

```
step_sizes = [100, 10, 1, 0.1, 0.01, 0.001, 0.0001, 0.00001]
```

It is possible that certain step sizes will result in invalid inputs for our function. So we'll need to create a "safe apply" function that returns infinity (which should never be the minimum of anything) for invalid inputs:

```
def safe(f):
    """return a new function that's the same as f,
    except that it outputs infinity whenever f produces an error"""
    def safe_f(*args, **kwargs):
        try:
            return f(*args, **kwargs)
        except:
            return float('inf')         # this means "infinity" in Python
    return safe_f
```

Putting It All Together

In the general case, we have some `target_fn` that we want to minimize, and we also have its `gradient_fn`. For example, the `target_fn` could represent the errors in a model as a function of its parameters, and we might want to find the parameters that make the errors as small as possible.

Furthermore, let's say we have (somehow) chosen a starting value for the parameters `theta_0`. Then we can implement gradient descent as:

```
def minimize_batch(target_fn, gradient_fn, theta_0, tolerance=0.000001):
    """use gradient descent to find theta that minimizes target function"""

    step_sizes = [100, 10, 1, 0.1, 0.01, 0.001, 0.0001, 0.00001]

    theta = theta_0                      # set theta to initial value
    target_fn = safe(target_fn)          # safe version of target_fn
    value = target_fn(theta)             # value we're minimizing

    while True:
        gradient = gradient_fn(theta)
        next_thetas = [step(theta, gradient, -step_size)
                       for step_size in step_sizes]
```

```
        # choose the one that minimizes the error function
        next_theta = min(next_thetas, key=target_fn)
        next_value = target_fn(next_theta)

        # stop if we're "converging"
        if abs(value - next_value) < tolerance:
            return theta
        else:
            theta, value = next_theta, next_value
```

We called it `minimize_batch` because, for each gradient step, it looks at the entire data set (because `target_fn` returns the error on the whole data set). In the next section, we'll see an alternative approach that only looks at one data point at a time.

Sometimes we'll instead want to *maximize* a function, which we can do by minimizing its negative (which has a corresponding negative gradient):

```
def negate(f):
    """return a function that for any input x returns -f(x)"""
    return lambda *args, **kwargs: -f(*args, **kwargs)

def negate_all(f):
    """the same when f returns a list of numbers"""
    return lambda *args, **kwargs: [-y for y in f(*args, **kwargs)]

def maximize_batch(target_fn, gradient_fn, theta_0, tolerance=0.000001):
    return minimize_batch(negate(target_fn),
                          negate_all(gradient_fn),
                          theta_0,
                          tolerance)
```

Stochastic Gradient Descent

As we mentioned before, often we'll be using gradient descent to choose the parameters of a model in a way that minimizes some notion of error. Using the previous batch approach, each gradient step requires us to make a prediction and compute the gradient for the whole data set, which makes each step take a long time.

Now, usually these error functions are *additive*, which means that the predictive error on the whole data set is simply the sum of the predictive errors for each data point.

When this is the case, we can instead apply a technique called *stochastic gradient descent*, which computes the gradient (and takes a step) for only one point at a time. It cycles over our data repeatedly until it reaches a stopping point.

During each cycle, we'll want to iterate through our data in a random order:

```
def in_random_order(data):
    """generator that returns the elements of data in random order"""
    indexes = [i for i, _ in enumerate(data)]  # create a list of indexes
    random.shuffle(indexes)                    # shuffle them
```

```
    for i in indexes:                       # return the data in that order
        yield data[i]
```

And we'll want to take a gradient step for each data point. This approach leaves the possibility that we might circle around near a minimum forever, so whenever we stop getting improvements we'll decrease the step size and eventually quit:

```
def minimize_stochastic(target_fn, gradient_fn, x, y, theta_0, alpha_0=0.01):

    data = zip(x, y)
    theta = theta_0                             # initial guess
    alpha = alpha_0                             # initial step size
    min_theta, min_value = None, float("inf")   # the minimum so far
    iterations_with_no_improvement = 0

    # if we ever go 100 iterations with no improvement, stop
    while iterations_with_no_improvement < 100:
        value = sum( target_fn(x_i, y_i, theta) for x_i, y_i in data )

        if value < min_value:
            # if we've found a new minimum, remember it
            # and go back to the original step size
            min_theta, min_value = theta, value
            iterations_with_no_improvement = 0
            alpha = alpha_0
        else:
            # otherwise we're not improving, so try shrinking the step size
            iterations_with_no_improvement += 1
            alpha *= 0.9

        # and take a gradient step for each of the data points
        for x_i, y_i in in_random_order(data):
            gradient_i = gradient_fn(x_i, y_i, theta)
            theta = vector_subtract(theta, scalar_multiply(alpha, gradient_i))

    return min_theta
```

The stochastic version will typically be a lot faster than the batch version. Of course, we'll want a version that maximizes as well:

```
def maximize_stochastic(target_fn, gradient_fn, x, y, theta_0, alpha_0=0.01):
    return minimize_stochastic(negate(target_fn),
                               negate_all(gradient_fn),
                               x, y, theta_0, alpha_0)
```

For Further Exploration

- Keep reading! We'll be using gradient descent to solve problems throughout the rest of the book.

- At this point, you're undoubtedly sick of me recommending that you read textbooks. If it's any consolation, Active Calculus (*http://gvsu.edu/s/xr/*) seems nicer than the calculus textbooks I learned from.

- scikit-learn has a Stochastic Gradient Descent module (*http://scikit-learn.org/stable/modules/sgd.html*) that is not as general as ours in some ways and more general in other ways. Really, though, in most real-world situations you'll be using libraries in which the optimization is already taken care of behind the scenes, and you won't have to worry about it yourself (other than when it doesn't work correctly, which one day, inevitably, it won't).

## CHAPTER 9

Getting Data

To write it, it took three months; to conceive it, three minutes; to collect the data in it, all my
life.
—F. Scott Fitzgerald

In order to be a data scientist you need data. In fact, as a data scientist you will spend an embarrassingly large fraction of your time acquiring, cleaning, and transforming data. In a pinch, you can always type the data in yourself (or if you have minions, make them do it), but usually this is not a good use of your time. In this chapter, we'll look at different ways of getting data into Python and into the right formats.

stdin and stdout

If you run your Python scripts at the command line, you can *pipe* data through them using `sys.stdin` and `sys.stdout`. For example, here is a script that reads in lines of text and spits back out the ones that match a regular expression:

```
# egrep.py
import sys, re

# sys.argv is the list of command-line arguments
# sys.argv[0] is the name of the program itself
# sys.argv[1] will be the regex specified at the command line
regex = sys.argv[1]

# for every line passed into the script
for line in sys.stdin:
    # if it matches the regex, write it to stdout
    if re.search(regex, line):
        sys.stdout.write(line)
```

And here's one that counts the lines it receives and then writes out the count:

```
# line_count.py
import sys

count = 0
for line in sys.stdin:
    count += 1

# print goes to sys.stdout
print count
```

You could then use these to count how many lines of a file contain numbers. In Windows, you'd use:

```
type SomeFile.txt | python egrep.py "[0-9]" | python line_count.py
```

whereas in a Unix system you'd use:

```
cat SomeFile.txt | python egrep.py "[0-9]" | python line_count.py
```

The | is the pipe character, which means "use the output of the left command as the input of the right command." You can build pretty elaborate data-processing pipelines this way.

If you are using Windows, you can probably leave out the python part of this command:

```
type SomeFile.txt | egrep.py "[0-9]" | line_count.py
```

If you are on a Unix system, doing so might require a little more work (*http://bit.ly/1L2Wgb7*).

Similarly, here's a script that counts the words in its input and writes out the most common ones:

```
# most_common_words.py
import sys
from collections import Counter

# pass in number of words as first argument
try:
    num_words = int(sys.argv[1])
except:
    print "usage: most_common_words.py num_words"
    sys.exit(1)    # non-zero exit code indicates error

counter = Counter(word.lower()                      # lowercase words
                  for line in sys.stdin             #
                  for word in line.strip().split()  # split on spaces
                  if word)                          # skip empty 'words'

for word, count in counter.most_common(num_words):
    sys.stdout.write(str(count))
    sys.stdout.write("\t")
```

```
    sys.stdout.write(word)
    sys.stdout.write("\n")
```

after which you could do something like:

```
C:\DataScience>type the_bible.txt | python most_common_words.py 10
64193    the
51380    and
34753    of
13643    to
12799    that
12560    in
10263    he
9840     shall
8987     unto
8836     for
```

 If you are a seasoned Unix programmer, you are probably familiar with a wide variety of command-line tools (for example, egrep) that are built into your operating system and that are probably preferable to building your own from scratch. Still, it's good to know you can if you need to.

Reading Files

You can also explicitly read from and write to files directly in your code. Python makes working with files pretty simple.

The Basics of Text Files

The first step to working with a text file is to obtain a *file object* using open:

```
# 'r' means read-only
file_for_reading = open('reading_file.txt', 'r')

# 'w' is write -- will destroy the file if it already exists!
file_for_writing = open('writing_file.txt', 'w')

# 'a' is append -- for adding to the end of the file
file_for_appending = open('appending_file.txt', 'a')

# don't forget to close your files when you're done
file_for_writing.close()
```

Because it is easy to forget to close your files, you should always use them in a with block, at the end of which they will be closed automatically:

```
with open(filename,'r') as f:
    data = function_that_gets_data_from(f)
```

```
# at this point f has already been closed, so don't try to use it
process(data)
```

If you need to read a whole text file, you can just iterate over the lines of the file using for:

```
starts_with_hash = 0

with open('input.txt','r') as f:
    for line in file:             # look at each line in the file
        if re.match("^#",line):   # use a regex to see if it starts with '#'
            starts_with_hash += 1  # if it does, add 1 to the count
```

Every line you get this way ends in a newline character, so you'll often want to strip() it before doing anything with it.

For example, imagine you have a file full of email addresses, one per line, and that you need to generate a histogram of the domains. The rules for correctly extracting domains are somewhat subtle (e.g., the Public Suffix List (*https://publicsuffix.org*)), but a good first approximation is to just take the parts of the email addresses that come after the @. (Which gives the wrong answer for email addresses like `joel@mail.datasciencester.com`.)

```
def get_domain(email_address):
    """split on '@' and return the last piece"""
    return email_address.lower().split("@")[-1]

with open('email_addresses.txt', 'r') as f:
    domain_counts = Counter(get_domain(line.strip())
                            for line in f
                            if "@" in line)
```

Delimited Files

The hypothetical email addresses file we just processed had one address per line. More frequently you'll work with files with lots of data on each line. These files are very often either *comma-separated* or *tab-separated*. Each line has several fields, with a comma (or a tab) indicating where one field ends and the next field starts.

This starts to get complicated when you have fields with commas and tabs and newlines in them (which you inevitably do). For this reason, it's pretty much always a mistake to try to parse them yourself. Instead, you should use Python's csv module (or the pandas library). For technical reasons that you should feel free to blame on Microsoft, you should always work with csv files in *binary* mode by including a *b* after the *r* or *w* (see Stack Overflow (*http://bit.ly/1L2Y7wl*)).

If your file has no headers (which means you probably want each row as a list, and which places the burden on you to know what's in each column), you can use csv.reader to iterate over the rows, each of which will be an appropriately split list.

For example, if we had a tab-delimited file of stock prices:

```
6/20/2014    AAPL    90.91
6/20/2014    MSFT    41.68
6/20/2014    FB  64.5
6/19/2014    AAPL    91.86
6/19/2014    MSFT    41.51
6/19/2014    FB  64.34
```

we could process them with:

```
import csv

with open('tab_delimited_stock_prices.txt', 'rb') as f:
    reader = csv.reader(f, delimiter='\t')
    for row in reader:
        date = row[0]
        symbol = row[1]
        closing_price = float(row[2])
        process(date, symbol, closing_price)
```

If your file has headers:

```
date:symbol:closing_price
6/20/2014:AAPL:90.91
6/20/2014:MSFT:41.68
6/20/2014:FB:64.5
```

you can either skip the header row (with an initial call to reader.next()) or get each row as a dict (with the headers as keys) by using csv.DictReader:

```
with open('colon_delimited_stock_prices.txt', 'rb') as f:
    reader = csv.DictReader(f, delimiter=':')
    for row in reader:
        date = row["date"]
        symbol = row["symbol"]
        closing_price = float(row["closing_price"])
        process(date, symbol, closing_price)
```

Even if your file doesn't have headers you can still use DictReader by passing it the keys as a fieldnames parameter.

You can similarly write out delimited data using csv.writer:

```
today_prices = { 'AAPL' : 90.91, 'MSFT' : 41.68, 'FB' : 64.5 }

with open('comma_delimited_stock_prices.txt','wb') as f:
    writer = csv.writer(f, delimiter=',')
    for stock, price in today_prices.items():
        writer.writerow([stock, price])
```

csv.writer will do the right thing if your fields themselves have commas in them. Your own hand-rolled writer probably won't. For example, if you attempt:

```
results = [["test1", "success", "Monday"],
           ["test2", "success, kind of", "Tuesday"],
           ["test3", "failure, kind of", "Wednesday"],
           ["test4", "failure, utter", "Thursday"]]

# don't do this!
with open('bad_csv.txt', 'wb') as f:
    for row in results:
        f.write(",".join(map(str, row))) # might have too many commas in it!
        f.write("\n")                    # row might have newlines as well!
```

You will end up with a csv file that looks like:

```
test1,success,Monday
test2,success, kind of,Tuesday
test3,failure, kind of,Wednesday
test4,failure, utter,Thursday
```

and that no one will ever be able to make sense of.

Scraping the Web

Another way to get data is by scraping it from web pages. Fetching web pages, it turns out, is pretty easy; getting meaningful structured information out of them less so.

HTML and the Parsing Thereof

Pages on the Web are written in HTML, in which text is (ideally) marked up into elements and their attributes:

```
<html>
  <head>
    <title>A web page</title>
  </head>
  <body>
    <p id="author">Joel Grus</p>
    <p id="subject">Data Science</p>
  </body>
</html>
```

In a perfect world, where all web pages are marked up semantically for our benefit, we would be able to extract data using rules like "find the <p> element whose id is subject and return the text it contains." In the actual world, HTML is not generally well-formed, let alone annotated. This means we'll need help making sense of it.

To get data out of HTML, we will use the BeautifulSoup library (*http://www.crummy.com/software/BeautifulSoup/*), which builds a tree out of the various elements on a web page and provides a simple interface for accessing them. As I write this, the latest version is Beautiful Soup 4.3.2 (pip install beautifulsoup4), which is what we'll be using. We'll also be using the requests library (*http://docs.python-*

---

requests.org/en/latest/) (`pip install requests`), which is a much nicer way of making HTTP requests than anything that's built into Python.

Python's built-in HTML parser is not that lenient, which means that it doesn't always cope well with HTML that's not perfectly formed. For that reason, we'll use a different parser, which we need to install:

```
pip install html5lib
```

To use Beautiful Soup, we'll need to pass some HTML into the `BeautifulSoup()` function. In our examples, this will be the result of a call to `requests.get`:

```
from bs4 import BeautifulSoup
import requests
html = requests.get("http://www.example.com").text
soup = BeautifulSoup(html, 'html5lib')
```

after which we can get pretty far using a few simple methods.

We'll typically work with `Tag` objects, which correspond to the tags representing the structure of an HTML page.

For example, to find the first `<p>` tag (and its contents) you can use:

```
first_paragraph = soup.find('p')        # or just soup.p
```

You can get the text contents of a `Tag` using its `text` property:

```
first_paragraph_text = soup.p.text
first_paragraph_words = soup.p.text.split()
```

And you can extract a tag's attributes by treating it like a `dict`:

```
first_paragraph_id = soup.p['id']       # raises KeyError if no 'id'
first_paragraph_id2 = soup.p.get('id')  # returns None if no 'id'
```

You can get multiple tags at once:

```
all_paragraphs = soup.find_all('p')  # or just soup('p')
paragraphs_with_ids = [p for p in soup('p') if p.get('id')]
```

Frequently you'll want to find tags with a specific `class`:

```
important_paragraphs = soup('p', {'class' : 'important'})
important_paragraphs2 = soup('p', 'important')
important_paragraphs3 = [p for p in soup('p')
                           if 'important' in p.get('class', [])]
```

And you can combine these to implement more elaborate logic. For example, if you want to find every `<span>` element that is contained inside a `<div>` element, you could do this:

```
# warning, will return the same span multiple times
# if it sits inside multiple divs
# be more clever if that's the case
```

```
spans_inside_divs = [span
                      for div in soup('div')     # for each <div> on the page
                      for span in div('span')]   # find each <span> inside it
```

Just this handful of features will allow us to do quite a lot. If you end up needing to do more-complicated things (or if you're just curious), check the documentation.

Of course, whatever data is important won't typically be labeled as `class="impor tant"`. You'll need to carefully inspect the source HTML, reason through your selection logic, and worry about edge cases to make sure your data is correct. Let's look at an example.

Example: O'Reilly Books About Data

A potential investor in DataSciencester thinks data is just a fad. To prove him wrong, you decide to examine how many data books O'Reilly has published over time. After digging through its website, you find that it has many pages of data books (and videos), reachable through 30-items-at-a-time directory pages with URLs like:

```
http://shop.oreilly.com/category/browse-subjects/data.do?
sortby=publicationDate&page=1
```

Unless you want to be a jerk (and unless you want your scraper to get banned), whenever you want to scrape data from a website you should first check to see if it has some sort of access policy. Looking at:

```
http://oreilly.com/terms/
```

there seems to be nothing prohibiting this project. In order to be good citizens, we should also check for a *robots.txt* file that tells webcrawlers how to behave. The important lines in *http://shop.oreilly.com/robots.txt* are:

```
Crawl-delay: 30
Request-rate: 1/30
```

The first tells us that we should wait 30 seconds between requests, the second that we should request only one page every 30 seconds. So basically they're two different ways of saying the same thing. (There are other lines that indicate directories not to scrape, but they don't include our URL, so we're OK there.)

 There's always the possibility that O'Reilly will at some point revamp its website and break all the logic in this section. I will do what I can to prevent that, of course, but I don't have a ton of influence over there. Although, if every one of you were to convince everyone you know to buy a copy of this book…

To figure out how to extract the data, let's download one of those pages and feed it to Beautiful Soup:

```
# you don't have to split the url like this unless it needs to fit in a book
url = "http://shop.oreilly.com/category/browse-subjects/" + \
    "data.do?sortby=publicationDate&page=1"
soup = BeautifulSoup(requests.get(url).text, 'html5lib')
```

If you view the source of the page (in your browser, right-click and select "View source" or "View page source" or whatever option looks the most like that), you'll see that each book (or video) seems to be uniquely contained in a <td> table cell element whose class is thumbtext. Here is (an abridged version of) the relevant HTML for one book:

```
<td class="thumbtext">
  <div class="thumbcontainer">
    <div class="thumbdiv">
      <a href="/product/9781118903407.do">
        <img src="..."/>
      </a>
    </div>
  </div>
  <div class="widthchange">
    <div class="thumbheader">
      <a href="/product/9781118903407.do">Getting a Big Data Job For Dummies</a>
    </div>
    <div class="AuthorName">By Jason Williamson</div>
    <span class="directorydate">          December 2014     </span>
    <div style="clear:both;">
      <div id="146350">
        <span class="pricelabel">
                      Ebook:

                      <span class="price"> $29.99</span>
        </span>
      </div>
    </div>
  </div>
</td>
```

A good first step is to find all of the td thumbtext tag elements:

```
tds = soup('td', 'thumbtext')
print len(tds)
# 30
```

Next we'd like to filter out the videos. (The would-be investor is only impressed by books.) If we inspect the HTML further, we see that each td contains one or more span elements whose class is pricelabel, and whose text looks like Ebook: or Video: or Print:. It appears that the videos contain only one pricelabel, whose text starts with Video (after removing leading spaces). This means we can test for videos with:

```
def is_video(td):
    """it's a video if it has exactly one pricelabel, and if
```

```
        the stripped text inside that pricelabel starts with 'Video'"""
    pricelabels = td('span', 'pricelabel')
    return (len(pricelabels) == 1 and
            pricelabels[0].text.strip().startswith("Video"))

print len([td for td in tds if not is_video(td)])
# 21 for me, might be different for you
```

Now we're ready to start pulling data out of the td elements. It looks like the book title is the text inside the `<a>` tag inside the `<div class="thumbheader">`:

```
title = td.find("div", "thumbheader").a.text
```

The author(s) are in the text of the `AuthorName` `<div>`. They are prefaced by a By (which we want to get rid of) and separated by commas (which we want to split out, after which we'll need to get rid of spaces):

```
author_name = td.find('div', 'AuthorName').text
authors = [x.strip() for x in re.sub("^By ", "", author_name).split(",")]
```

The ISBN seems to be contained in the link that's in the `thumbheader` `<div>`:

```
isbn_link = td.find("div", "thumbheader").a.get("href")

# re.match captures the part of the regex in parentheses
isbn = re.match("/product/(.*)\.do", isbn_link).group(1)
```

And the date is just the contents of the `<span class="directorydate">`:

```
date = td.find("span", "directorydate").text.strip()
```

Let's put this all together into a function:

```
def book_info(td):
    """given a BeautifulSoup <td> Tag representing a book,
    extract the book's details and return a dict"""

    title = td.find("div", "thumbheader").a.text
    by_author = td.find('div', 'AuthorName').text
    authors = [x.strip() for x in re.sub("^By ", "", by_author).split(",")]
    isbn_link = td.find("div", "thumbheader").a.get("href")
    isbn = re.match("/product/(.*)\.do", isbn_link).groups()[0]
    date = td.find("span", "directorydate").text.strip()

    return {
        "title" : title,
        "authors" : authors,
        "isbn" : isbn,
        "date" : date
    }
```

And now we're ready to scrape:

```
from bs4 import BeautifulSoup
import requests
```

```
from time import sleep
base_url = "http://shop.oreilly.com/category/browse-subjects/" + \
           "data.do?sortby=publicationDate&page="

books = []

NUM_PAGES = 31      # at the time of writing, probably more by now

for page_num in range(1, NUM_PAGES + 1):
    print "souping page", page_num, ",", len(books), " found so far"
    url = base_url + str(page_num)
    soup = BeautifulSoup(requests.get(url).text, 'html5lib')

    for td in soup('td', 'thumbtext'):
        if not is_video(td):
            books.append(book_info(td))

    # now be a good citizen and respect the robots.txt!
    sleep(30)
```

 Extracting data from HTML like this is more data art than data science. There are countless other find-the-books and find-the-title logics that would have worked just as well.

Now that we've collected the data, we can plot the number of books published each year (Figure 9-1):

```
def get_year(book):
    """book["date"] looks like 'November 2014' so we need to
    split on the space and then take the second piece"""
    return int(book["date"].split()[1])

# 2014 is the last complete year of data (when I ran this)
year_counts = Counter(get_year(book) for book in books
                      if get_year(book) <= 2014)

import matplotlib.pyplot as plt
years = sorted(year_counts)
book_counts = [year_counts[year] for year in years]
plt.plot(years, book_counts)
plt.ylabel("# of data books")
plt.title("Data is Big!")
plt.show()
```

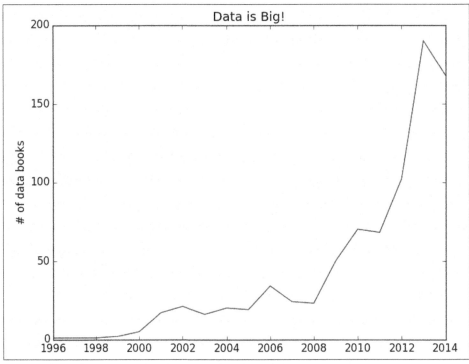

Figure 9-1. Number of data books per year

Unfortunately, the would-be investor looks at the graph and decides that 2013 was "peak data."

Using APIs

Many websites and web services provide application programming interfaces (APIs), which allow you to explicitly request data in a structured format. This saves you the trouble of having to scrape them!

JSON (and XML)

Because HTTP is a protocol for transferring *text*, the data you request through a web API needs to be *serialized* into a string format. Often this serialization uses JavaScript Object Notation (JSON). JavaScript objects look quite similar to Python dicts, which makes their string representations easy to interpret:

```
{ "title" : "Data Science Book",
  "author" : "Joel Grus",
  "publicationYear" : 2014,
  "topics" : [ "data", "science", "data science"] }
```

We can parse JSON using Python's `json` module. In particular, we will use its `loads` function, which deserializes a string representing a JSON object into a Python object:

```
import json
serialized = """{ "title" : "Data Science Book",
                  "author" : "Joel Grus",
                  "publicationYear" : 2014,
                  "topics" : [ "data", "science", "data science"] }"""

# parse the JSON to create a Python dict
deserialized = json.loads(serialized)
if "data science" in deserialized["topics"]:
    print deserialized
```

Sometimes an API provider hates you and only provides responses in XML:

```
<Book>
  <Title>Data Science Book</Title>
  <Author>Joel Grus</Author>
  <PublicationYear>2014</PublicationYear>
  <Topics>
    <Topic>data</Topic>
    <Topic>science</Topic>
    <Topic>data science</Topic>
  </Topics>
</Book>
```

You can use `BeautifulSoup` to get data from XML similarly to how we used it to get data from HTML; check its documentation for details.

Using an Unauthenticated API

Most APIs these days require you to first authenticate yourself in order to use them. While we don't begrudge them this policy, it creates a lot of extra boilerplate that muddies up our exposition. Accordingly, we'll first take a look at GitHub's API (*http://developer.github.com/v3/*), with which you can do some simple things unauthenticated:

```
import requests, json
endpoint = "https://api.github.com/users/joelgrus/repos"

repos = json.loads(requests.get(endpoint).text)
```

At this point `repos` is a `list` of Python `dicts`, each representing a public repository in my GitHub account. (Feel free to substitute your username and get your GitHub repository data instead. You do have a GitHub account, right?)

We can use this to figure out which months and days of the week I'm most likely to create a repository. The only issue is that the dates in the response are (Unicode) strings:

```
u'created_at': u'2013-07-05T02:02:28Z'
```

Python doesn't come with a great date parser, so we'll need to install one:

```
pip install python-dateutil
```

from which you'll probably only ever need the `dateutil.parser.parse` function:

```
from dateutil.parser import parse

dates = [parse(repo["created_at"]) for repo in repos]
month_counts = Counter(date.month for date in dates)
weekday_counts = Counter(date.weekday() for date in dates)
```

Similarly, you can get the languages of my last five repositories:

```
last_5_repositories = sorted(repos,
                             key=lambda r: r["created_at"],
                             reverse=True)[:5]

last_5_languages = [repo["language"]
                    for repo in last_5_repositories]
```

Typically we won't be working with APIs at this low "make the requests and parse the responses ourselves" level. One of the benefits of using Python is that someone has already built a library for pretty much any API you're interested in accessing. When they're done well, these libraries can save you a lot of the trouble of figuring out the hairier details of API access. (When they're not done well, or when it turns out they're based on defunct versions of the corresponding APIs, they can cause you enormous headaches.)

Nonetheless, you'll occasionally have to roll your own API-access library (or, more likely, debug why someone else's isn't working), so it's good to know some of the details.

Finding APIs

If you need data from a specific site, look for a developers or API section of the site for details, and try searching the Web for "python __ api" to find a library. There is a Rotten Tomatoes API for Python. There are multiple Python wrappers for the Klout API, for the Yelp API, for the IMDB API, and so on.

If you're looking for lists of APIs that have Python wrappers, two directories are at Python API (*http://www.pythonapi.com*) and Python for Beginners (*http://bit.ly/1L35VOR*).

If you want a directory of web APIs more broadly (without Python wrappers necessarily), a good resource is Programmable Web (*http://www.programmableweb.com*), which has a huge directory of categorized APIs.

And if after all that you can't find what you need, there's always scraping, the last refuge of the data scientist.

Example: Using the Twitter APIs

Twitter is a fantastic source of data to work with. You can use it to get real-time news. You can use it to measure reactions to current events. You can use it to find links related to specific topics. You can use it for pretty much anything you can imagine, just as long as you can get access to its data. And you can get access to its data through its API.

To interact with the Twitter APIs we'll be using the Twython library (*https://github.com/ryanmcgrath/twython*) (`pip install twython`). There are quite a few Python Twitter libraries out there, but this is the one that I've had the most success working with. You are encouraged to explore the others as well!

Getting Credentials

In order to use Twitter's APIs, you need to get some credentials (for which you need a Twitter account, which you should have anyway so that you can be part of the lively and friendly Twitter `#datascience` community). Like all instructions that relate to websites that I don't control, these may go obsolete at some point but will hopefully work for a while. (Although they have already changed at least once while I was writing this book, so good luck!)

1. Go to *https://apps.twitter.com/*.
2. If you are not signed in, click Sign in and enter your Twitter username and password.
3. Click Create New App.
4. Give it a name (such as "Data Science") and a description, and put any URL as the website (it doesn't matter which one).
5. Agree to the Terms of Service and click Create.
6. Take note of the consumer key and consumer secret.
7. Click "Create my access token."
8. Take note of the access token and access token secret (you may have to refresh the page).

The consumer key and consumer secret tell Twitter what application is accessing its APIs, while the access token and access token secret tell Twitter *who* is accessing its APIs. If you have ever used your Twitter account to log in to some other site, the "click to authorize" page was generating an access token for that site to use to convince Twitter that it was you (or, at least, acting on your behalf). As we don't need this "let anyone log in" functionality, we can get by with the statically generated access token and access token secret.

 The consumer key/secret and access token key/secret should be treated like *passwords*. You shouldn't share them, you shouldn't publish them in your book, and you shouldn't check them into your public GitHub repository. One simple solution is to store them in a *credentials.json* file that doesn't get checked in, and to have your code use `json.loads` to retrieve them.

Using Twython

First we'll look at the Search API (*https://dev.twitter.com/docs/api/1.1/get/search/ tweets*), which requires only the consumer key and secret, not the access token or secret:

```
from twython import Twython

twitter = Twython(CONSUMER_KEY, CONSUMER_SECRET)

# search for tweets containing the phrase "data science"
for status in twitter.search(q='"data science"')["statuses"]:
    user = status["user"]["screen_name"].encode('utf-8')
    text = status["text"].encode('utf-8')
    print user, ":", text
    print
```

 The `.encode("utf-8")` is necessary to deal with the fact that tweets often contain Unicode characters that `print` can't deal with. (If you leave it out, you will very likely get a `UnicodeEncodeError`.)

It is almost certain that at some point in your data science career you will run into some serious Unicode problems, at which point you will need to refer to the Python documentation (*http://bit.ly/ 1ycODJw*) or else grudgingly start using Python 3, which plays much more nicely with Unicode text.

If you run this, you should get some tweets back like:

```
haithemnyc: Data scientists with the technical savvy &amp; analytical chops to
derive meaning from big data are in demand. http://t.co/HsF9Q0dShP

RPubsRecent: Data Science http://t.co/6hcHUz2PHM

spleonard1: Using #dplyr in #R to work through a procrastinated assignment for
@rdpeng in @coursera data science specialization.  So easy and Awesome.
```

This isn't that interesting, largely because the Twitter Search API just shows you whatever handful of recent results it feels like. When you're doing data science, more often you want a lot of tweets. This is where the Streaming API (*http://bit.ly/ 1ycOEgG*) is useful. It allows you to connect to (a sample of) the great Twitter fire-hose. To use it, you'll need to authenticate using your access tokens.

In order to access the Streaming API with Twython, we need to define a class that inherits from `TwythonStreamer` and that overrides its `on_success` method (and possibly its `on_error` method):

```python
from twython import TwythonStreamer

# appending data to a global variable is pretty poor form
# but it makes the example much simpler
tweets = []

class MyStreamer(TwythonStreamer):
    """our own subclass of TwythonStreamer that specifies
    how to interact with the stream"""

    def on_success(self, data):
        """what do we do when twitter sends us data?
        here data will be a Python dict representing a tweet"""

        # only want to collect English-language tweets
        if data['lang'] == 'en':
            tweets.append(data)
            print "received tweet #", len(tweets)

        # stop when we've collected enough
        if len(tweets) >= 1000:
            self.disconnect()

    def on_error(self, status_code, data):
        print status_code, data
        self.disconnect()
```

MyStreamer will connect to the Twitter stream and wait for Twitter to feed it data. Each time it receives some data (here, a Tweet represented as a Python object) it passes it to the `on_success` method, which appends it to our `tweets` list if its language is English, and then disconnects the streamer after it's collected 1,000 tweets.

All that's left is to initialize it and start it running:

```python
stream = MyStreamer(CONSUMER_KEY, CONSUMER_SECRET,
                    ACCESS_TOKEN, ACCESS_TOKEN_SECRET)

# starts consuming public statuses that contain the keyword 'data'
stream.statuses.filter(track='data')
```

```
# if instead we wanted to start consuming a sample of *all* public statuses
# stream.statuses.sample()
```

This will run until it collects 1,000 tweets (or until it encounters an error) and stop, at which point you can start analyzing those tweets. For instance, you could find the most common hashtags with:

```
top_hashtags = Counter(hashtag['text'].lower()
                       for tweet in tweets
                       for hashtag in tweet["entities"]["hashtags"])

print top_hashtags.most_common(5)
```

Each tweet contains a lot of data. You can either poke around yourself or dig through the Twitter API documentation (*https://dev.twitter.com/overview/api/tweets*).

 In a non-toy project you probably wouldn't want to rely on an in-memory list for storing the tweets. Instead you'd want to save them to a file or a database, so that you'd have them permanently.

For Further Exploration

- pandas (*http://pandas.pydata.org/*) is the primary library that data science types use for working with (and, in particular, importing) data.

- Scrapy (*http://scrapy.org/*) is a more full-featured library for building more complicated web scrapers that do things like follow unknown links.

## CHAPTER 10

Working with Data

Experts often possess more data than judgment.
—Colin Powell

Working with data is both an art and a science. We've mostly been talking about the science part, but in this chapter we'll look at some of the art.

Exploring Your Data

After you've identified the questions you're trying to answer and have gotten your hands on some data, you might be tempted to dive in and immediately start building models and getting answers. But you should resist this urge. Your first step should be to *explore* your data.

Exploring One-Dimensional Data

The simplest case is when you have a one-dimensional data set, which is just a collection of numbers. For example, these could be the daily average number of minutes each user spends on your site, the number of times each of a collection of data science tutorial videos was watched, or the number of pages of each of the data science books in your data science library.

An obvious first step is to compute a few summary statistics. You'd like to know how many data points you have, the smallest, the largest, the mean, and the standard deviation.

But even these don't necessarily give you a great understanding. A good next step is to create a histogram, in which you group your data into discrete *buckets* and count how many points fall into each bucket:

```
def bucketize(point, bucket_size):
    """floor the point to the next lower multiple of bucket_size"""
    return bucket_size * math.floor(point / bucket_size)

def make_histogram(points, bucket_size):
    """buckets the points and counts how many in each bucket"""
    return Counter(bucketize(point, bucket_size) for point in points)

def plot_histogram(points, bucket_size, title=""):
    histogram = make_histogram(points, bucket_size)
    plt.bar(histogram.keys(), histogram.values(), width=bucket_size)
    plt.title(title)
    plt.show()
```

For example, consider the two following sets of data:

```
random.seed(0)

# uniform between -100 and 100
uniform = [200 * random.random() - 100 for _ in range(10000)]

# normal distribution with mean 0, standard deviation 57
normal = [57 * inverse_normal_cdf(random.random())
          for _ in range(10000)]
```

Both have means close to 0 and standard deviations close to 58. However, they have very different distributions. Figure 10-1 shows the distribution of uniform:

```
plot_histogram(uniform, 10, "Uniform Histogram")
```

while Figure 10-2 shows the distribution of normal:

```
plot_histogram(normal, 10, "Normal Histogram")
```

In this case, both distributions had pretty different max and min, but even knowing that wouldn't have been sufficient to understand *how* they differed.

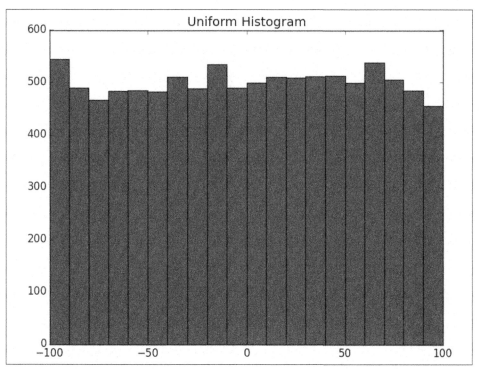

Figure 10-1. Histogram of uniform

Two Dimensions

Now imagine you have a data set with two dimensions. Maybe in addition to daily minutes you have years of data science experience. Of course you'd want to understand each dimension individually. But you probably also want to scatter the data.

For example, consider another fake data set:

```
def random_normal():
    """returns a random draw from a standard normal distribution"""
    return inverse_normal_cdf(random.random())

xs = [random_normal() for _ in range(1000)]
ys1 = [ x + random_normal() / 2 for x in xs]
ys2 = [-x + random_normal() / 2 for x in xs]
```

If you were to run `plot_histogram` on `ys1` and `ys2` you'd get very similar looking plots (indeed, both are normally distributed with the same mean and standard deviation).

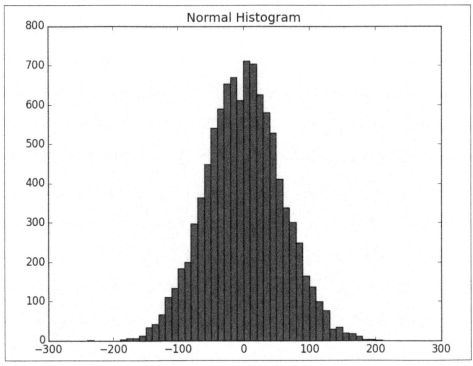

Figure 10-2. Histogram of normal

But each has a very different joint distribution with xs, as shown in Figure 10-3:

```
plt.scatter(xs, ys1, marker='.', color='black', label='ys1')
plt.scatter(xs, ys2, marker='.', color='gray',  label='ys2')
plt.xlabel('xs')
plt.ylabel('ys')
plt.legend(loc=9)
plt.title("Very Different Joint Distributions")
plt.show()
```

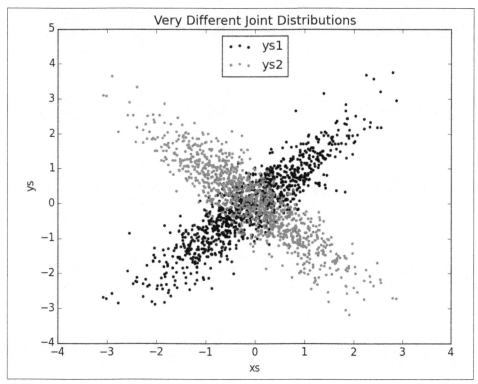

Figure 10-3. Scattering two different ys

This difference would also be apparent if you looked at the correlations:

```
print correlation(xs, ys1)      #  0.9
print correlation(xs, ys2)      # -0.9
```

Many Dimensions

With many dimensions, you'd like to know how all the dimensions relate to one another. A simple approach is to look at the *correlation matrix*, in which the entry in row *i* and column *j* is the correlation between the *i*th dimension and the *j*th dimension of the data:

```
def correlation_matrix(data):
    """returns the num_columns x num_columns matrix whose (i, j)th entry
    is the correlation between columns i and j of data"""

    _, num_columns = shape(data)

    def matrix_entry(i, j):
        return correlation(get_column(data, i), get_column(data, j))

    return make_matrix(num_columns, num_columns, matrix_entry)
```

A more visual approach (if you don't have too many dimensions) is to make a *scatter-plot matrix* (Figure 10-4) showing all the pairwise scatterplots. To do that we'll use `plt.subplots()`, which allows us to create subplots of our chart. We give it the number of rows and the number of columns, and it returns a `figure` object (which we won't use) and a two-dimensional array of `axes` objects (each of which we'll plot to):

```
import matplotlib.pyplot as plt

_, num_columns = shape(data)
fig, ax = plt.subplots(num_columns, num_columns)

for i in range(num_columns):
    for j in range(num_columns):

        # scatter column_j on the x-axis vs column_i on the y-axis
        if i != j: ax[i][j].scatter(get_column(data, j), get_column(data, i))

        # unless i == j, in which case show the series name
        else: ax[i][j].annotate("series " + str(i), (0.5, 0.5),
                                xycoords='axes fraction',
                                ha="center", va="center")

        # then hide axis labels except left and bottom charts
        if i < num_columns - 1: ax[i][j].xaxis.set_visible(False)
        if j > 0: ax[i][j].yaxis.set_visible(False)

# fix the bottom right and top left axis labels, which are wrong because
# their charts only have text in them
ax[-1][-1].set_xlim(ax[0][-1].get_xlim())
ax[0][0].set_ylim(ax[0][1].get_ylim())

plt.show()
```

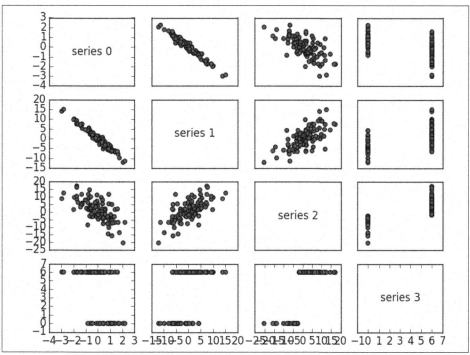

Figure 10-4. Scatterplot matrix

Looking at the scatterplots, you can see that series 1 is very negatively correlated with series 0, series 2 is positively correlated with series 1, and series 3 only takes on the values 0 and 6, with 0 corresponding to small values of series 2 and 6 corresponding to large values.

This is a quick way to get a rough sense of which of your variables are correlated (unless you spend hours tweaking `matplotlib` to display things exactly the way you want them to, in which case it's not a quick way).

Cleaning and Munging

Real-world data is *dirty*. Often you'll have to do some work on it before you can use it. We've seen examples of this in Chapter 9. We have to convert strings to `floats` or `ints` before we can use them. Previously, we did that right before using the data:

```
closing_price = float(row[2])
```

But it's probably less error-prone to do the parsing on the way in, which we can do by creating a function that wraps `csv.reader`. We'll give it a list of parsers, each specifying how to parse one of the columns. And we'll use `None` to represent "don't do anything to this column":

```
def parse_row(input_row, parsers):
    """given a list of parsers (some of which may be None)
    apply the appropriate one to each element of the input_row"""

    return [parser(value) if parser is not None else value
            for value, parser in zip(input_row, parsers)]

def parse_rows_with(reader, parsers):
    """wrap a reader to apply the parsers to each of its rows"""
    for row in reader:
        yield parse_row(row, parsers)
```

What if there's bad data? A "float" value that doesn't actually represent a number? We'd usually rather get a None than crash our program. We can do this with a helper function:

```
def try_or_none(f):
    """wraps f to return None if f raises an exception
    assumes f takes only one input"""
    def f_or_none(x):
        try: return f(x)
        except: return None
    return f_or_none
```

after which we can rewrite parse_row to use it:

```
def parse_row(input_row, parsers):
    return [try_or_none(parser)(value) if parser is not None else value
            for value, parser in zip(input_row, parsers)]
```

For example, if we have comma-delimited stock prices with bad data:

```
6/20/2014,AAPL,90.91
6/20/2014,MSFT,41.68
6/20/3014,FB,64.5
6/19/2014,AAPL,91.86
6/19/2014,MSFT,n/a
6/19/2014,FB,64.34
```

we can now read and parse in a single step:

```
import dateutil.parser
data = []

with open("comma_delimited_stock_prices.csv", "rb") as f:
    reader = csv.reader(f)
    for line in parse_rows_with(reader, [dateutil.parser.parse, None, float]):
        data.append(line)
```

after which we just need to check for None rows:

```
for row in data:
    if any(x is None for x in row):
        print row
```

and decide what we want to do about them. (Generally speaking, the three options are to get rid of them, to go back to the source and try to fix the bad/missing data, or to do nothing and cross our fingers.)

We could create similar helpers for csv.DictReader. In that case, you'd probably want to supply a dict of parsers by field name. For example:

```
def try_parse_field(field_name, value, parser_dict):
    """try to parse value using the appropriate function from parser_dict"""
    parser = parser_dict.get(field_name)   # None if no such entry
    if parser is not None:
        return try_or_none(parser)(value)
    else:
        return value

def parse_dict(input_dict, parser_dict):
    return { field_name : try_parse_field(field_name, value, parser_dict)
            for field_name, value in input_dict.iteritems() }
```

A good next step is to check for outliers, using techniques from "Exploring Your Data" on page 121 or by ad hoc investigating. For example, did you notice that one of the dates in the stocks file had the year 3014? That won't (necessarily) give you an error, but it's quite plainly wrong, and you'll get screwy results if you don't catch it. Real-world data sets have missing decimal points, extra zeroes, typographical errors, and countless other problems that it's your job to catch. (Maybe it's not officially your job, but who else is going to do it?)

Manipulating Data

One of the most important skills of a data scientist is *manipulating data*. It's more of a general approach than a specific technique, so we'll just work through a handful of examples to give you the flavor of it.

Imagine we're working with dicts of stock prices that look like:

```
data = [
    {'closing_price': 102.06,
     'date': datetime.datetime(2014, 8, 29, 0, 0),
     'symbol': 'AAPL'},
    # ...
]
```

Conceptually we'll think of them as rows (as in a spreadsheet).

Let's start asking questions about this data. Along the way we'll try to notice patterns in what we're doing and abstract out some tools to make the manipulation easier.

For instance, suppose we want to know the highest-ever closing price for AAPL. Let's break this down into concrete steps:

1. Restrict ourselves to AAPL rows.

2. Grab the `closing_price` from each row.

3. Take the `max` of those prices.

We can do all three at once using a list comprehension:

```
max_aapl_price = max(row["closing_price"]
                     for row in data
                     if row["symbol"] == "AAPL")
```

More generally, we might want to know the highest-ever closing price for each stock in our data set. One way to do this is:

1. Group together all the rows with the same `symbol`.

2. Within each group, do the same as before:

```
# group rows by symbol
by_symbol = defaultdict(list)
for row in data:
    by_symbol[row["symbol"]].append(row)

# use a dict comprehension to find the max for each symbol
max_price_by_symbol = { symbol : max(row["closing_price"]
                                     for row in grouped_rows)
                        for symbol, grouped_rows in by_symbol.iteritems() }
```

There are some patterns here already. In both examples, we needed to pull the `clos ing_price` value out of every dict. So let's create a function to pick a field out of a dict, and another function to pluck the same field out of a collection of dicts:

```
def picker(field_name):
    """returns a function that picks a field out of a dict"""
    return lambda row: row[field_name]

def pluck(field_name, rows):
    """turn a list of dicts into the list of field_name values"""
    return map(picker(field_name), rows)
```

We can also create a function to group rows by the result of a `grouper` function and to optionally apply some sort of `value_transform` to each group:

```
def group_by(grouper, rows, value_transform=None):
    # key is output of grouper, value is list of rows
    grouped = defaultdict(list)
    for row in rows:
        grouped[grouper(row)].append(row)

    if value_transform is None:
        return grouped
    else:
```

```
    return { key : value_transform(rows)
             for key, rows in grouped.iteritems() }
```

This allows us to rewrite our previous examples quite simply. For example:

```
max_price_by_symbol = group_by(picker("symbol"),
                               data,
                               lambda rows: max(pluck("closing_price", rows)))
```

We can now start to ask more complicated things, like what are the largest and smallest one-day percent changes in our data set. The percent change is `price_today /
price_yesterday - 1`, which means we need some way of associating today's price
and yesterday's price. One approach is to group the prices by symbol, then, within
each group:

1. Order the prices by date.

2. Use `zip` to get pairs (previous, current).

3. Turn the pairs into new "percent change" rows.

We'll start by writing a function to do all the within-each-group work:

```
def percent_price_change(yesterday, today):
    return today["closing_price"] / yesterday["closing_price"] - 1

def day_over_day_changes(grouped_rows):
    # sort the rows by date
    ordered = sorted(grouped_rows, key=picker("date"))

    # zip with an offset to get pairs of consecutive days
    return [{ "symbol" : today["symbol"],
             "date" : today["date"],
             "change" : percent_price_change(yesterday, today) }
           for yesterday, today in zip(ordered, ordered[1:])]
```

Then we can just use this as the `value_transform` in a `group_by`:

```
# key is symbol, value is list of "change" dicts
changes_by_symbol = group_by(picker("symbol"), data, day_over_day_changes)

# collect all "change" dicts into one big list
all_changes = [change
               for changes in changes_by_symbol.values()
               for change in changes]
```

At which point it's easy to find the largest and smallest:

```
max(all_changes, key=picker("change"))
# {'change': 0.3283582089552237,
#  'date': datetime.datetime(1997, 8, 6, 0, 0),
#  'symbol': 'AAPL'}
# see, e.g. http://news.cnet.com/2100-1001-202143.html
```

```
min(all_changes, key=picker("change"))
# {'change': -0.5193370165745856,
#  'date': datetime.datetime(2000, 9, 29, 0, 0),
#  'symbol': 'AAPL'}
# see, e.g. http://money.cnn.com/2000/09/29/markets/techwrap/
```

We can now use this new `all_changes` data set to find which month is the best to invest in tech stocks. First we group the changes by month; then we compute the overall change within each group.

Once again, we write an appropriate `value_transform` and then use `group_by`:

```
# to combine percent changes, we add 1 to each, multiply them, and subtract 1
# for instance, if we combine +10% and -20%, the overall change is
#     (1 + 10%) * (1 - 20%) - 1 = 1.1 * .8 - 1 = -12%
def combine_pct_changes(pct_change1, pct_change2):
    return (1 + pct_change1) * (1 + pct_change2) - 1

def overall_change(changes):
    return reduce(combine_pct_changes, pluck("change", changes))

overall_change_by_month = group_by(lambda row: row['date'].month,
                                   all_changes,
                                   overall_change)
```

We'll be doing these sorts of manipulations throughout the book, usually without calling too much explicit attention to them.

Rescaling

Many techniques are sensitive to the *scale* of your data. For example, imagine that you have a data set consisting of the heights and weights of hundreds of data scientists, and that you are trying to identify *clusters* of body sizes.

Intuitively, we'd like clusters to represent points near each other, which means that we need some notion of distance between points. We already have a Euclidean `distance` function, so a natural approach might be to treat (height, weight) pairs as points in two-dimensional space. Consider the people listed in Table 10-1.

Table 10-1. Heights and Weights

Person	Height (inches)	Height (centimeters)	Weight
A	63 inches	160 cm	150 pounds
B	67 inches	170.2 cm	160 pounds
C	70 inches	177.8 cm	171 pounds

If we measure height in inches, then B's nearest neighbor is A:

```
a_to_b = distance([63, 150], [67, 160])        # 10.77
a_to_c = distance([63, 150], [70, 171])        # 22.14
b_to_c = distance([67, 160], [70, 171])        # 11.40
```

However, if we measure height in centimeters, then B's nearest neighbor is instead C:

```
a_to_b = distance([160, 150], [170.2, 160])    # 14.28
a_to_c = distance([160, 150], [177.8, 171])    # 27.53
b_to_c = distance([170.2, 160], [177.8, 171])  # 13.37
```

Obviously it's problematic if changing units can change results like this. For this reason, when dimensions aren't comparable with one another, we will sometimes *rescale* our data so that each dimension has mean 0 and standard deviation 1. This effectively gets rid of the units, converting each dimension to "standard deviations from the mean."

To start with, we'll need to compute the mean and the standard_deviation for each column:

```
def scale(data_matrix):
    """returns the means and standard deviations of each column"""
    num_rows, num_cols = shape(data_matrix)
    means = [mean(get_column(data_matrix,j))
             for j in range(num_cols)]
    stdevs = [standard_deviation(get_column(data_matrix,j))
              for j in range(num_cols)]
    return means, stdevs
```

And then use them to create a new data matrix:

```
def rescale(data_matrix):
    """rescales the input data so that each column
    has mean 0 and standard deviation 1
    leaves alone columns with no deviation"""
    means, stdevs = scale(data_matrix)

    def rescaled(i, j):
        if stdevs[j] > 0:
            return (data_matrix[i][j] - means[j]) / stdevs[j]
        else:
            return data_matrix[i][j]

    num_rows, num_cols = shape(data_matrix)
    return make_matrix(num_rows, num_cols, rescaled)
```

As always, you need to use your judgment. If you were to take a huge data set of heights and weights and filter it down to only the people with heights between 69.5 inches and 70.5 inches, it's quite likely (depending on the question you're trying to answer) that the variation remaining is simply *noise*, and you might not want to put its standard deviation on equal footing with other dimensions' deviations.

Dimensionality Reduction

Sometimes the "actual" (or useful) dimensions of the data might not correspond to the dimensions we have. For example, consider the data set pictured in Figure 10-5.

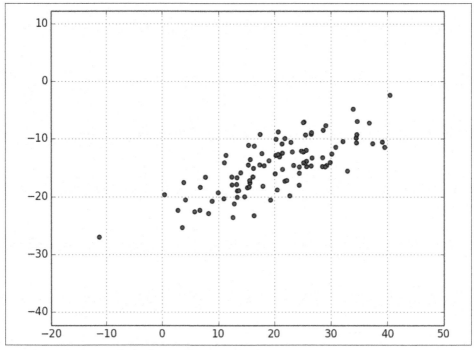

Figure 10-5. Data with the "wrong" axes

Most of the variation in the data seems to be along a single dimension that doesn't correspond to either the x-axis or the y-axis.

When this is the case, we can use a technique called *principal component analysis* to extract one or more dimensions that capture as much of the variation in the data as possible.

 In practice, you wouldn't use this technique on such a low-dimensional data set. Dimensionality reduction is mostly useful when your data set has a large number of dimensions and you want to find a small subset that captures most of the variation. Unfortunately, that case is difficult to illustrate in a two-dimensional book format.

As a first step, we'll need to translate the data so that each dimension has mean zero:

```
def de_mean_matrix(A):
    """returns the result of subtracting from every value in A the mean
    value of its column. the resulting matrix has mean 0 in every column"""
    nr, nc = shape(A)
    column_means, _ = scale(A)
    return make_matrix(nr, nc, lambda i, j: A[i][j] - column_means[j])
```

(If we don't do this, our techniques are likely to identify the mean itself rather than the variation in the data.)

Figure 10-6 shows the example data after de-meaning.

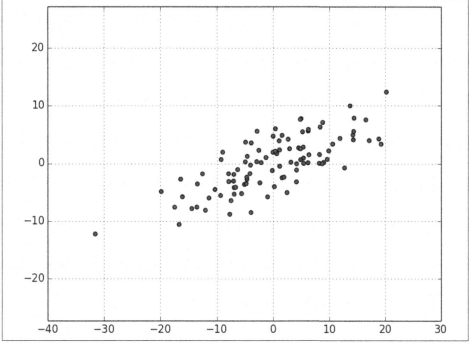

Figure 10-6. Data after de-meaning

Now, given a de-meaned matrix X, we can ask which is the direction that captures the greatest variance in the data?

Specifically, given a direction d (a vector of magnitude 1), each row x in the matrix extends dot(x, d) in the d direction. And every nonzero vector w determines a direction if we rescale it to have magnitude 1:

```
def direction(w):
    mag = magnitude(w)
    return [w_i / mag for w_i in w]
```

Therefore, given a nonzero vector *w*, we can compute the variance of our data set in the direction determined by *w*:

```
def directional_variance_i(x_i, w):
    """the variance of the row x_i in the direction determined by w"""
    return dot(x_i, direction(w)) ** 2

def directional_variance(X, w):
    """the variance of the data in the direction determined w"""
    return sum(directional_variance_i(x_i, w)
               for x_i in X)
```

We'd like to find the direction that maximizes this variance. We can do this using gradient descent, as soon as we have the gradient function:

```
def directional_variance_gradient_i(x_i, w):
    """the contribution of row x_i to the gradient of
    the direction-w variance"""
    projection_length = dot(x_i, direction(w))
    return [2 * projection_length * x_ij for x_ij in x_i]

def directional_variance_gradient(X, w):
    return vector_sum(directional_variance_gradient_i(x_i,w)
                      for x_i in X)
```

The first principal component is just the direction that maximizes the `direc tional_variance` function:

```
def first_principal_component(X):
    guess = [1 for _ in X[0]]
    unscaled_maximizer = maximize_batch(
        partial(directional_variance, X),          # is now a function of w
        partial(directional_variance_gradient, X), # is now a function of w
        guess)
    return direction(unscaled_maximizer)
```

Or, if you'd rather use stochastic gradient descent:

```
# here there is no "y", so we just pass in a vector of Nones
# and functions that ignore that input
def first_principal_component_sgd(X):
    guess = [1 for _ in X[0]]
    unscaled_maximizer = maximize_stochastic(
        lambda x, _, w: directional_variance_i(x, w),
        lambda x, _, w: directional_variance_gradient_i(x, w),
        X,
        [None for _ in X],   # the fake "y"
        guess)
    return direction(unscaled_maximizer)
```

On the de-meaned data set, this returns the direction [0.924, 0.383], which does appear to capture the primary axis along which our data varies (Figure 10-7).

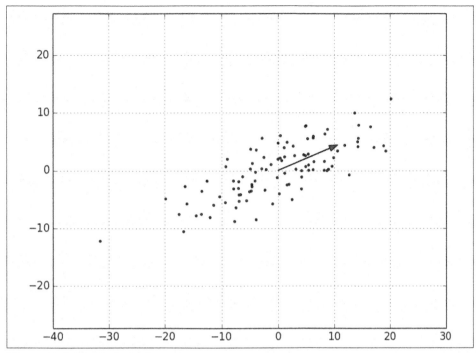

Figure 10-7. First principal component

Once we've found the direction that's the first principal component, we can project our data onto it to find the values of that component:

```
def project(v, w):
    """return the projection of v onto the direction w"""
    projection_length = dot(v, w)
    return scalar_multiply(projection_length, w)
```

If we want to find further components, we first remove the projections from the data:

```
def remove_projection_from_vector(v, w):
    """projects v onto w and subtracts the result from v"""
    return vector_subtract(v, project(v, w))

def remove_projection(X, w):
    """for each row of X
    projects the row onto w, and subtracts the result from the row"""
    return [remove_projection_from_vector(x_i, w) for x_i in X]
```

Because this example data set is only two-dimensional, after we remove the first component, what's left will be effectively one-dimensional (Figure 10-8).

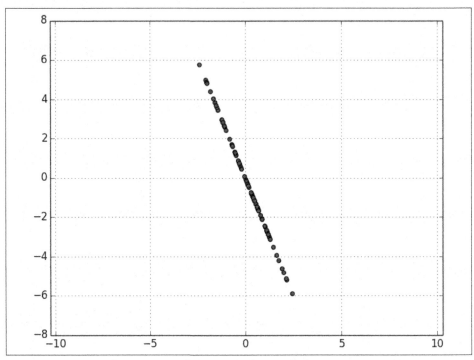

Figure 10-8. Data after removing first principal component

At that point, we can find the next principal component by repeating the process on the result of remove_projection (Figure 10-9).

On a higher-dimensional data set, we can iteratively find as many components as we want:

```
def principal_component_analysis(X, num_components):
    components = []
    for _ in range(num_components):
        component = first_principal_component(X)
        components.append(component)
        X = remove_projection(X, component)

    return components
```

We can then *transform* our data into the lower-dimensional space spanned by the components:

```
def transform_vector(v, components):
    return [dot(v, w) for w in components]

def transform(X, components):
    return [transform_vector(x_i, components) for x_i in X]
```

This technique is valuable for a couple of reasons. First, it can help us clean our data by eliminating noise dimensions and consolidating dimensions that are highly correlated.

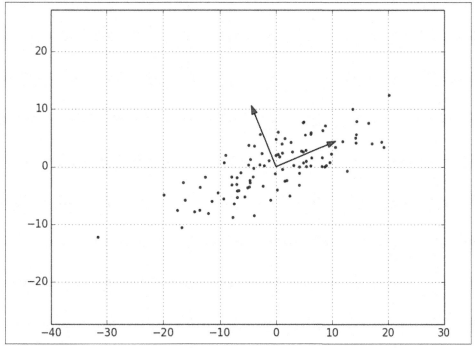

Figure 10-9. First two principal components

Second, after extracting a low-dimensional representation of our data, we can use a variety of techniques that don't work as well on high-dimensional data. We'll see examples of such techniques throughout the book.

At the same time, while it can help you build better models, it can also make those models harder to interpret. It's easy to understand conclusions like "every extra year of experience adds an average of $10k in salary." It's much harder to make sense of "every increase of 0.1 in the third principal component adds an average of $10k in salary."

For Further Exploration

- As we mentioned at the end of Chapter 9, pandas (*http://pandas.pydata.org/*) is probably the primary Python tool for cleaning, munging, manipulating, and working with data. All the examples we did by hand in this chapter could be done much more simply using pandas. *Python for Data Analysis* (O'Reilly) is probably the best way to learn pandas.

- scikit-learn has a wide variety of matrix decomposition (*http://bit.ly/1ycOLJd*) functions, including PCA.

## CHAPTER 11

Machine Learning

I am always ready to learn although I do not always like being taught.
—Winston Churchill

Many people imagine that data science is mostly machine learning and that data scientists mostly build and train and tweak machine-learning models all day long. (Then again, many of those people don't actually know what machine learning *is*.) In fact, data science is mostly turning business problems into data problems and collecting data and understanding data and cleaning data and formatting data, after which machine learning is almost an afterthought. Even so, it's an interesting and essential afterthought that you pretty much have to know about in order to do data science.

Modeling

Before we can talk about machine learning we need to talk about *models*.

What is a model? It's simply a specification of a mathematical (or probabilistic) relationship that exists between different variables.

For instance, if you're trying to raise money for your social networking site, you might build a *business model* (likely in a spreadsheet) that takes inputs like "number of users" and "ad revenue per user" and "number of employees" and outputs your annual profit for the next several years. A cookbook recipe entails a model that relates inputs like "number of eaters" and "hungriness" to quantities of ingredients needed. And if you've ever watched poker on television, you know that they estimate each player's "win probability" in real time based on a model that takes into account the cards that have been revealed so far and the distribution of cards in the deck.

The business model is probably based on simple mathematical relationships: profit is revenue minus expenses, revenue is units sold times average price, and so on. The recipe model is probably based on trial and error—someone went in a kitchen and tried different combinations of ingredients until they found one they liked. And the poker model is based on probability theory, the rules of poker, and some reasonably innocuous assumptions about the random process by which cards are dealt.

What Is Machine Learning?

Everyone has her own exact definition, but we'll use *machine learning* to refer to creating and using models that are *learned from data*. In other contexts this might be called *predictive modeling* or *data mining*, but we will stick with machine learning. Typically, our goal will be to use existing data to develop models that we can use to *predict* various outcomes for new data, such as:

- Predicting whether an email message is spam or not
- Predicting whether a credit card transaction is fraudulent
- Predicting which advertisement a shopper is most likely to click on
- Predicting which football team is going to win the Super Bowl

We'll look at both *supervised* models (in which there is a set of data labeled with the correct answers to learn from), and *unsupervised* models (in which there are no such labels). There are various other types like *semisupervised* (in which only some of the data are labeled) and *online* (in which the model needs to continuously adjust to newly arriving data) that we won't cover in this book.

Now, in even the simplest situation there are entire universes of models that might describe the relationship we're interested in. In most cases we will ourselves choose a *parameterized* family of models and then use data to learn parameters that are in some way optimal.

For instance, we might assume that a person's height is (roughly) a linear function of his weight and then use data to learn what that linear function is. Or we might assume that a decision tree is a good way to diagnose what diseases our patients have and then use data to learn the "optimal" such tree. Throughout the rest of the book we'll be investigating different families of models that we can learn.

But before we can do that, we need to better understand the fundamentals of machine learning. For the rest of the chapter, we'll discuss some of those basic concepts, before we move on to the models themselves.

Overfitting and Underfitting

A common danger in machine learning is *overfitting*—producing a model that performs well on the data you train it on but that generalizes poorly to any new data.

This could involve learning *noise* in the data. Or it could involve learning to identify specific inputs rather than whatever factors are actually predictive for the desired output.

The other side of this is *underfitting*, producing a model that doesn't perform well even on the training data, although typically when this happens you decide your model isn't good enough and keep looking for a better one.

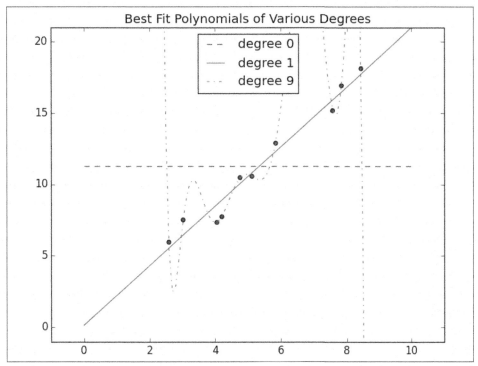

Figure 11-1. Overfitting and underfitting

In Figure 11-1, I've fit three polynomials to a sample of data. (Don't worry about how; we'll get to that in later chapters.)

The horizontal line shows the best fit degree 0 (i.e., constant) polynomial. It severely *underfits* the training data. The best fit degree 9 (i.e., 10-parameter) polynomial goes through every training data point exactly, but it very severely *overfits*—if we were to pick a few more data points it would quite likely miss them by a lot. And the degree 1 line strikes a nice balance—it's pretty close to every point, and (if these data are representative) the line will likely be close to new data points as well.

Clearly models that are too complex lead to overfitting and don't generalize well beyond the data they were trained on. So how do we make sure our models aren't too complex? The most fundamental approach involves using different data to train the model and to test the model.

The simplest way to do this is to split your data set, so that (for example) two-thirds of it is used to train the model, after which we measure the model's performance on the remaining third:

```
def split_data(data, prob):
    """split data into fractions [prob, 1 - prob]"""
    results = [], []
    for row in data:
        results[0 if random.random() < prob else 1].append(row)
    return results
```

Often, we'll have a matrix x of input variables and a vector y of output variables. In that case, we need to make sure to put corresponding values together in either the training data or the test data:

```
def train_test_split(x, y, test_pct):
    data = zip(x, y)                              # pair corresponding values
    train, test = split_data(data, 1 - test_pct) # split the data set of pairs
    x_train, y_train = zip(*train)               # magical un-zip trick
    x_test, y_test = zip(*test)
    return x_train, x_test, y_train, y_test
```

so that you might do something like:

```
model = SomeKindOfModel()
x_train, x_test, y_train, y_test = train_test_split(xs, ys, 0.33)
model.train(x_train, y_train)
performance = model.test(x_test, y_test)
```

If the model was overfit to the training data, then it will hopefully perform really poorly on the (completely separate) test data. Said differently, if it performs well on the test data, then you can be more confident that it's *fitting* rather than *overfitting*.

However, there are a couple of ways this can go wrong.

The first is if there are common patterns in the test and train data that wouldn't generalize to a larger data set.

For example, imagine that your data set consists of user activity, one row per user per week. In such a case, most users will appear in both the training data and the test data, and certain models might learn to *identify* users rather than discover relationships involving *attributes*. This isn't a huge worry, although it did happen to me once.

A bigger problem is if you use the test/train split not just to judge a model but also to *choose* from among many models. In that case, although each individual model may not be overfit, the "choose a model that performs best on the test set" is a meta-training that makes the test set function as a second training set. (Of course the model that performed best on the test set is going to perform well on the test set.)

In such a situation, you should split the data into three parts: a *training* set for build-ing models, a *validation* set for choosing among trained models, and a *test* set for judging the final model.

Correctness

When I'm not doing data science, I dabble in medicine. And in my spare time I've come up with a cheap, noninvasive test that can be given to a newborn baby that pre-dicts—with greater than 98% accuracy — whether the newborn will ever develop leu-kemia. My lawyer has convinced me the test is unpatentable, so I'll share with you the details here: predict leukemia if and only if the baby is named Luke (which sounds sort of like "leukemia").

As we'll see below, this test is indeed more than 98% accurate. Nonetheless, it's an incredibly stupid test, and a good illustration of why we don't typically use "accuracy" to measure how good a model is.

Imagine building a model to make a *binary* judgment. Is this email spam? Should we hire this candidate? Is this air traveler secretly a terrorist?

Given a set of labeled data and such a predictive model, every data point lies in one of four categories:

- True positive: "This message is spam, and we correctly predicted spam."
- False positive (Type 1 Error): "This message is not spam, but we predicted spam."
- False negative (Type 2 Error): "This message is spam, but we predicted not spam."
- True negative: "This message is not spam, and we correctly predicted not spam."

We often represent these as counts in a *confusion matrix*:

	Spam	not Spam
predict "Spam"	True Positive	False Positive
predict "Not Spam"	False Negative	True Negative

Let's see how my leukemia test fits into this framework. These days approximately 5 babies out of 1,000 are named Luke (*http://bit.ly/1CchAqt*). And the lifetime preva-lence of leukemia is about 1.4%, or 14 out of every 1,000 people (*http://1.usa.gov/1ycORjO*).

If we believe these two factors are independent and apply my "Luke is for leukemia" test to 1 million people, we'd expect to see a confusion matrix like:

	leukemia	no leukemia	total
"Luke"	70	4,930	5,000
not "Luke"	13,930	981,070	995,000
total	14,000	986,000	1,000,000

We can then use these to compute various statistics about model performance. For example, *accuracy* is defined as the fraction of correct predictions:

```
def accuracy(tp, fp, fn, tn):
    correct = tp + tn
    total = tp + fp + fn + tn
    return correct / total

print accuracy(70, 4930, 13930, 981070)     # 0.98114
```

That seems like a pretty impressive number. But clearly this is not a good test, which means that we probably shouldn't put a lot of credence in raw accuracy.

It's common to look at the combination of *precision* and *recall*. Precision measures how accurate our *positive* predictions were:

```
def precision(tp, fp, fn, tn):
    return tp / (tp + fp)

print precision(70, 4930, 13930, 981070)     # 0.014
```

And recall measures what fraction of the positives our model identified:

```
def recall(tp, fp, fn, tn):
    return tp / (tp + fn)

print recall(70, 4930, 13930, 981070)     # 0.005
```

These are both terrible numbers, reflecting that this is a terrible model.

Sometimes precision and recall are combined into the *F1 score*, which is defined as:

```
def f1_score(tp, fp, fn, tn):
    p = precision(tp, fp, fn, tn)
    r = recall(tp, fp, fn, tn)

    return 2 * p * r / (p + r)
```

This is the *harmonic mean* (*http://en.wikipedia.org/wiki/Harmonic_mean*) of precision and recall and necessarily lies between them.

Usually the choice of a model involves a trade-off between precision and recall. A model that predicts "yes" when it's even a little bit confident will probably have a high recall but a low precision; a model that predicts "yes" only when it's extremely confident is likely to have a low recall and a high precision.

Alternatively, you can think of this as a trade-off between false positives and false negatives. Saying "yes" too often will give you lots of false positives; saying "no" too often will give you lots of false negatives.

Imagine that there were 10 risk factors for leukemia, and that the more of them you had the more likely you were to develop leukemia. In that case you can imagine a continuum of tests: "predict leukemia if at least one risk factor," "predict leukemia if at least two risk factors," and so on. As you increase the threshold, you increase the test's precision (since people with more risk factors are more likely to develop the disease), and you decrease the test's recall (since fewer and fewer of the eventual disease-sufferers will meet the threshhold). In cases like this, choosing the right threshhold is a matter of finding the right trade-off.

The Bias-Variance Trade-off

Another way of thinking about the overfitting problem is as a trade-off between bias and variance.

Both are measures of what would happen if you were to retrain your model many times on different sets of training data (from the same larger population).

For example, the degree 0 model in "Overfitting and Underfitting" on page 142 will make a lot of mistakes for pretty much any training set (drawn from the same population), which means that it has a high *bias*. However, any two randomly chosen training sets should give pretty similar models (since any two randomly chosen training sets should have pretty similar average values). So we say that it has a low *variance*. High bias and low variance typically correspond to underfitting.

On the other hand, the degree 9 model fit the training set perfectly. It has very low bias but very high variance (since any two training sets would likely give rise to very different models). This corresponds to overfitting.

Thinking about model problems this way can help you figure out what do when your model doesn't work so well.

If your model has high bias (which means it performs poorly even on your training data) then one thing to try is adding more features. Going from the degree 0 model in "Overfitting and Underfitting" on page 142 to the degree 1 model was a big improvement.

If your model has high variance, then you can similarly *remove* features. But another solution is to obtain more data (if you can).

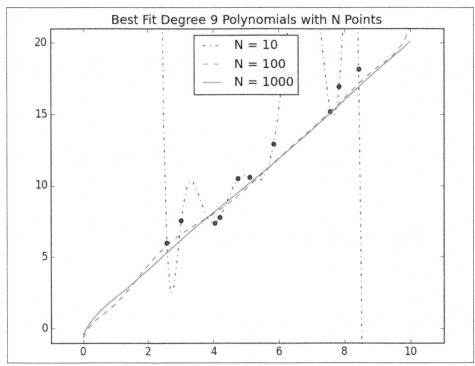

Figure 11-2. Reducing variance with more data

In Figure 11-2, we fit a degree 9 polynomial to different size samples. The model fit based on 10 data points is all over the place, as we saw before. If we instead trained on 100 data points, there's much less overfitting. And the model trained from 1,000 data points looks very similar to the degree 1 model.

Holding model complexity constant, the more data you have, the harder it is to overfit.

On the other hand, more data won't help with bias. If your model doesn't use enough features to capture regularities in the data, throwing more data at it won't help.

Feature Extraction and Selection

As we mentioned, when your data doesn't have enough features, your model is likely to underfit. And when your data has too many features, it's easy to overfit. But what are features and where do they come from?

Features are whatever inputs we provide to our model.

In the simplest case, features are simply given to you. If you want to predict someone's salary based on her years of experience, then years of experience is the only feature you have.

(Although, as we saw in "Overfitting and Underfitting" on page 142, you might also consider adding years of experience squared, cubed, and so on if that helps you build a better model.)

Things become more interesting as your data becomes more complicated. Imagine trying to build a spam filter to predict whether an email is junk or not. Most models won't know what to do with a raw email, which is just a collection of text. You'll have to extract features. For example:

- Does the email contain the word "Viagra"?
- How many times does the letter d appear?
- What was the domain of the sender?

The first is simply a yes or no, which we typically encode as a 1 or 0. The second is a number. And the third is a choice from a discrete set of options.

Pretty much always, we'll extract features from our data that fall into one of these three categories. What's more, the type of features we have constrains the type of models we can use.

The Naive Bayes classifier we'll build in Chapter 13 is suited to yes-or-no features, like the first one in the preceding list.

Regression models, as we'll study in Chapter 14 and Chapter 16, require numeric features (which could include dummy variables that are 0s and 1s).

And decision trees, which we'll look at in Chapter 17, can deal with numeric or categorical data.

Although in the spam filter example we looked for ways to create features, sometimes we'll instead look for ways to remove features.

For example, your inputs might be vectors of several hundred numbers. Depending on the situation, it might be appropriate to distill these down to handful of important dimensions (as in "Dimensionality Reduction" on page 134) and use only those small number of features. Or it might be appropriate to use a technique (like regularization, which we'll look at in "Regularization" on page 186) that penalizes models the more features they use.

How do we choose features? That's where a combination of *experience* and *domain expertise* comes into play. If you've received lots of emails, then you probably have a sense that the presence of certain words might be a good indicator of spamminess. And you might also have a sense that the number of d's is likely not a good indicator of spamminess. But in general you'll have to try different things, which is part of the fun.

For Further Exploration

- Keep reading! The next several chapters are about different families of machine-learning models.
- The Coursera Machine Learning (*https://www.coursera.org/course/ml*) course is the original MOOC and is a good place to get a deeper understanding of the basics of machine learning. The Caltech Machine Learning (*http://bit.ly/1ycOTIx*) MOOC is also good.
- *The Elements of Statistical Learning* is a somewhat canonical textbook that can be downloaded online for free (*http://stanford.io/1ycOXbo*). But be warned: it's *very* mathy.

k-Nearest Neighbors

If you want to annoy your neighbors, tell the truth about them.
—Pietro Aretino

Imagine that you're trying to predict how I'm going to vote in the next presidential election. If you know nothing else about me (and if you have the data), one sensible approach is to look at how my *neighbors* are planning to vote. Living in downtown Seattle, as I do, my neighbors are invariably planning to vote for the Democratic candidate, which suggests that "Democratic candidate" is a good guess for me as well.

Now imagine you know more about me than just geography—perhaps you know my age, my income, how many kids I have, and so on. To the extent my behavior is influenced (or characterized) by those things, looking just at my neighbors who are close to me among all those dimensions seems likely to be an even better predictor than looking at all my neighbors. This is the idea behind *nearest neighbors classification*.

The Model

Nearest neighbors is one of the simplest predictive models there is. It makes no mathematical assumptions, and it doesn't require any sort of heavy machinery. The only things it requires are:

- Some notion of distance
- An assumption that points that are close to one another are similar

Most of the techniques we'll look at in this book look at the data set as a whole in order to learn patterns in the data. Nearest neighbors, on the other hand, quite consciously neglects a lot of information, since the prediction for each new point depends only on the handful of points closest to it.

What's more, nearest neighbors is probably not going to help you understand the drivers of whatever phenomenon you're looking at. Predicting my votes based on my neighbors' votes doesn't tell you much about what causes me to vote the way I do, whereas some alternative model that predicted my vote based on (say) my income and marital status very well might.

In the general situation, we have some data points and we have a corresponding set of labels. The labels could be True and False, indicating whether each input satisfies some condition like "is spam?" or "is poisonous?" or "would be enjoyable to watch?" Or they could be categories, like movie ratings (G, PG, PG-13, R, NC-17). Or they could be the names of presidential candidates. Or they could be favorite programming languages.

In our case, the data points will be vectors, which means that we can use the distance function from Chapter 4.

Let's say we've picked a number *k* like 3 or 5. Then when we want to classify some new data point, we find the k nearest labeled points and let them vote on the new output.

To do this, we'll need a function that counts votes. One possibility is:

```python
def raw_majority_vote(labels):
    votes = Counter(labels)
    winner, _ = votes.most_common(1)[0]
    return winner
```

But this doesn't do anything intelligent with ties. For example, imagine we're rating movies and the five nearest movies are rated G, G, PG, PG, and R. Then G has two votes and PG also has two votes. In that case, we have several options:

- Pick one of the winners at random.

- Weight the votes by distance and pick the weighted winner.

- Reduce *k* until we find a unique winner.

We'll implement the third:

```python
def majority_vote(labels):
    """assumes that labels are ordered from nearest to farthest"""
    vote_counts = Counter(labels)
    winner, winner_count = vote_counts.most_common(1)[0]
    num_winners = len([count
                       for count in vote_counts.values()
                       if count == winner_count])

    if num_winners == 1:
        return winner                        # unique winner, so return it
    else:
        return majority_vote(labels[:-1]) # try again without the farthest
```

This approach is sure to work eventually, since in the worst case we go all the way down to just one label, at which point that one label wins.

With this function it's easy to create a classifier:

```
def knn_classify(k, labeled_points, new_point):
    """each labeled point should be a pair (point, label)"""

    # order the labeled points from nearest to farthest
    by_distance = sorted(labeled_points,
                         key=lambda (point, _): distance(point, new_point))

    # find the labels for the k closest
    k_nearest_labels = [label for _, label in by_distance[:k]]

    # and let them vote
    return majority_vote(k_nearest_labels)
```

Let's take a look at how this works.

Example: Favorite Languages

The results of the first DataSciencester user survey are back, and we've found the preferred programming languages of our users in a number of large cities:

```
# each entry is ([longitude, latitude], favorite_language)

cities = [([-122.3 , 47.53], "Python"),   # Seattle
          ([ -96.85, 32.85], "Java"),     # Austin
          ([ -89.33, 43.13], "R"),        # Madison
          # ... and so on
         ]
```

The VP of Community Engagement wants to know if we can use these results to predict the favorite programming languages for places that weren't part of our survey.

As usual, a good first step is plotting the data (Figure 12-1):

```
# key is language, value is pair (longitudes, latitudes)
plots = { "Java" : ([], []), "Python" : ([], []), "R" : ([], []) }

# we want each language to have a different marker and color
markers = { "Java" : "o", "Python" : "s", "R" : "^" }
colors  = { "Java" : "r", "Python" : "b", "R" : "g" }

for (longitude, latitude), language in cities:
    plots[language][0].append(longitude)
    plots[language][1].append(latitude)

# create a scatter series for each language
for language, (x, y) in plots.iteritems():
    plt.scatter(x, y, color=colors[language], marker=markers[language],
```

```
                           label=language, zorder=10)

plot_state_borders(plt)        # pretend we have a function that does this

plt.legend(loc=0)              # let matplotlib choose the location
plt.axis([-130,-60,20,55])     # set the axes

plt.title("Favorite Programming Languages")
plt.show()
```

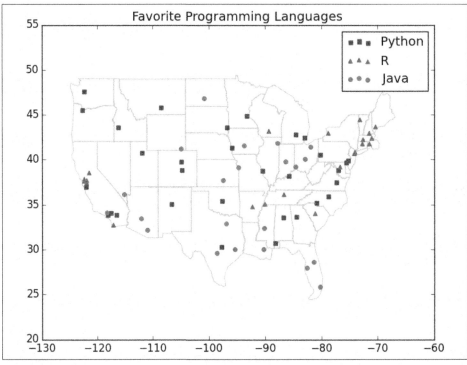

Figure 12-1. Favorite programming languages

 You may have noticed the call to `plot_state_borders()`, a function that we haven't actually defined. There's an implementation on the book's GitHub page (*http://bit.ly/1ycP2M8*), but it's a good exercise to try to do it yourself:

1. Search the Web for something like *state boundaries latitude longitude*.

2. Convert whatever data you can find into a list of segments [(long1, lat1), (long2, lat2)].

3. Use `plt.plot()` to draw the segments.

Since it looks like nearby places tend to like the same language, *k*-nearest neighbors seems like a reasonable choice for a predictive model.

To start with, let's look at what happens if we try to predict each city's preferred language using its neighbors other than itself:

```
# try several different values for k
for k in [1, 3, 5, 7]:
    num_correct = 0

    for city in cities:
        location, actual_language = city
        other_cities = [other_city
                        for other_city in cities
                        if other_city != city]

        predicted_language = knn_classify(k, other_cities, location)

        if predicted_language == actual_language:
            num_correct += 1

    print k, "neighbor[s]:", num_correct, "correct out of", len(cities)
```

It looks like 3-nearest neighbors performs the best, giving the correct result about 59% of the time:

```
1 neighbor[s]: 40 correct out of 75
3 neighbor[s]: 44 correct out of 75
5 neighbor[s]: 41 correct out of 75
7 neighbor[s]: 35 correct out of 75
```

Now we can look at what regions would get classified to which languages under each nearest neighbors scheme. We can do that by classifying an entire grid worth of points, and then plotting them as we did the cities:

```
plots = { "Java" : ([], []), "Python" : ([], []), "R" : ([], []) }

k = 1 # or 3, or 5, or ...

for longitude in range(-130, -60):
    for latitude in range(20, 55):
        predicted_language = knn_classify(k, cities, [longitude, latitude])
        plots[predicted_language][0].append(longitude)
        plots[predicted_language][1].append(latitude)
```

For instance, Figure 12-2 shows what happens when we look at just the nearest neighbor (*k* = 1).

We see lots of abrupt changes from one language to another with sharp boundaries. As we increase the number of neighbors to three, we see smoother regions for each language (Figure 12-3).

And as we increase the neighbors to five, the boundaries get smoother still (Figure 12-4).

Here our dimensions are roughly comparable, but if they weren't you might want to rescale the data as we did in "Rescaling" on page 132.

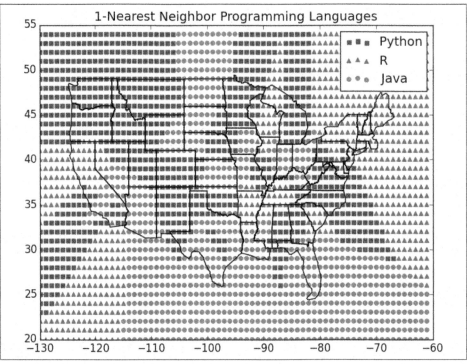

Figure 12-2. 1-Nearest neighbor programming languages

The Curse of Dimensionality

k-nearest neighbors runs into trouble in higher dimensions thanks to the "curse of dimensionality," which boils down to the fact that high-dimensional spaces are *vast*. Points in high-dimensional spaces tend not to be close to one another at all. One way to see this is by randomly generating pairs of points in the d-dimensional "unit cube" in a variety of dimensions, and calculating the distances between them.

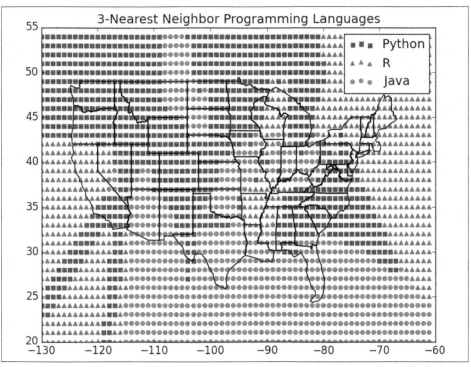

Figure 12-3. 3-Nearest neighbor programming languages

Generating random points should be second nature by now:

```
def random_point(dim):
    return [random.random() for _ in range(dim)]
```

as is writing a function to generate the distances:

```
def random_distances(dim, num_pairs):
    return [distance(random_point(dim), random_point(dim))
            for _ in range(num_pairs)]
```

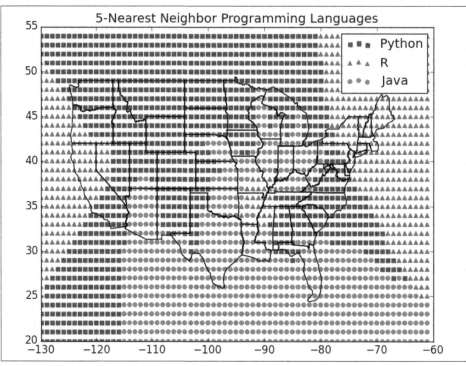

Figure 12-4. 5-Nearest neighbor programming languages

For every dimension from 1 to 100, we'll compute 10,000 distances and use those to compute the average distance between points and the minimum distance between points in each dimension (Figure 12-5):

```
dimensions = range(1, 101)

avg_distances = []
min_distances = []

random.seed(0)
for dim in dimensions:
    distances = random_distances(dim, 10000)    # 10,000 random pairs
    avg_distances.append(mean(distances))       # track the average
    min_distances.append(min(distances))        # track the minimum
```

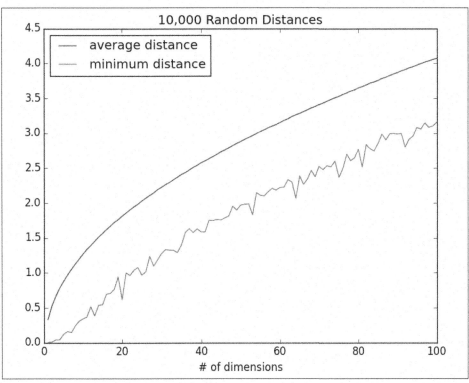

Figure 12-5. The curse of dimensionality

As the number of dimensions increases, the average distance between points increases. But what's more problematic is the ratio between the closest distance and the average distance (Figure 12-6):

```
min_avg_ratio = [min_dist / avg_dist
                 for min_dist, avg_dist in zip(min_distances, avg_distances)]
```

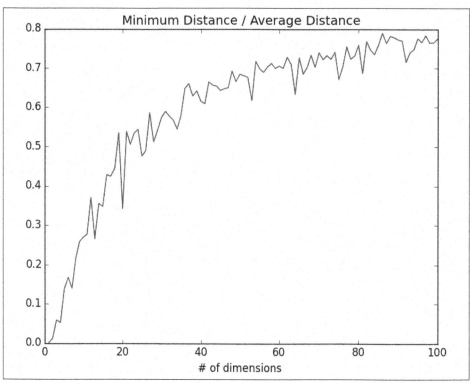

Figure 12-6. The curse of dimensionality again

In low-dimensional data sets, the closest points tend to be much closer than average. But two points are close only if they're close in every dimension, and every extra dimension—even if just noise—is another opportunity for each point to be further away from every other point. When you have a lot of dimensions, it's likely that the closest points aren't much closer than average, which means that two points being close doesn't mean very much (unless there's a lot of structure in your data that makes it behave as if it were much lower-dimensional).

A different way of thinking about the problem involves the sparsity of higher-dimensional spaces.

If you pick 50 random numbers between 0 and 1, you'll probably get a pretty good sample of the unit interval (Figure 12-7).

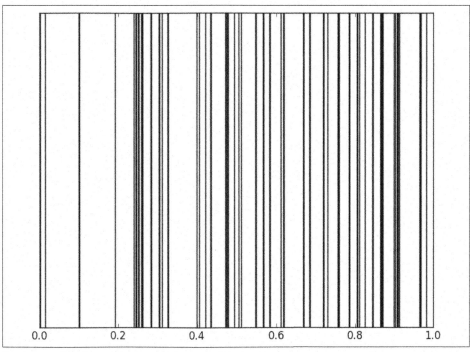

Figure 12-7. Fifty random points in one dimension

If you pick 50 random points in the unit square, you'll get less coverage (Figure 12-8).

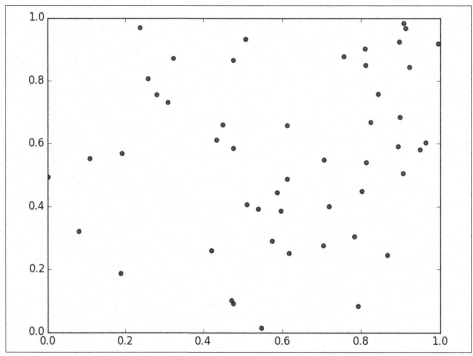

Figure 12-8. Fifty random points in two dimensions

And in three dimensions less still (Figure 12-9).

`matplotlib` doesn't graph four dimensions well, so that's as far as we'll go, but you can see already that there are starting to be large empty spaces with no points near them. In more dimensions—unless you get exponentially more data—those large empty spaces represent regions far from all the points you want to use in your predictions.

So if you're trying to use nearest neighbors in higher dimensions, it's probably a good idea to do some kind of dimensionality reduction first.

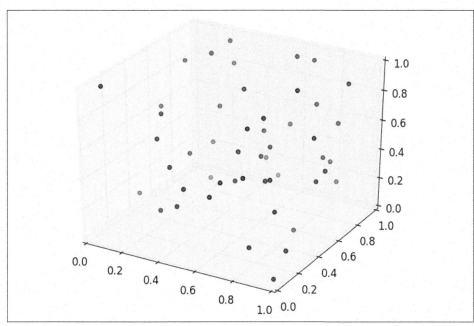

Figure 12-9. Fifty random points in three dimensions

For Further Exploration

scikit-learn has many nearest neighbor (*http://bit.ly/1ycP5rj*) models.

## CHAPTER 13

Naive Bayes

It is well for the heart to be naive and for the mind not to be.
—Anatole France

A social network isn't much good if people can't network. Accordingly, DataSciencester has a popular feature that allows members to send messages to other members. And while most of your members are responsible citizens who send only well-received "how's it going?" messages, a few miscreants persistently spam other members about get-rich schemes, no-prescription-required pharmaceuticals, and for-profit data science credentialing programs. Your users have begun to complain, and so the VP of Messaging has asked you to use data science to figure out a way to filter out these spam messages.

A Really Dumb Spam Filter

Imagine a "universe" that consists of receiving a message chosen randomly from all possible messages. Let S be the event "the message is spam" and V be the event "the message contains the word *viagra*." Then Bayes's Theorem tells us that the probability that the message is spam conditional on containing the word *viagra* is:

$$P(S \mid V) = [P(V \mid S)P(S)]/[P(V \mid S)P(S) + P(V \mid \neg S)P(\neg S)]$$

The numerator is the probability that a message is spam *and* contains *viagra*, while the denominator is just the probability that a message contains *viagra*. Hence you can think of this calculation as simply representing the proportion of *viagra* messages that are spam.

If we have a large collection of messages we know are spam, and a large collection of messages we know are not spam, then we can easily estimate $P(V \mid S)$ and $P(V \mid \neg S)$. If we further assume that any message is equally likely to be spam or not-spam (so that $P(S) = P(\neg S) = 0.5$), then:

$$P(S|V) = P(V|S)/[P(V|S) + P(V|\neg S)]$$

For example, if 50% of spam messages have the word *viagra*, but only 1% of nonspam messages do, then the probability that any given *viagra*-containing email is spam is:

$$0.5/(0.5 + 0.01) = 98\%$$

A More Sophisticated Spam Filter

Imagine now that we have a vocabulary of many words $w_1, ..., w_n$. To move this into the realm of probability theory, we'll write X_i for the event "a message contains the word w_i." Also imagine that (through some unspecified-at-this-point process) we've come up with an estimate $P(X_i|S)$ for the probability that a spam message contains the ith word, and a similar estimate $P(X_i|\neg S)$ for the probability that a nonspam message contains the ith word.

The key to Naive Bayes is making the (big) assumption that the presences (or absences) of each word are independent of one another, conditional on a message being spam or not. Intuitively, this assumption means that knowing whether a certain spam message contains the word "viagra" gives you no information about whether that same message contains the word "rolex." In math terms, this means that:

$$P\big(X_1 = x_1, \ldots, X_n = x_n | S\big) = P\big(X_1 = x_1 | S\big) \times \cdots \times P\big(X_n = x_n | S\big)$$

This is an extreme assumption. (There's a reason the technique has "naive" in its name.) Imagine that our vocabulary consists *only* of the words "viagra" and "rolex," and that half of all spam messages are for "cheap viagra" and that the other half are for "authentic rolex." In this case, the Naive Bayes estimate that a spam message contains both "viagra" and "rolex" is:

$$P\big(X_1 = 1, X_2 = 1 | S\big) = P\big(X_1 = 1 | S\big)P\big(X_2 = 1 | S\big) = .5 \times .5 = .25$$

since we've assumed away the knowledge that "viagra" and "rolex" actually never occur together. Despite the unrealisticness of this assumption, this model often performs well and is used in actual spam filters.

The same Bayes's Theorem reasoning we used for our "viagra-only" spam filter tells us that we can calculate the probability a message is spam using the equation:

$$P(S \mid X = x) = P(X = x \mid S) / [P(X = x \mid S) + P(X = x \mid \neg S)]$$

The Naive Bayes assumption allows us to compute each of the probabilities on the right simply by multiplying together the individual probability estimates for each vocabulary word.

In practice, you usually want to avoid multiplying lots of probabilities together, to avoid a problem called *underflow*, in which computers don't deal well with floating-point numbers that are too close to zero. Recalling from algebra that $\log(ab) = \log a + \log b$ and that $\exp(\log x) = x$, we usually compute $p_1 * \cdots * p_n$ as the equivalent (but floating-point-friendlier):

$$\exp\left(\log(p_1) + \cdots + \log(p_n)\right)$$

The only challenge left is coming up with estimates for $P(X_i \mid S)$ and $P(X_i \mid \neg S)$, the probabilities that a spam message (or nonspam message) contains the word w_i. If we have a fair number of "training" messages labeled as spam and not-spam, an obvious first try is to estimate $P(X_i \mid S)$ simply as the fraction of spam messages containing word w_i.

This causes a big problem, though. Imagine that in our training set the vocabulary word "data" only occurs in nonspam messages. Then we'd estimate $P(\text{"data"} \mid S) = 0$. The result is that our Naive Bayes classifier would always assign spam probability 0 to *any* message containing the word "data," even a message like "data on cheap viagra and authentic rolex watches." To avoid this problem, we usually use some kind of smoothing.

In particular, we'll choose a *pseudocount—k—*and estimate the probability of seeing the *i*th word in a spam as:

$$P(X_i \mid S) = \left(k + \text{number of spams containing } w_i\right) / (2k + \text{number of spams})$$

Similarly for $P(X_i \mid \neg S)$. That is, when computing the spam probabilities for the *i*th word, we assume we also saw k additional spams containing the word and k additional spams not containing the word.

For example, if "data" occurs in 0/98 spam documents, and if k is 1, we estimate $P(\text{"data"} \mid S)$ as 1/100 = 0.01, which allows our classifier to still assign some nonzero spam probability to messages that contain the word "data."

Implementation

Now we have all the pieces we need to build our classifier. First, let's create a simple function to tokenize messages into distinct words. We'll first convert each message to lowercase; use re.findall() to extract "words" consisting of letters, numbers, and apostrophes; and finally use set() to get just the distinct words:

```
def tokenize(message):
    message = message.lower()                       # convert to lowercase
    all_words = re.findall("[a-z0-9']+", message)   # extract the words
    return set(all_words)                           # remove duplicates
```

Our second function will count the words in a labeled training set of messages. We'll have it return a dictionary whose keys are words, and whose values are two-element lists [spam_count, non_spam_count] corresponding to how many times we saw that word in both spam and nonspam messages:

```
def count_words(training_set):
    """training set consists of pairs (message, is_spam)"""
    counts = defaultdict(lambda: [0, 0])
    for message, is_spam in training_set:
        for word in tokenize(message):
            counts[word][0 if is_spam else 1] += 1
    return counts
```

Our next step is to turn these counts into estimated probabilities using the smoothing we described before. Our function will return a list of triplets containing each word, the probability of seeing that word in a spam message, and the probability of seeing that word in a nonspam message:

```
def word_probabilities(counts, total_spams, total_non_spams, k=0.5):
    """turn the word_counts into a list of triplets
    w, p(w | spam) and p(w | ~spam)"""
    return [(w,
             (spam + k) / (total_spams + 2 * k),
             (non_spam + k) / (total_non_spams + 2 * k))
            for w, (spam, non_spam) in counts.iteritems()]
```

The last piece is to use these word probabilities (and our Naive Bayes assumptions) to assign probabilities to messages:

```
def spam_probability(word_probs, message):
    message_words = tokenize(message)
    log_prob_if_spam = log_prob_if_not_spam = 0.0

    # iterate through each word in our vocabulary
    for word, prob_if_spam, prob_if_not_spam in word_probs:

        # if *word* appears in the message,
        # add the log probability of seeing it
        if word in message_words:
```

```
            log_prob_if_spam += math.log(prob_if_spam)
            log_prob_if_not_spam += math.log(prob_if_not_spam)

        # if *word* doesn't appear in the message
        # add the log probability of _not_ seeing it
        # which is log(1 - probability of seeing it)
        else:
            log_prob_if_spam += math.log(1.0 - prob_if_spam)
            log_prob_if_not_spam += math.log(1.0 - prob_if_not_spam)

    prob_if_spam = math.exp(log_prob_if_spam)
    prob_if_not_spam = math.exp(log_prob_if_not_spam)
    return prob_if_spam / (prob_if_spam + prob_if_not_spam)
```

We can put this all together into our Naive Bayes Classifier:

```
class NaiveBayesClassifier:

    def __init__(self, k=0.5):
        self.k = k
        self.word_probs = []

    def train(self, training_set):

        # count spam and non-spam messages
        num_spams = len([is_spam
                        for message, is_spam in training_set
                        if is_spam])
        num_non_spams = len(training_set) - num_spams

        # run training data through our "pipeline"
        word_counts = count_words(training_set)
        self.word_probs = word_probabilities(word_counts,
                                             num_spams,
                                             num_non_spams,
                                             self.k)

    def classify(self, message):
        return spam_probability(self.word_probs, message)
```

Testing Our Model

A good (if somewhat old) data set is the SpamAssassin public corpus (*https://spamas sassin.apache.org/publiccorpus/*). We'll look at the files prefixed with *20021010*. (On Windows, you might need a program like 7-Zip (*http://www.7-zip.org/*) to decompress and extract them.)

After extracting the data (to, say, *C:\spam*) you should have three folders: *spam*, *easy_ham*, and *hard_ham*. Each folder contains many emails, each contained in a single file. To keep things *really* simple, we'll just look at the subject lines of each email.

How do we identify the subject line? Looking through the files, they all seem to start with "Subject:". So we'll look for that:

```
import glob, re

# modify the path with wherever you've put the files
path = r"C:\spam\*\*"

data = []

# glob.glob returns every filename that matches the wildcarded path
for fn in glob.glob(path):
    is_spam = "ham" not in fn

    with open(fn,'r') as file:
        for line in file:
            if line.startswith("Subject:"):
                # remove the leading "Subject: " and keep what's left
                subject = re.sub(r"^Subject: ", "", line).strip()
                data.append((subject, is_spam))
```

Now we can split the data into training data and test data, and then we're ready to build a classifier:

```
random.seed(0)      # just so you get the same answers as me
train_data, test_data = split_data(data, 0.75)

classifier = NaiveBayesClassifier()
classifier.train(train_data)
```

And then we can check how our model does:

```
# triplets (subject, actual is_spam, predicted spam probability)
classified = [(subject, is_spam, classifier.classify(subject))
              for subject, is_spam in test_data]

# assume that spam_probability > 0.5 corresponds to spam prediction
# and count the combinations of (actual is_spam, predicted is_spam)
counts = Counter((is_spam, spam_probability > 0.5)
                 for _, is_spam, spam_probability in classified)
```

This gives 101 true positives (spam classified as "spam"), 33 false positives (ham classified as "spam"), 704 true negatives (ham classified as "ham"), and 38 false negatives (spam classified as "ham"). This means our precision is 101 / (101 + 33) = 75%, and our recall is 101 / (101 + 38) = 73%, which are not bad numbers for such a simple model.

It's also interesting to look at the most misclassified:

```
# sort by spam_probability from smallest to largest
classified.sort(key=lambda row: row[2])

# the highest predicted spam probabilities among the non-spams
```

```
    spammiest_hams = filter(lambda row: not row[1], classified)[-5:]

    # the lowest predicted spam probabilities among the actual spams
    hammiest_spams = filter(lambda row: row[1], classified)[:5]
```

The two spammiest hams both have the words "needed" (77 times more likely to appear in spam), "insurance" (30 times more likely to appear in spam), and "important" (10 times more likely to appear in spam).

The hammiest spam is too short ("Re: girls") to make much of a judgment, and the second-hammiest is a credit card solicitation most of whose words weren't in the training set.

We can similarly look at the spammiest *words*:

```
def p_spam_given_word(word_prob):
    """uses bayes's theorem to compute p(spam | message contains word)"""

    # word_prob is one of the triplets produced by word_probabilities
    word, prob_if_spam, prob_if_not_spam = word_prob
    return prob_if_spam / (prob_if_spam + prob_if_not_spam)

words = sorted(classifier.word_probs, key=p_spam_given_word)

spammiest_words = words[-5:]
hammiest_words = words[:5]
```

The spammiest words are "money," "systemworks," "rates," "sale," and "year," all of which seem related to trying to get people to buy things. And the hammiest words are "spambayes," "users," "razor," "zzzzteana," and "sadev," most of which seem related to spam prevention, oddly enough.

How could we get better performance? One obvious way would be to get more data to train on. There are a number of ways to improve the model as well. Here are some possibilities that you might try:

- Look at the message content, not just the subject line. You'll have to be careful how you deal with the message headers.

- Our classifier takes into account every word that appears in the training set, even words that appear only once. Modify the classifier to accept an optional min_count threshhold and ignore tokens that don't appear at least that many times.

- The tokenizer has no notion of similar words (e.g., "cheap" and "cheapest"). Modify the classifier to take an optional stemmer function that converts words to *equivalence classes* of words. For example, a really simple stemmer function might be:

```
def drop_final_s(word):
    return re.sub("s$", "", word)
```

Creating a good stemmer function is hard. People frequently use the Porter Stemmer (*http://tartarus.org/martin/PorterStemmer/*).

- Although our features are all of the form "message contains word w_i," there's no reason why this has to be the case. In our implementation, we could add extra features like "message contains a number" by creating phony tokens like *contains:number* and modifying the `tokenizer` to emit them when appropriate.

For Further Exploration

- Paul Graham's articles "A Plan for Spam" (*http://bit.ly/1ycPcmA*) and "Better Bayesian Filtering" (*http://bit.ly/1ycPbiy*) (are interesting and) give more insight into the ideas behind building spam filters.
- `scikit-learn` (*http://bit.ly/1ycP9ar*) contains a `BernoulliNB` model that implements the same Naive Bayes algorithm we implemented here, as well as other variations on the model.

## CHAPTER 14

Simple Linear Regression

Art, like morality, consists in drawing the line somewhere.
—G. K. Chesterton

In Chapter 5, we used the `correlation` function to measure the strength of the linear relationship between two variables. For most applications, knowing that such a linear relationship exists isn't enough. We'll want to be able to understand the nature of the relationship. This is where we'll use simple linear regression.

The Model

Recall that we were investigating the relationship between a DataSciencester user's number of friends and the amount of time he spent on the site each day. Let's assume that you've convinced yourself that having more friends *causes* people to spend more time on the site, rather than one of the alternative explanations we discussed.

The VP of Engagement asks you to build a model describing this relationship. Since you found a pretty strong linear relationship, a natural place to start is a linear model.

In particular, you hypothesize that there are constants α (alpha) and β (beta) such that:

$$y_i = \beta x_i + \alpha + \varepsilon_i$$

where y_i is the number of minutes user i spends on the site daily, x_i is the number of friends user i has, and ε_i is a (hopefully small) error term representing the fact that there are other factors not accounted for by this simple model.

Assuming we've determined such an `alpha` and `beta`, then we make predictions simply with:

```
def predict(alpha, beta, x_i):
    return beta * x_i + alpha
```

How do we choose `alpha` and `beta`? Well, any choice of `alpha` and `beta` gives us a predicted output for each input `x_i`. Since we know the actual output `y_i` we can compute the error for each pair:

```
def error(alpha, beta, x_i, y_i):
    """the error from predicting beta * x_i + alpha
    when the actual value is y_i"""
    return y_i - predict(alpha, beta, x_i)
```

What we'd really like to know is the total error over the entire data set. But we don't want to just add the errors—if the prediction for `x_1` is too high and the prediction for `x_2` is too low, the errors may just cancel out.

So instead we add up the *squared* errors:

```
def sum_of_squared_errors(alpha, beta, x, y):
    return sum(error(alpha, beta, x_i, y_i) ** 2
               for x_i, y_i in zip(x, y))
```

The *least squares solution* is to choose the `alpha` and `beta` that make `sum_of_squared_errors` as small as possible.

Using calculus (or tedious algebra), the error-minimizing alpha and beta are given by:

```
def least_squares_fit(x, y):
    """given training values for x and y,
    find the least-squares values of alpha and beta"""
    beta = correlation(x, y) * standard_deviation(y) / standard_deviation(x)
    alpha = mean(y) - beta * mean(x)
    return alpha, beta
```

Without going through the exact mathematics, let's think about why this might be a reasonable solution. The choice of `alpha` simply says that when we see the average value of the independent variable x, we predict the average value of the dependent variable y.

The choice of `beta` means that when the input value increases by `standard_devia tion(x)`, the prediction increases by `correlation(x, y) * standard_devia tion(y)`. In the case when x and y are perfectly correlated, a one standard deviation increase in x results in a one-standard-deviation-of-y increase in the prediction. When they're perfectly anticorrelated, the increase in x results in a *decrease* in the prediction. And when the correlation is zero, `beta` is zero, which means that changes in x don't affect the prediction at all.

It's easy to apply this to the outlierless data from Chapter 5:

```
alpha, beta = least_squares_fit(num_friends_good, daily_minutes_good)
```

This gives values of alpha = 22.95 and beta = 0.903. So our model says that we expect a user with n friends to spend `22.95 + n * 0.903` minutes on the site each day. That is, we predict that a user with no friends on DataSciencester would still spend about 23 minutes a day on the site. And for each additional friend, we expect a user to spend almost a minute more on the site each day.

In Figure 14-1, we plot the prediction line to get a sense of how well the model fits the observed data.

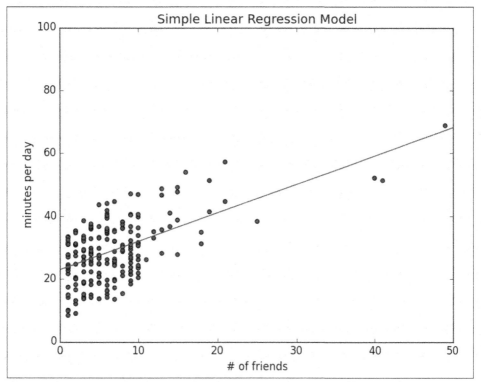

Figure 14-1. Our simple linear model

Of course, we need a better way to figure out how well we've fit the data than staring at the graph. A common measure is the *coefficient of determination* (or *R-squared*), which measures the fraction of the total variation in the dependent variable that is captured by the model:

```
def total_sum_of_squares(y):
    """the total squared variation of y_i's from their mean"""
    return sum(v ** 2 for v in de_mean(y))

def r_squared(alpha, beta, x, y):
```

```
    """the fraction of variation in y captured by the model, which equals
    1 - the fraction of variation in y not captured by the model"""

    return 1.0 - (sum_of_squared_errors(alpha, beta, x, y) /
                    total_sum_of_squares(y))

r_squared(alpha, beta, num_friends_good, daily_minutes_good)    # 0.329
```

Now, we chose the `alpha` and `beta` that minimized the sum of the squared prediction errors. One linear model we could have chosen is "always predict `mean(y)`" (corresponding to `alpha = mean(y)` and `beta = 0`), whose sum of squared errors exactly equals its total sum of squares. This means an R-squared of zero, which indicates a model that (obviously, in this case) performs no better than just predicting the mean.

Clearly, the least squares model must be at least as good as that one, which means that the sum of the squared errors is *at most* the total sum of squares, which means that the R-squared must be at least zero. And the sum of squared errors must be at least 0, which means that the R-squared can be at most 1.

The higher the number, the better our model fits the data. Here we calculate an R-squared of 0.329, which tells us that our model is only sort of okay at fitting the data, and that clearly there are other factors at play.

Using Gradient Descent

If we write `theta = [alpha, beta]`, then we can also solve this using gradient descent:

```
def squared_error(x_i, y_i, theta):
    alpha, beta = theta
    return error(alpha, beta, x_i, y_i) ** 2

def squared_error_gradient(x_i, y_i, theta):
    alpha, beta = theta
    return [-2 * error(alpha, beta, x_i, y_i),       # alpha partial derivative
            -2 * error(alpha, beta, x_i, y_i) * x_i] # beta partial derivative

# choose random value to start
random.seed(0)
theta = [random.random(), random.random()]
alpha, beta = minimize_stochastic(squared_error,
                                  squared_error_gradient,
                                  num_friends_good,
                                  daily_minutes_good,
                                  theta,
                                  0.0001)
print alpha, beta
```

Using the same data we get alpha = 22.93, beta = 0.905, which are very close to the exact answers.

Maximum Likelihood Estimation

Why choose least squares? One justification involves *maximum likelihood estimation*.

Imagine that we have a sample of data $v_1, ..., v_n$ that comes from a distribution that depends on some unknown parameter θ:

$$p(v_1, ..., v_n | \theta)$$

If we didn't know theta, we could turn around and think of this quantity as the *likelihood* of θ given the sample:

$$L(\theta | v_1, ..., v_n)$$

Under this approach, the most likely θ is the value that maximizes this likelihood function; that is, the value that makes the observed data the most probable. In the case of a continuous distribution, in which we have a probability distribution function rather than a probability mass function, we can do the same thing.

Back to regression. One assumption that's often made about the simple regression model is that the regression errors are normally distributed with mean 0 and some (known) standard deviation σ. If that's the case, then the likelihood based on seeing a pair (x_i, y_i) is:

$$L(\alpha, \beta | x_i, y_i, \sigma) = \frac{1}{\sqrt{2\pi}\sigma} \exp\left(-(y_i - \alpha - \beta x_i)^2 / 2\sigma^2\right)$$

The likelihood based on the entire data set is the product of the individual likelihoods, which is largest precisely when `alpha` and `beta` are chosen to minimize the sum of squared errors. That is, in this case (and with these assumptions), minimizing the sum of squared errors is equivalent to maximizing the likelihood of the observed data.

For Further Exploration

Continue reading about multiple regression in Chapter 15!

Multiple Regression

I don't look at a problem and put variables in there that don't affect it.
—Bill Parcells

Although the VP is pretty impressed with your predictive model, she thinks you can do better. To that end, you've collected additional data: for each of your users, you know how many hours he works each day, and whether he has a PhD. You'd like to use this additional data to improve your model.

Accordingly, you hypothesize a linear model with more independent variables:

$$\text{minutes} = \alpha + \beta_1 \text{friends} + \beta_2 \text{work hours} + \beta_3 \text{phd} + \varepsilon$$

Obviously, whether a user has a PhD is not a number, but—as we mentioned in Chapter 11—we can introduce a *dummy variable* that equals 1 for users with PhDs and 0 for users without, after which it's just as numeric as the other variables.

The Model

Recall that in Chapter 14 we fit a model of the form:

$$y_i = \alpha + \beta x_i + \varepsilon_i$$

Now imagine that each input x_i is not a single number but rather a vector of k numbers $x_{i1}, ..., x_{ik}$. The multiple regression model assumes that:

$$y_i = \alpha + \beta_1 x_{i1} + \ . \ . \ . \ + \beta_k x_{ik} + \varepsilon_i$$

In multiple regression the vector of parameters is usually called β. We'll want this to include the constant term as well, which we can achieve by adding a column of ones to our data:

```
beta = [alpha, beta_1, ..., beta_k]
```

and:

```
x_i = [1, x_i1, ..., x_ik]
```

Then our model is just:

```
def predict(x_i, beta):
    """assumes that the first element of each x_i is 1"""
    return dot(x_i, beta)
```

In this particular case, our independent variable x will be a list of vectors, each of which looks like this:

```
[1,     # constant term
 49,    # number of friends
 4,     # work hours per day
 0]     # doesn't have PhD
```

Further Assumptions of the Least Squares Model

There are a couple of further assumptions that are required for this model (and our solution) to make sense.

The first is that the columns of *x* are *linearly independent*—that there's no way to write any one as a weighted sum of some of the others. If this assumption fails, it's impossible to estimate beta. To see this in an extreme case, imagine we had an extra field num_acquaintances in our data that for every user was exactly equal to num_friends.

Then, starting with any beta, if we add *any* amount to the num_friends coefficient and subtract that same amount from the num_acquaintances coefficient, the model's predictions will remain unchanged. Which means that there's no way to find *the* coefficient for num_friends. (Usually violations of this assumption won't be so obvious.)

The second important assumption is that the columns of *x* are all uncorrelated with the errors ε. If this fails to be the case, our estimates of beta will be systematically wrong.

For instance, in Chapter 14, we built a model that predicted that each additional friend was associated with an extra 0.90 daily minutes on the site.

Imagine that it's also the case that:

- People who work more hours spend less time on the site.

- People with more friends tend to work more hours.

That is, imagine that the "actual" model is:

$$\text{minutes} = \alpha + \beta_1 \text{friends} + \beta_2 \text{work hours} + \varepsilon$$

and that work hours and friends are positively correlated. In that case, when we minimize the errors of the single variable model:

$$\text{minutes} = \alpha + \beta_1 \text{friends} + \varepsilon$$

we will underestimate β_1.

Think about what would happen if we made predictions using the single variable model with the "actual" value of β_1. (That is, the value that arises from minimizing the errors of what we called the "actual" model.) The predictions would tend to be too small for users who work many hours and too large for users who work few hours, because $\beta_2 > 0$ and we "forgot" to include it. Because work hours is positively correlated with number of friends, this means the predictions tend to be too small for users with many friends and too large for users with few friends.

The result of this is that we can reduce the errors (in the single-variable model) by decreasing our estimate of β_1, which means that the error-minimizing β_1 is smaller than the "actual" value. That is, in this case the single-variable least squares solution is biased to underestimate β_1. And, in general, whenever the independent variables are correlated with the errors like this, our least squares solution will give us a biased estimate of β.

Fitting the Model

As we did in the simple linear model, we'll choose `beta` to minimize the sum of squared errors. Finding an exact solution is not simple to do by hand, which means we'll need to use gradient descent. We'll start by creating an error function to minimize. For stochastic gradient descent, we'll just want the squared error corresponding to a single prediction:

```
def error(x_i, y_i, beta):
    return y_i - predict(x_i, beta)

def squared_error(x_i, y_i, beta):
    return error(x_i, y_i, beta) ** 2
```

If you know calculus, you can compute:

```
def squared_error_gradient(x_i, y_i, beta):
    """the gradient (with respect to beta)
    corresponding to the ith squared error term"""
    return [-2 * x_ij * error(x_i, y_i, beta)
            for x_ij in x_i]
```

Otherwise, you'll need to take my word for it.

At this point, we're ready to find the optimal beta using stochastic gradient descent:

```
def estimate_beta(x, y):
    beta_initial = [random.random() for x_i in x[0]]
    return minimize_stochastic(squared_error,
                               squared_error_gradient,
                               x, y,
                               beta_initial,
                               0.001)

random.seed(0)
beta = estimate_beta(x, daily_minutes_good) # [30.63, 0.972, -1.868, 0.911]
```

This means our model looks like:

$$\text{minutes} = 30.63 + 0.972\ \text{friends} - 1.868\ \text{work hours} + 0.911\ \text{phd}$$

Interpreting the Model

You should think of the coefficients of the model as representing all-else-being-equal estimates of the impacts of each factor. All else being equal, each additional friend corresponds to an extra minute spent on the site each day. All else being equal, each additional hour in a user's workday corresponds to about two fewer minutes spent on the site each day. All else being equal, having a PhD is associated with spending an extra minute on the site each day.

What this doesn't (directly) tell us is anything about the interactions among the variables. It's possible that the effect of work hours is different for people with many friends than it is for people with few friends. This model doesn't capture that. One way to handle this case is to introduce a new variable that is the *product* of "friends" and "work hours." This effectively allows the "work hours" coefficient to increase (or decrease) as the number of friends increases.

Or it's possible that the more friends you have, the more time you spend on the site *up to a point*, after which further friends cause you to spend less time on the site. (Perhaps with too many friends the experience is just too overwhelming?) We could try to capture this in our model by adding another variable that's the *square* of the number of friends.

Once we start adding variables, we need to worry about whether their coefficients "matter." There are no limits to the numbers of products, logs, squares, and higher powers we could add.

Goodness of Fit

Again we can look at the R-squared, which has now increased to 0.68:

```
def multiple_r_squared(x, y, beta):
    sum_of_squared_errors = sum(error(x_i, y_i, beta) ** 2
                                for x_i, y_i in zip(x, y))
    return 1.0 - sum_of_squared_errors / total_sum_of_squares(y)
```

Keep in mind, however, that adding new variables to a regression will *necessarily* increase the R-squared. After all, the simple regression model is just the special case of the multiple regression model where the coefficients on "work hours" and "PhD" both equal 0. The optimal multiple regression model will necessarily have an error at least as small as that one.

Because of this, in a multiple regression, we also need to look at the *standard errors* of the coefficients, which measure how certain we are about our estimates of each β_i. The regression as a whole may fit our data very well, but if some of the independent variables are correlated (or irrelevant), their coefficients might not *mean* much.

The typical approach to measuring these errors starts with another assumption—that the errors ε_i are independent normal random variables with mean 0 and some shared (unknown) standard deviation σ. In that case, we (or, more likely, our statistical software) can use some linear algebra to find the standard error of each coefficient. The larger it is, the less sure our model is about that coefficient. Unfortunately, we're not set up to do that kind of linear algebra from scratch.

Digression: The Bootstrap

Imagine we have a sample of n data points, generated by some (unknown to us) distribution:

```
data = get_sample(num_points=n)
```

In Chapter 5, we wrote a function to compute the `median` of the observed data, which we can use as an estimate of the median of the distribution itself.

But how confident can we be about our estimate? If all the data in the sample are very close to 100, then it seems likely that the actual median is close to 100. If approximately half the data in the sample is close to 0 and the other half is close to 200, then we can't be nearly as certain about the median.

If we could repeatedly get new samples, we could compute the median of each and look at the distribution of those medians. Usually we can't. What we can do instead is *bootstrap* new data sets by choosing *n* data points *with replacement* from our data and then compute the medians of those synthetic data sets:

```
def bootstrap_sample(data):
    """randomly samples len(data) elements with replacement"""
    return [random.choice(data) for _ in data]

def bootstrap_statistic(data, stats_fn, num_samples):
    """evaluates stats_fn on num_samples bootstrap samples from data"""
    return [stats_fn(bootstrap_sample(data))
            for _ in range(num_samples)]
```

For example, consider the two following data sets:

```
# 101 points all very close to 100
close_to_100 = [99.5 + random.random() for _ in range(101)]

# 101 points, 50 of them near 0, 50 of them near 200
far_from_100 = ([99.5 + random.random()] +
                [random.random() for _ in range(50)] +
                [200 + random.random() for _ in range(50)])
```

If you compute the `median` of each, both will be very close to 100. However, if you look at:

```
bootstrap_statistic(close_to_100, median, 100)
```

you will mostly see numbers really close to 100. Whereas if you look at:

```
bootstrap_statistic(far_from_100, median, 100)
```

you will see a lot of numbers close to 0 and a lot of numbers close to 200.

The `standard_deviation` of the first set of medians is close to 0, while the `standard_deviation` of the second set of medians is close to 100. (This extreme a case would be pretty easy to figure out by manually inspecting the data, but in general that won't be true.)

Standard Errors of Regression Coefficients

We can take the same approach to estimating the standard errors of our regression coefficients. We repeatedly take a `bootstrap_sample` of our data and estimate `beta` based on that sample. If the coefficient corresponding to one of the independent variables (say `num_friends`) doesn't vary much across samples, then we can be confident that our estimate is relatively tight. If the coefficient varies greatly across samples, then we can't be at all confident in our estimate.

The only subtlety is that, before sampling, we'll need to `zip` our x data and y data to make sure that corresponding values of the independent and dependent variables are sampled together. This means that `bootstrap_sample` will return a list of pairs (x_i, y_i), which we'll need to reassemble into an x_sample and a y_sample:

```
def estimate_sample_beta(sample):
    """sample is a list of pairs (x_i, y_i)"""
    x_sample, y_sample = zip(*sample) # magic unzipping trick
    return estimate_beta(x_sample, y_sample)

random.seed(0) # so that you get the same results as me

bootstrap_betas = bootstrap_statistic(zip(x, daily_minutes_good),
                                      estimate_sample_beta,
                                      100)
```

After which we can estimate the standard deviation of each coefficient:

```
bootstrap_standard_errors = [
    standard_deviation([beta[i] for beta in bootstrap_betas])
    for i in range(4)]

# [1.174,      # constant term, actual error = 1.19
#  0.079,      # num_friends,   actual error = 0.080
#  0.131,      # unemployed,    actual error = 0.127
#  0.990]      # phd,           actual error = 0.998
```

We can use these to test hypotheses such as "does β_i equal zero?" Under the null hypothesis $\beta_i = 0$ (and with our other assumptions about the distribution of ε_i) the statistic:

$$t_j = \widehat{\beta_j} / \widehat{\sigma_j}$$

which is our estimate of β_j divided by our estimate of its standard error, follows a *Student's t-distribution* with "$n - k$ degrees of freedom."

If we had a `students_t_cdf` function, we could compute *p*-values for each least-squares coefficient to indicate how likely we would be to observe such a value if the actual coefficient were zero. Unfortunately, we don't have such a function. (Although we would if we weren't working from scratch.)

However, as the degrees of freedom get large, the *t*-distribution gets closer and closer to a standard normal. In a situation like this, where *n* is much larger than *k*, we can use `normal_cdf` and still feel good about ourselves:

```
def p_value(beta_hat_j, sigma_hat_j):
    if beta_hat_j > 0:
        # if the coefficient is positive, we need to compute twice the
        # probability of seeing an even *larger* value
```

```
        return 2 * (1 - normal_cdf(beta_hat_j / sigma_hat_j))
    else:
        # otherwise twice the probability of seeing a *smaller* value
        return 2 * normal_cdf(beta_hat_j / sigma_hat_j)

p_value(30.63, 1.174)     # ~0   (constant term)
p_value(0.972, 0.079)     # ~0   (num_friends)
p_value(-1.868, 0.131)    # ~0   (work_hours)
p_value(0.911, 0.990)     # 0.36 (phd)
```

(In a situation not like this, we would probably be using statistical software that knows how to compute the *t*-distribution, as well as how to compute the exact standard errors.)

While most of the coefficients have very small *p*-values (suggesting that they are indeed nonzero), the coefficient for "PhD" is not "significantly" different from zero, which makes it likely that the coefficient for "PhD" is random rather than meaningful.

In more elaborate regression scenarios, you sometimes want to test more elaborate hypotheses about the data, such as "at least one of the β_j is non-zero" or "β_1 equals β_2 and β_3 equals β_4," which you can do with an *F-test*, which, alas, falls outside the scope of this book.

Regularization

In practice, you'd often like to apply linear regression to data sets with large numbers of variables. This creates a couple of extra wrinkles. First, the more variables you use, the more likely you are to overfit your model to the training set. And second, the more nonzero coefficients you have, the harder it is to make sense of them. If the goal is to *explain* some phenomenon, a sparse model with three factors might be more useful than a slightly better model with hundreds.

Regularization is an approach in which we add to the error term a penalty that gets larger as beta gets larger. We then minimize the combined error and penalty. The more importance we place on the penalty term, the more we discourage large coefficients.

For example, in *ridge regression*, we add a penalty proportional to the sum of the squares of the beta_i. (Except that typically we don't penalize beta_0, the constant term.)

```
# alpha is a *hyperparameter* controlling how harsh the penalty is
# sometimes it's called "lambda" but that already means something in Python
def ridge_penalty(beta, alpha):
  return alpha * dot(beta[1:], beta[1:])

def squared_error_ridge(x_i, y_i, beta, alpha):
```

```
    """estimate error plus ridge penalty on beta"""
    return error(x_i, y_i, beta) ** 2 + ridge_penalty(beta, alpha)
```

which you can then plug into gradient descent in the usual way:

```
def ridge_penalty_gradient(beta, alpha):
    """gradient of just the ridge penalty"""
    return [0] + [2 * alpha * beta_j for beta_j in beta[1:]]

def squared_error_ridge_gradient(x_i, y_i, beta, alpha):
    """the gradient corresponding to the ith squared error term
    including the ridge penalty"""
    return vector_add(squared_error_gradient(x_i, y_i, beta),
                      ridge_penalty_gradient(beta, alpha))

def estimate_beta_ridge(x, y, alpha):
    """use gradient descent to fit a ridge regression
    with penalty alpha"""
    beta_initial = [random.random() for x_i in x[0]]
    return minimize_stochastic(partial(squared_error_ridge, alpha=alpha),
                               partial(squared_error_ridge_gradient,
                                       alpha=alpha),
                               x, y,
                               beta_initial,
                               0.001)
```

With `alpha` set to zero, there's no penalty at all and we get the same results as before:

```
random.seed(0)
beta_0 = estimate_beta_ridge(x, daily_minutes_good, alpha=0.0)
# [30.6, 0.97, -1.87, 0.91]
dot(beta_0[1:], beta_0[1:]) # 5.26
multiple_r_squared(x, daily_minutes_good, beta_0) # 0.680
```

As we increase `alpha`, the goodness of fit gets worse, but the size of `beta` gets smaller:

```
beta_0_01 = estimate_beta_ridge(x, daily_minutes_good, alpha=0.01)
# [30.6, 0.97, -1.86, 0.89]
dot(beta_0_01[1:], beta_0_01[1:])  # 5.19
multiple_r_squared(x, daily_minutes_good, beta_0_01)  # 0.680

beta_0_1 = estimate_beta_ridge(x, daily_minutes_good, alpha=0.1)
# [30.8, 0.95, -1.84, 0.54]
dot(beta_0_1[1:], beta_0_1[1:])  # 4.60
multiple_r_squared(x, daily_minutes_good, beta_0_1)  # 0.680

beta_1 = estimate_beta_ridge(x, daily_minutes_good, alpha=1)
# [30.7, 0.90, -1.69, 0.085]
dot(beta_1[1:], beta_1[1:])  # 3.69
multiple_r_squared(x, daily_minutes_good, beta_1)  # 0.676

beta_10 = estimate_beta_ridge(x, daily_minutes_good, alpha=10)
# [28.3, 0.72, -0.91, -0.017]
```

```
dot(beta_10[1:], beta_10[1:])  # 1.36
multiple_r_squared(x, daily_minutes_good, beta_10)  # 0.573
```

In particular, the coefficient on "PhD" vanishes as we increase the penalty, which accords with our previous result that it wasn't significantly different from zero.

 Usually you'd want to rescale your data before using this approach. After all, if you changed years of experience to centuries of experience, its least squares coefficient would increase by a factor of 100 and suddenly get penalized much more, even though it's the same model.

Another approach is *lasso* regression, which uses the penalty:

```
def lasso_penalty(beta, alpha):
    return alpha * sum(abs(beta_i) for beta_i in beta[1:])
```

Whereas the ridge penalty shrank the coefficients overall, the lasso penalty tends to force coefficients to be zero, which makes it good for learning sparse models. Unfortunately, it's not amenable to gradient descent, which means that we won't be able to solve it from scratch.

For Further Exploration

- Regression has a rich and expansive theory behind it. This is another place where you should consider reading a textbook or at least a lot of Wikipedia articles.

- scikit-learn has a linear_model module (*http://bit.ly/1ycPg63*) that provides a Lin earRegression model similar to ours, as well as Ridge regression, Lasso regression, and other types of regularization too.

- Statsmodels (*http://statsmodels.sourceforge.net*) is another Python module that contains (among other things) linear regression models.

## CHAPTER 16

Logistic Regression

A lot of people say there's a fine line between genius and insanity. I don't think there's a fine line, I actually think there's a yawning gulf.

—Bill Bailey

In Chapter 1, we briefly looked at the problem of trying to predict which DataSciencester users paid for premium accounts. Here we'll revisit that problem.

The Problem

We have an anonymized data set of about 200 users, containing each user's salary, her years of experience as a data scientist, and whether she paid for a premium account (Figure 16-1). As is usual with categorical variables, we represent the dependent variable as either 0 (no premium account) or 1 (premium account).

As usual, our data is in a matrix where each row is a list [experience, salary, paid_account]. Let's turn it into the format we need:

```
x = [[1] + row[:2] for row in data]   # each element is [1, experience, salary]
y = [row[2] for row in data]          # each element is paid_account
```

An obvious first attempt is to use linear regression and find the best model:

$$\text{paid account} = \beta_0 + \beta_1 \text{experience} + \beta_2 \text{salary} + \varepsilon$$

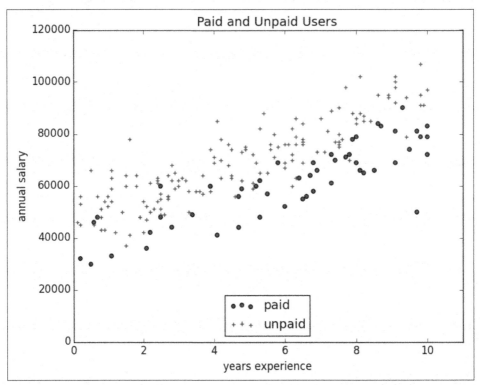

Figure 16-1. Paid and unpaid users

And certainly, there's nothing preventing us from modeling the problem this way. The results are shown in Figure 16-2:

```
rescaled_x = rescale(x)
beta = estimate_beta(rescaled_x, y)  # [0.26, 0.43, -0.43]
predictions = [predict(x_i, beta) for x_i in rescaled_x]

plt.scatter(predictions, y)
plt.xlabel("predicted")
plt.ylabel("actual")
plt.show()
```

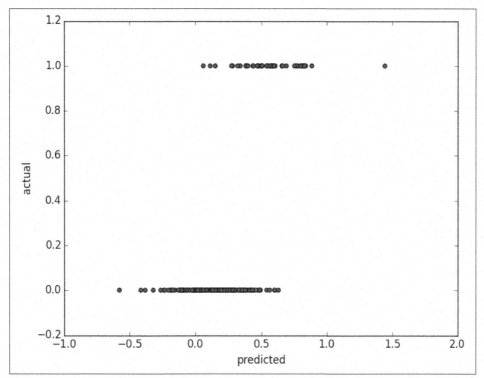

Figure 16-2. Using linear regression to predict premium accounts

But this approach leads to a couple of immediate problems:

- We'd like for our predicted outputs to be 0 or 1, to indicate class membership. It's fine if they're between 0 and 1, since we can interpret these as probabilities—an output of 0.25 could mean 25% chance of being a paid member. But the outputs of the linear model can be huge positive numbers or even negative numbers, which it's not clear how to interpret. Indeed, here a lot of our predictions were negative.

- The linear regression model assumed that the errors were uncorrelated with the columns of x. But here, the regression coefficent for `experience` is 0.43, indicating that more experience leads to a greater likelihood of a premium account. This means that our model outputs very large values for people with lots of experience. But we know that the actual values must be at most 1, which means that necessarily very large outputs (and therefore very large values of `experience`) correspond to very large negative values of the error term. Because this is the case, our estimate of `beta` is biased.

What we'd like instead is for large positive values of `dot(x_i, beta)` to correspond to probabilities close to 1, and for large negative values to correspond to probabilities close to 0. We can accomplish this by applying another function to the result.

The Logistic Function

In the case of logistic regression, we use the *logistic function*, pictured in Figure 16-3:

```
def logistic(x):
    return 1.0 / (1 + math.exp(-x))
```

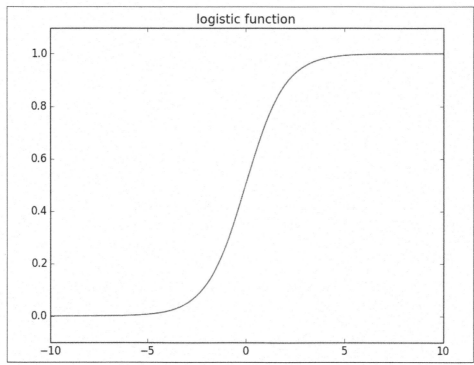

Figure 16-3. The logistic function

As its input gets large and positive, it gets closer and closer to 1. As its input gets large and negative, it gets closer and closer to 0. Additionally, it has the convenient property that its derivative is given by:

```
def logistic_prime(x):
    return logistic(x) * (1 - logistic(x))
```

which we'll make use of in a bit. We'll use this to fit a model:

$$y_i = f(x_i\beta) + \varepsilon_i$$

where f is the `logistic` function.

Recall that for linear regression we fit the model by minimizing the sum of squared errors, which ended up choosing the β that maximized the likelihood of the data.

Here the two aren't equivalent, so we'll use gradient descent to maximize the likelihood directly. This means we need to calculate the likelihood function and its gradient.

Given some β, our model says that each y_i should equal 1 with probability $f(x_i\beta)$ and 0 with probability $1 - f(x_i\beta)$.

In particular, the pdf for y_i can be written as:

$$p(y_i | x_i, \beta) = f(x_i\beta)^{y_i}(1 - f(x_i\beta))^{1 - y_i}$$

since if y_i is 0, this equals:

$$1 - f(x_i\beta)$$

and if y_i is 1, it equals:

$$f(x_i\beta)$$

It turns out that it's actually simpler to maximize the *log likelihood*:

$$\log L(\beta | x_i, y_i) = y_i \log f(x_i\beta) + (1 - y_i) \log (1 - f(x_i\beta))$$

Because log is strictly increasing function, any `beta` that maximizes the log likelihood also maximizes the likelihood, and vice versa.

```
def logistic_log_likelihood_i(x_i, y_i, beta):
    if y_i == 1:
        return math.log(logistic(dot(x_i, beta)))
    else:
        return math.log(1 - logistic(dot(x_i, beta)))
```

If we assume different data points are independent from one another, the overall likelihood is just the product of the individual likelihoods. Which means the overall log likelihood is the sum of the individual log likelihoods:

```
def logistic_log_likelihood(x, y, beta):
    return sum(logistic_log_likelihood_i(x_i, y_i, beta)
              for x_i, y_i in zip(x, y))
```

A little bit of calculus gives us the gradient:

```
def logistic_log_partial_ij(x_i, y_i, beta, j):
    """here i is the index of the data point,
    j the index of the derivative"""

    return (y_i - logistic(dot(x_i, beta))) * x_i[j]

def logistic_log_gradient_i(x_i, y_i, beta):
    """the gradient of the log likelihood
    corresponding to the ith data point"""

    return [logistic_log_partial_ij(x_i, y_i, beta, j)
            for j, _ in enumerate(beta)]

def logistic_log_gradient(x, y, beta):
    return reduce(vector_add,
                  [logistic_log_gradient_i(x_i, y_i, beta)
                   for x_i, y_i in zip(x,y)])
```

at which point we have all the pieces we need.

Applying the Model

We'll want to split our data into a training set and a test set:

```
random.seed(0)
x_train, x_test, y_train, y_test = train_test_split(rescaled_x, y, 0.33)

# want to maximize log likelihood on the training data
fn = partial(logistic_log_likelihood, x_train, y_train)
gradient_fn = partial(logistic_log_gradient, x_train, y_train)

# pick a random starting point
beta_0 = [random.random() for _ in range(3)]

# and maximize using gradient descent
beta_hat = maximize_batch(fn, gradient_fn, beta_0)
```

Alternatively, you could use stochastic gradient descent:

```
beta_hat = maximize_stochastic(logistic_log_likelihood_i,
                               logistic_log_gradient_i,
                               x_train, y_train, beta_0)
```

Either way we find approximately:

```
beta_hat = [-1.90, 4.05, -3.87]
```

These are coefficients for the rescaled data, but we can transform them back to the original data as well:

```
beta_hat_unscaled = [7.61, 1.42, -0.000249]
```

Unfortunately, these are not as easy to interpret as linear regression coefficients. All else being equal, an extra year of experience adds 1.42 to the input of `logistic`. All else being equal, an extra $10,000 of salary subtracts 2.49 from the input of `logistic`.

The impact on the output, however, depends on the other inputs as well. If `dot(beta, x_i)` is already large (corresponding to a probability close to 1), increasing it even by a lot cannot affect the probability very much. If it's close to 0, increasing it just a little might increase the probability quite a bit.

What we can say is that—all else being equal—people with more experience are more likely to pay for accounts. And that—all else being equal—people with higher salaries are less likely to pay for accounts. (This was also somewhat apparent when we plotted the data.)

Goodness of Fit

We haven't yet used the test data that we held out. Let's see what happens if we predict *paid account* whenever the probability exceeds 0.5:

```
true_positives = false_positives = true_negatives = false_negatives = 0

for x_i, y_i in zip(x_test, y_test):
    predict = logistic(dot(beta_hat, x_i))

    if y_i == 1 and predict >= 0.5:  # TP: paid and we predict paid
        true_positives += 1
    elif y_i == 1:                   # FN: paid and we predict unpaid
        false_negatives += 1
    elif predict >= 0.5:            # FP: unpaid and we predict paid
        false_positives += 1
    else:                           # TN: unpaid and we predict unpaid
        true_negatives += 1

precision = true_positives / (true_positives + false_positives)
recall = true_positives / (true_positives + false_negatives)
```

This gives a precision of 93% ("when we predict *paid account* we're right 93% of the time") and a recall of 82% ("when a user has a paid account we predict *paid account* 82% of the time"), both of which are pretty respectable numbers.

We can also plot the predictions versus the actuals (Figure 16-4), which also shows that the model performs well:

```
predictions = [logistic(dot(beta_hat, x_i)) for x_i in x_test]
plt.scatter(predictions, y_test)
plt.xlabel("predicted probability")
plt.ylabel("actual outcome")
plt.title("Logistic Regression Predicted vs. Actual")
plt.show()
```

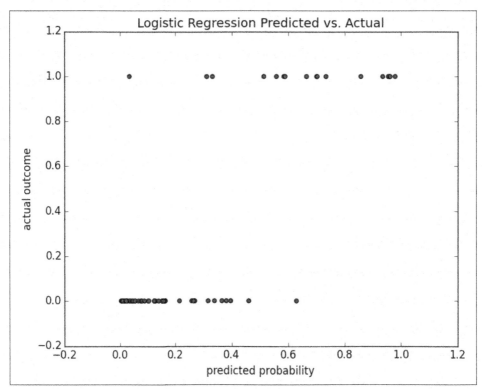

Figure 16-4. Logistic regression predicted versus actual

Support Vector Machines

The set of points where `dot(beta_hat, x_i)` equals 0 is the boundary between our classes. We can plot this to see exactly what our model is doing (Figure 16-5).

This boundary is a *hyperplane* that splits the parameter space into two half-spaces corresponding to *predict paid* and *predict unpaid*. We found it as a side-effect of finding the most likely logistic model.

An alternative approach to classification is to just look for the hyperplane that "best" separates the classes in the training data. This is the idea behind the *support vector machine*, which finds the hyperplane that maximizes the distance to the nearest point in each class (Figure 16-6).

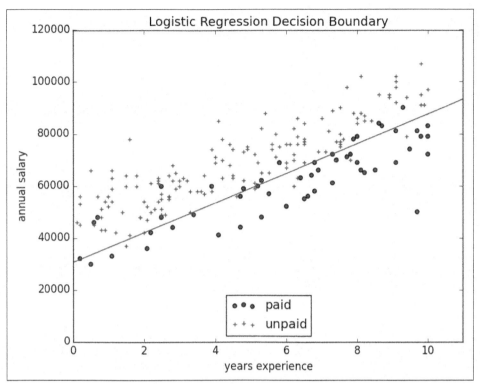

Figure 16-5. Paid and unpaid users with decision boundary

Finding such a hyperplane is an optimization problem that involves techniques that are too advanced for us. A different problem is that a separating hyperplane might not exist at all. In our "who pays?" data set there simply is no line that perfectly separates the paid users from the unpaid users.

We can (sometimes) get around this by transforming the data into a higher-dimensional space. For example, consider the simple one-dimensional data set shown in Figure 16-7.

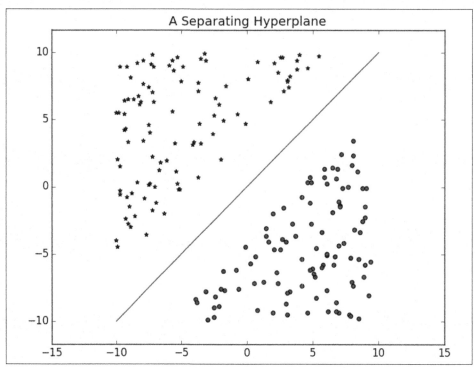

Figure 16-6. A separating hyperplane

It's clear that there's no hyperplane that separates the positive examples from the negative ones. However, look at what happens when we map this data set to two dimensions by sending the point x to (x, x**2). Suddenly it's possible to find a hyperplane that splits the data (Figure 16-8).

This is usually called the *kernel trick* because rather than actually mapping the points into the higher-dimensional space (which could be expensive if there are a lot of points and the mapping is complicated), we can use a "kernel" function to compute dot products in the higher-dimensional space and use those to find a hyperplane.

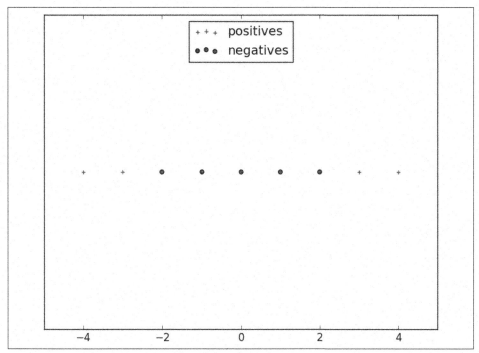

Figure 16-7. A nonseparable one-dimensional data set

It's hard (and probably not a good idea) to *use* support vector machines without rely-ing on specialized optimization software written by people with the appropriate expertise, so we'll have to leave our treatment here.

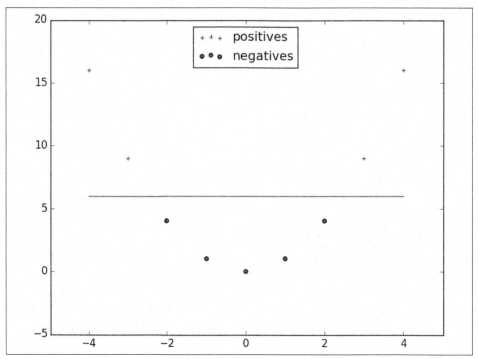

Figure 16-8. Data set becomes separable in higher dimensions

For Further Investigation

- scikit-learn has modules for both Logistic Regression (*http://bit.ly/1xkbywA*) and Support Vector Machines (*http://bit.ly/1xkbBZj*).
- libsvm (*http://bit.ly/1xkbA7t*) is the support vector machine implementation that scikit-learn is using behind the scenes. Its website has a variety of useful documentation about support vector machines.

## CHAPTER 17

Decision Trees

A tree is an incomprehensible mystery.
—Jim Woodring

DataSciencester's VP of Talent has interviewed a number of job candidates from the site, with varying degrees of success. He's collected a data set consisting of several (qualitative) attributes of each candidate, as well as whether that candidate interviewed well or poorly. Could you, he asks, use this data to build a model identifying which candidates will interview well, so that he doesn't have to waste time conducting interviews?

This seems like a good fit for a *decision tree*, another predictive modeling tool in the data scientist's kit.

What Is a Decision Tree?

A decision tree uses a tree structure to represent a number of possible *decision paths* and an outcome for each path.

If you have ever played the game Twenty Questions (*http://en.wikipedia.org/wiki/Twenty_Questions*), then it turns out you are familiar with decision trees. For example:

- "I am thinking of an animal."
- "Does it have more than five legs?"
- "No."
- "Is it delicious?"
- "No."

- "Does it appear on the back of the Australian five-cent coin?"
- "Yes."
- "Is it an echidna?"
- "Yes, it is!"

This corresponds to the path:

"Not more than 5 legs" → "Not delicious" → "On the 5-cent coin" → "Echidna!"

in an idiosyncratic (and not very comprehensive) "guess the animal" decision tree (Figure 17-1).

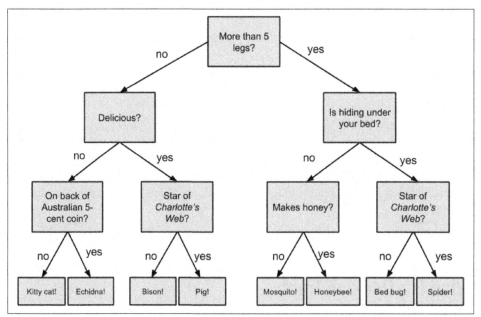

Figure 17-1. A "guess the animal" decision tree

Decision trees have a lot to recommend them. They're very easy to understand and interpret, and the process by which they reach a prediction is completely transparent. Unlike the other models we've looked at so far, decision trees can easily handle a mix of numeric (e.g., number of legs) and categorical (e.g., delicious/not delicious) attributes and can even classify data for which attributes are missing.

At the same time, finding an "optimal" decision tree for a set of training data is computationally a very hard problem. (We will get around this by trying to build a good-enough tree rather than an optimal one, although for large data sets this can still be a lot of work.) More important, it is very easy (and very bad) to build decision trees that are *overfitted* to the training data, and that don't generalize well to unseen data. We'll look at ways to address this.

Most people divide decision trees into *classification trees* (which produce categorical outputs) and *regression trees* (which produce numeric outputs). In this chapter, we'll focus on classification trees, and we'll work through the ID3 algorithm for learning a decision tree from a set of labeled data, which should help us understand how decision trees actually work. To make things simple, we'll restrict ourselves to problems with binary outputs like "should I hire this candidate?" or "should I show this website visitor advertisement A or advertisement B?" or "will eating this food I found in the office fridge make me sick?"

Entropy

In order to build a decision tree, we will need to decide what questions to ask and in what order. At each stage of the tree there are some possibilities we've eliminated and some that we haven't. After learning that an animal doesn't have more than five legs, we've eliminated the possibility that it's a grasshopper. We haven't eliminated the possibility that it's a duck. Every possible question partitions the remaining possibilities according to their answers.

Ideally, we'd like to choose questions whose answers give a lot of information about what our tree should predict. If there's a single yes/no question for which "yes" answers always correspond to `True` outputs and "no" answers to `False` outputs (or vice versa), this would be an awesome question to pick. Conversely, a yes/no question for which neither answer gives you much new information about what the prediction should be is probably not a good choice.

We capture this notion of "how much information" with *entropy*. You have probably heard this used to mean disorder. We use it to represent the uncertainty associated with data.

Imagine that we have a set S of data, each member of which is labeled as belonging to one of a finite number of classes $C_1, ..., C_n$. If all the data points belong to a single class, then there is no real uncertainty, which means we'd like there to be low entropy. If the data points are evenly spread across the classes, there is a lot of uncertainty and we'd like there to be high entropy.

In math terms, if p_i is the proportion of data labeled as class c_i, we define the entropy as:

$$H(S) = -p_1 \log_2 p_1 - ... - p_n \log_2 p_n$$

with the (standard) convention that $0 \log 0 = 0$.

Without worrying too much about the grisly details, each term $-p_i \log_2 p_i$ is nonnegative and is close to zero precisely when p_i is either close to zero or close to one (Figure 17-2).

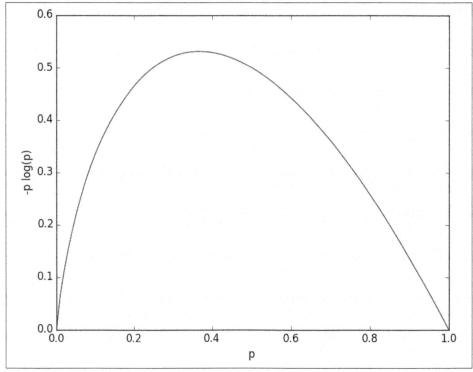

Figure 17-2. A graph of -p log p

This means the entropy will be small when every p_i is close to 0 or 1 (i.e., when most of the data is in a single class), and it will be larger when many of the p_i's are not close to 0 (i.e., when the data is spread across multiple classes). This is exactly the behavior we desire.

It is easy enough to roll all of this into a function:

```
def entropy(class_probabilities):
    """given a list of class probabilities, compute the entropy"""
    return sum(-p * math.log(p, 2)
               for p in class_probabilities
               if p)                        # ignore zero probabilities
```

Our data will consist of pairs (input, label), which means that we'll need to compute the class probabilities ourselves. Observe that we don't actually care which label is associated with each probability, only what the probabilities are:

```
def class_probabilities(labels):
    total_count = len(labels)
    return [count / total_count
            for count in Counter(labels).values()]

def data_entropy(labeled_data):
    labels = [label for _, label in labeled_data]
    probabilities = class_probabilities(labels)
    return entropy(probabilities)
```

The Entropy of a Partition

What we've done so far is compute the entropy (think "uncertainty") of a single set of labeled data. Now, each stage of a decision tree involves asking a question whose answer partitions data into one or (hopefully) more subsets. For instance, our "does it have more than five legs?" question partitions animals into those who have more than five legs (e.g., spiders) and those that don't (e.g., echidnas).

Correspondingly, we'd like some notion of the entropy that results from partitioning a set of data in a certain way. We want a partition to have low entropy if it splits the data into subsets that themselves have low entropy (i.e., are highly certain), and high entropy if it contains subsets that (are large and) have high entropy (i.e., are highly uncertain).

For example, my "Australian five-cent coin" question was pretty dumb (albeit pretty lucky!), as it partitioned the remaining animals at that point into S_1 = {echidna} and S_2 = {everything else}, where S_2 is both large and high-entropy. (S_1 has no entropy but it represents a small fraction of the remaining "classes.")

Mathematically, if we partition our data S into subsets $S_1, ..., S_m$ containing proportions $q_1, ..., q_m$ of the data, then we compute the entropy of the partition as a weighted sum:

$$H = q_1 H(S_1) + \ldots + q_m H(S_m)$$

which we can implement as:

```
def partition_entropy(subsets):
    """find the entropy from this partition of data into subsets
    subsets is a list of lists of labeled data"""

    total_count = sum(len(subset) for subset in subsets)

    return sum( data_entropy(subset) * len(subset) / total_count
                for subset in subsets )
```

One problem with this approach is that partitioning by an attribute with many different values will result in a very low entropy due to overfitting. For example, imagine you work for a bank and are trying to build a decision tree to predict which of your customers are likely to default on their mortgages, using some historical data as your training set. Imagine further that the data set contains each customer's Social Security number. Partitioning on SSN will produce one-person subsets, each of which necessarily has zero entropy. But a model that relies on SSN is *certain* not to generalize beyond the training set. For this reason, you should probably try to avoid (or bucket, if appropriate) attributes with large numbers of possible values when creating decision trees.

Creating a Decision Tree

The VP provides you with the interviewee data, consisting of (per your specification) pairs (input, label), where each input is a dict of candidate attributes, and each label is either True (the candidate interviewed well) or False (the candidate interviewed poorly). In particular, you are provided with each candidate's level, her preferred language, whether she is active on Twitter, and whether she has a PhD:

```
inputs = [
    ({'level':'Senior', 'lang':'Java', 'tweets':'no', 'phd':'no'},    False),
    ({'level':'Senior', 'lang':'Java', 'tweets':'no', 'phd':'yes'},   False),
    ({'level':'Mid', 'lang':'Python', 'tweets':'no', 'phd':'no'},      True),
    ({'level':'Junior', 'lang':'Python', 'tweets':'no', 'phd':'no'},   True),
    ({'level':'Junior', 'lang':'R', 'tweets':'yes', 'phd':'no'},       True),
    ({'level':'Junior', 'lang':'R', 'tweets':'yes', 'phd':'yes'},     False),
    ({'level':'Mid', 'lang':'R', 'tweets':'yes', 'phd':'yes'},         True),
    ({'level':'Senior', 'lang':'Python', 'tweets':'no', 'phd':'no'},  False),
    ({'level':'Senior', 'lang':'R', 'tweets':'yes', 'phd':'no'},       True),
    ({'level':'Junior', 'lang':'Python', 'tweets':'yes', 'phd':'no'},  True),
    ({'level':'Senior', 'lang':'Python', 'tweets':'yes', 'phd':'yes'}, True),
    ({'level':'Mid', 'lang':'Python', 'tweets':'no', 'phd':'yes'},     True),
    ({'level':'Mid', 'lang':'Java', 'tweets':'yes', 'phd':'no'},       True),
    ({'level':'Junior', 'lang':'Python', 'tweets':'no', 'phd':'yes'}, False)
]
```

Our tree will consist of *decision nodes* (which ask a question and direct us differently depending on the answer) and *leaf nodes* (which give us a prediction). We will build it using the relatively simple *ID3* algorithm, which operates in the following manner. Let's say we're given some labeled data, and a list of attributes to consider branching on.

- If the data all have the same label, then create a leaf node that predicts that label and then stop.

- If the list of attributes is empty (i.e., there are no more possible questions to ask), then create a leaf node that predicts the most common label and then stop.
- Otherwise, try partitioning the data by each of the attributes
- Choose the partition with the lowest partition entropy
- Add a decision node based on the chosen attribute
- Recur on each partitioned subset using the remaining attributes

This is what's known as a "greedy" algorithm because, at each step, it chooses the most immediately best option. Given a data set, there may be a better tree with a worse-looking first move. If so, this algorithm won't find it. Nonetheless, it is relatively easy to understand and implement, which makes it a good place to begin exploring decision trees.

Let's manually go through these steps on the interviewee data set. The data set has both True and False labels, and we have four attributes we can split on. So our first step will be to find the partition with the least entropy. We'll start by writing a function that does the partitioning:

```
def partition_by(inputs, attribute):
    """each input is a pair (attribute_dict, label).
    returns a dict : attribute_value -> inputs"""
    groups = defaultdict(list)
    for input in inputs:
        key = input[0][attribute]     # get the value of the specified attribute
        groups[key].append(input)     # then add this input to the correct list
    return groups
```

and one that uses it to compute entropy:

```
def partition_entropy_by(inputs, attribute):
    """computes the entropy corresponding to the given partition"""
    partitions = partition_by(inputs, attribute)
    return partition_entropy(partitions.values())
```

Then we just need to find the minimum-entropy partition for the whole data set:

```
for key in ['level','lang','tweets','phd']:
    print key, partition_entropy_by(inputs, key)

# level 0.693536138896
# lang 0.860131712855
# tweets 0.788450457308
# phd 0.892158928262
```

The lowest entropy comes from splitting on level, so we'll need to make a subtree for each possible level value. Every Mid candidate is labeled True, which means that the Mid subtree is simply a leaf node predicting True. For Senior candidates, we have a mix of Trues and Falses, so we need to split again:

```
senior_inputs = [(input, label)
                 for input, label in inputs if input["level"] == "Senior"]

for key in ['lang', 'tweets', 'phd']:
    print key, partition_entropy_by(senior_inputs, key)

# lang 0.4
# tweets 0.0
# phd 0.950977500433
```

This shows us that our next split should be on `tweets`, which results in a zero-entropy partition. For these Senior-level candidates, "yes" tweets always result in `True` while "no" tweets always result in `False`.

Finally, if we do the same thing for the `Junior` candidates, we end up splitting on phd, after which we find that no PhD always results in `True` and PhD always results in `False`.

Figure 17-3 shows the complete decision tree.

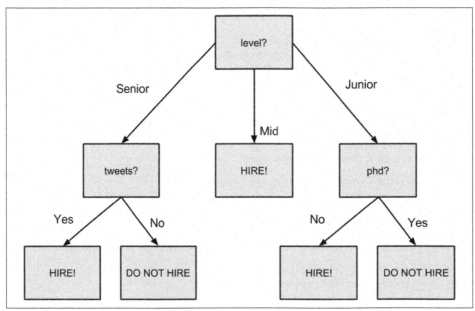

Figure 17-3. The decision tree for hiring

Putting It All Together

Now that we've seen how the algorithm works, we would like to implement it more generally. This means we need to decide how we want to represent trees. We'll use pretty much the most lightweight representation possible. We define a *tree* to be one of the following:

- True

- False

- a tuple (`attribute`, `subtree_dict`)

Here `True` represents a leaf node that returns `True` for any input, `False` represents a leaf node that returns `False` for any input, and a tuple represents a decision node that, for any input, finds its `attribute` value, and classifies the input using the corresponding subtree.

With this representation, our hiring tree would look like:

```
('level',
 {'Junior': ('phd', {'no': True, 'yes': False}),
  'Mid': True,
  'Senior': ('tweets', {'no': False, 'yes': True})})
```

There's still the question of what to do if we encounter an unexpected (or missing) attribute value. What should our hiring tree do if it encounters a candidate whose `level` is "Intern"? We'll handle this case by adding a `None` key that just predicts the most common label. (Although this would be a bad idea if `None` is actually a value that appears in the data.)

Given such a representation, we can classify an input with:

```python
def classify(tree, input):
    """classify the input using the given decision tree"""

    # if this is a leaf node, return its value
    if tree in [True, False]:
        return tree

    # otherwise this tree consists of an attribute to split on
    # and a dictionary whose keys are values of that attribute
    # and whose values of are subtrees to consider next
    attribute, subtree_dict = tree

    subtree_key = input.get(attribute)      # None if input is missing attribute

    if subtree_key not in subtree_dict:     # if no subtree for key,
        subtree_key = None                  # we'll use the None subtree

    subtree = subtree_dict[subtree_key]     # choose the appropriate subtree
    return classify(subtree, input)         # and use it to classify the input
```

All that's left is to build the tree representation from our training data:

```python
def build_tree_id3(inputs, split_candidates=None):

    # if this is our first pass,
    # all keys of the first input are split candidates
```

```
    if split_candidates is None:
        split_candidates = inputs[0][0].keys()

    # count Trues and Falses in the inputs
    num_inputs = len(inputs)
    num_trues = len([label for item, label in inputs if label])
    num_falses = num_inputs - num_trues

    if num_trues == 0: return False     # no Trues? return a "False" leaf
    if num_falses == 0: return True     # no Falses? return a "True" leaf

    if not split_candidates:            # if no split candidates left
        return num_trues >= num_falses  # return the majority leaf

    # otherwise, split on the best attribute
    best_attribute = min(split_candidates,
                        key=partial(partition_entropy_by, inputs))

    partitions = partition_by(inputs, best_attribute)
    new_candidates = [a for a in split_candidates
                        if a != best_attribute]

    # recursively build the subtrees
    subtrees = { attribute_value : build_tree_id3(subset, new_candidates)
                for attribute_value, subset in partitions.iteritems() }

    subtrees[None] = num_trues > num_falses      # default case

    return (best_attribute, subtrees)
```

In the tree we built, every leaf consisted entirely of `True` inputs or entirely of `False` inputs. This means that the tree predicts perfectly on the training data set. But we can also apply it to new data that wasn't in the training set:

```
tree = build_tree_id3(inputs)

classify(tree, { "level" : "Junior",
                 "lang" : "Java",
                 "tweets" : "yes",
                 "phd" : "no"} )         # True

classify(tree, { "level" : "Junior",
                 "lang" : "Java",
                 "tweets" : "yes",
                 "phd" : "yes"} )        # False
```

And also to data with missing or unexpected values:

```
classify(tree, { "level" : "Intern" } ) # True
classify(tree, { "level" : "Senior" } ) # False
```

Since our goal was mainly to demonstrate *how* to build a tree, we built the tree using the entire data set. As always, if we were really trying to create a good model for something, we would have (collected more data and) split the data into train/validation/test subsets.

Random Forests

Given how closely decision trees can fit themselves to their training data, it's not surprising that they have a tendency to overfit. One way of avoiding this is a technique called *random forests*, in which we build multiple decision trees and let them vote on how to classify inputs:

```
def forest_classify(trees, input):
    votes = [classify(tree, input) for tree in trees]
    vote_counts = Counter(votes)
    return vote_counts.most_common(1)[0][0]
```

Our tree-building process was deterministic, so how do we get random trees?

One piece involves bootstrapping data (recall "Digression: The Bootstrap" on page 183). Rather than training each tree on all the `inputs` in the training set, we train each tree on the result of `bootstrap_sample(inputs)`. Since each tree is built using different data, each tree will be different from every other tree. (A side benefit is that it's totally fair to use the nonsampled data to test each tree, which means you can get away with using all of your data as the training set if you are clever in how you measure performance.) This technique is known as *bootstrap aggregating* or *bagging*.

A second source of randomness involves changing the way we chose the `best_attribute` to split on. Rather than looking at all the remaining attributes, we first choose a random subset of them and then split on whichever of those is best:

```
# if there's already few enough split candidates, look at all of them
if len(split_candidates) <= self.num_split_candidates:
    sampled_split_candidates = split_candidates
# otherwise pick a random sample
else:
    sampled_split_candidates = random.sample(split_candidates,
                                             self.num_split_candidates)

# now choose the best attribute only from those candidates
best_attribute = min(sampled_split_candidates,
    key=partial(partition_entropy_by, inputs))

partitions = partition_by(inputs, best_attribute)
```

This is an example of a broader technique called *ensemble learning* in which we combine several *weak learners* (typically high-bias, low-variance models) in order to produce an overall strong model.

Random forests are one of the most popular and versatile models around.

For Further Exploration

- scikit-learn has many Decision Tree (*http://bit.ly/1ycPmuq*) models. It also has an ensemble (*http://bit.ly/1ycPom1*) module that includes a `RandomForestClassifier` as well as other ensemble methods.
- We barely scratched the surface of decision trees and their algorithms. Wikipedia (*http://bit.ly/1ycPn1j*) is a good starting point for broader exploration.

## CHAPTER 18

Neural Networks

I like nonsense; it wakes up the brain cells.
—Dr. Seuss

An *artificial neural network* (or neural network for short) is a predictive model motivated by the way the brain operates. Think of the brain as a collection of neurons wired together. Each neuron looks at the outputs of the other neurons that feed into it, does a calculation, and then either fires (if the calculation exceeds some threshold) or doesn't (if it doesn't).

Accordingly, artificial neural networks consist of artificial neurons, which perform similar calculations over their inputs. Neural networks can solve a wide variety of problems like handwriting recognition and face detection, and they are used heavily in deep learning, one of the trendiest subfields of data science. However, most neural networks are "black boxes"—inspecting their details doesn't give you much understanding of *how* they're solving a problem. And large neural networks can be difficult to train. For most problems you'll encounter as a budding data scientist, they're probably not the right choice. Someday, when you're trying to build an artificial intelligence to bring about the Singularity, they very well might be.

Perceptrons

Pretty much the simplest neural network is the *perceptron*, which approximates a single neuron with *n* binary inputs. It computes a weighted sum of its inputs and "fires" if that weighted sum is zero or greater:

```
def step_function(x):
    return 1 if x >= 0 else 0

def perceptron_output(weights, bias, x):
    """returns 1 if the perceptron 'fires', 0 if not"""
```

```
calculation = dot(weights, x) + bias
return step_function(calculation)
```

The perceptron is simply distinguishing between the half spaces separated by the hyperplane of points x for which:

```
dot(weights,x) + bias == 0
```

With properly chosen weights, perceptrons can solve a number of simple problems (Figure 18-1). For example, we can create an *AND gate* (which returns 1 if both its inputs are 1 but returns 0 if one of its inputs is 0) with:

```
weights = [2, 2]
bias = -3
```

If both inputs are 1, the `calculation` equals 2 + 2 - 3 = 1, and the output is 1. If only one of the inputs is 1, the `calculation` equals 2 + 0 - 3 = -1, and the output is 0. And if both of the inputs are 0, the `calculation` equals -3, and the output is 0.

Similarly, we could build an *OR gate* with:

```
weights = [2, 2]
bias = -1
```

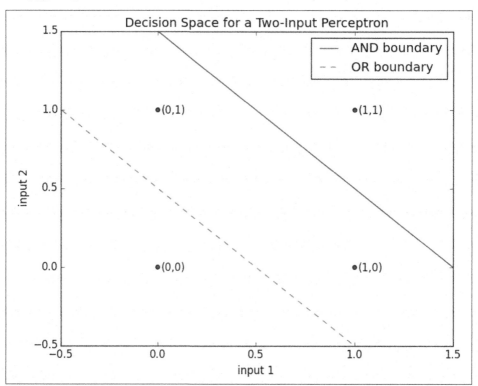

Figure 18-1. Decision space for a two-input perceptron

And we could build a *NOT gate* (which has one input and converts 1 to 0 and 0 to 1) with:

```
weights = [-2]
bias = 1
```

However, there are some problems that simply can't be solved by a single perceptron. For example, no matter how hard you try, you cannot use a perceptron to build an *XOR gate* that outputs 1 if exactly one of its inputs is 1 and 0 otherwise. This is where we start needing more-complicated neural networks.

Of course, you don't need to approximate a neuron in order to build a logic gate:

```
and_gate = min
or_gate = max
xor_gate = lambda x, y: 0 if x == y else 1
```

Like real neurons, artificial neurons start getting more interesting when you start connecting them together.

Feed-Forward Neural Networks

The topology of the brain is enormously complicated, so it's common to approximate it with an idealized *feed-forward* neural network that consists of discrete *layers* of neurons, each connected to the next. This typically entails an input layer (which receives inputs and feeds them forward unchanged), one or more "hidden layers" (each of which consists of neurons that take the outputs of the previous layer, performs some calculation, and passes the result to the next layer), and an output layer (which produces the final outputs).

Just like the perceptron, each (noninput) neuron has a weight corresponding to each of its inputs and a bias. To make our representation simpler, we'll add the bias to the end of our weights vector and give each neuron a *bias input* that always equals 1.

As with the perceptron, for each neuron we'll sum up the products of its inputs and its weights. But here, rather than outputting the `step_function` applied to that product, we'll output a smooth approximation of the step function. In particular, we'll use the `sigmoid` function (Figure 18-2):

```
def sigmoid(t):
    return 1 / (1 + math.exp(-t))
```

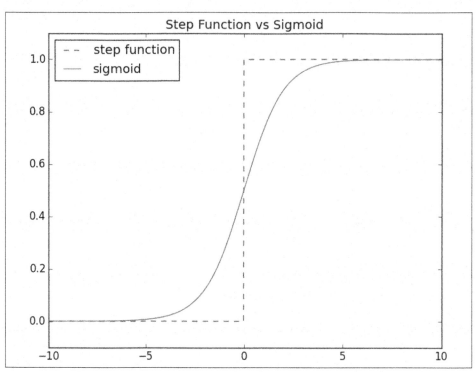

Figure 18-2. The sigmoid function

Why use `sigmoid` instead of the simpler `step_function`? In order to train a neural network, we'll need to use calculus, and in order to use calculus, we need *smooth* functions. The step function isn't even continuous, and sigmoid is a good smooth approximation of it.

 You may remember `sigmoid` from Chapter 16, where it was called `logistic`. Technically "sigmoid" refers to the *shape* of the function, "logistic" to this particular function although people often use the terms interchangeably.

We then calculate the output as:

```
def neuron_output(weights, inputs):
    return sigmoid(dot(weights, inputs))
```

Given this function, we can represent a neuron simply as a list of weights whose length is one more than the number of inputs to that neuron (because of the bias weight). Then we can represent a neural network as a list of (noninput) *layers*, where each layer is just a list of the neurons in that layer.

That is, we'll represent a neural network as a list (layers) of lists (neurons) of lists (weights).

Given such a representation, using the neural network is quite simple:

```
def feed_forward(neural_network, input_vector):
    """takes in a neural network
    (represented as a list of lists of lists of weights)
    and returns the output from forward-propagating the input"""

    outputs = []

    # process one layer at a time
    for layer in neural_network:
        input_with_bias = input_vector + [1]            # add a bias input
        output = [neuron_output(neuron, input_with_bias)  # compute the output
                  for neuron in layer]                   # for each neuron
        outputs.append(output)                          # and remember it

        # then the input to the next layer is the output of this one
        input_vector = output

    return outputs
```

Now it's easy to build the XOR gate that we couldn't build with a single perceptron. We just need to scale the weights up so that the neuron_outputs are either really close to 0 or really close to 1:

```
xor_network = [# hidden layer
               [[20, 20, -30],      # 'and' neuron
                [20, 20, -10]],     # 'or'  neuron
               # output layer
               [[-60, 60, -30]]]    # '2nd input but not 1st input' neuron

for x in [0, 1]:
    for y in [0, 1]:
        # feed_forward produces the outputs of every neuron
        # feed_forward[-1] is the outputs of the output-layer neurons
        print x, y, feed_forward(xor_network,[x, y])[-1]

# 0 0 [9.38314668300676e-14]
# 0 1 [0.9999999999999059]
# 1 0 [0.9999999999999059]
# 1 1 [9.383146683006828e-14]
```

By using a hidden layer, we are able to feed the output of an "and" neuron and the output of an "or" neuron into a "second input but not first input" neuron. The result is a network that performs "or, but not and," which is precisely XOR (Figure 18-3).

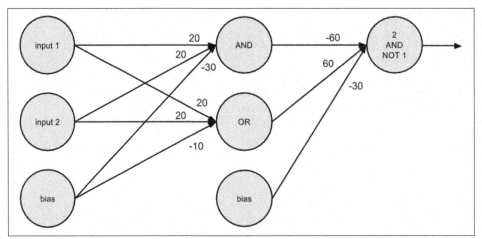

Figure 18-3. A neural network for XOR

Backpropagation

Usually we don't build neural networks by hand. This is in part because we use them to solve much bigger problems—an image recognition problem might involve hundreds or thousands of neurons. And it's in part because we usually won't be able to "reason out" what the neurons should be.

Instead (as usual) we use data to *train* neural networks. One popular approach is an algorithm called *backpropagation* that has similarities to the gradient descent algorithm we looked at earlier.

Imagine we have a training set that consists of input vectors and corresponding target output vectors. For example, in our previous `xor_network` example, the input vector `[1, 0]` corresponded to the target output `[1]`. And imagine that our network has some set of weights. We then adjust the weights using the following algorithm:

1. Run `feed_forward` on an input vector to produce the outputs of all the neurons in the network.

2. This results in an error for each output neuron—the difference between its output and its target.

3. Compute the gradient of this error as a function of the neuron's weights, and adjust its weights in the direction that most decreases the error.

4. "Propagate" these output errors backward to infer errors for the hidden layer.

5. Compute the gradients of these errors and adjust the hidden layer's weights in the same manner.

Typically we run this algorithm many times for our entire training set until the network converges:

```
def backpropagate(network, input_vector, targets):

    hidden_outputs, outputs = feed_forward(network, input_vector)

    # the output * (1 - output) is from the derivative of sigmoid
    output_deltas = [output * (1 - output) * (output - target)
                     for output, target in zip(outputs, targets)]

    # adjust weights for output layer, one neuron at a time
    for i, output_neuron in enumerate(network[-1]):
        # focus on the ith output layer neuron
        for j, hidden_output in enumerate(hidden_outputs + [1]):
            # adjust the jth weight based on both
            # this neuron's delta and its jth input
            output_neuron[j] -= output_deltas[i] * hidden_output

    # back-propagate errors to hidden layer
    hidden_deltas = [hidden_output * (1 - hidden_output) *
                     dot(output_deltas, [n[i] for n in output_layer])
                     for i, hidden_output in enumerate(hidden_outputs)]

    # adjust weights for hidden layer, one neuron at a time
    for i, hidden_neuron in enumerate(network[0]):
        for j, input in enumerate(input_vector + [1]):
            hidden_neuron[j] -= hidden_deltas[i] * input
```

This is pretty much doing the same thing as if you explicitly wrote the squared error as a function of the weights and used the `minimize_stochastic` function we built in Chapter 8.

In this case, explicitly writing out the gradient function turns out to be kind of a pain. If you know calculus and the chain rule, the mathematical details are relatively straightforward, but keeping the notation straight ("the partial derivative of the error function with respect to the weight that neuron i assigns to the input coming from neuron j") is not much fun.

Example: Defeating a CAPTCHA

To make sure that people registering for your site are actually people, the VP of Product Management wants to implement a CAPTCHA as part of the registration process. In particular, he'd like to show users a picture of a digit and require them to input that digit to prove they're human.

He doesn't believe you that computers can easily solve this problem, so you decide to convince him by creating a program that can easily solve the problem.

We'll represent each digit as a 5 × 5 image:

```
@@@@@   ..@..   @@@@@   @@@@@   @...@   @@@@@   @@@@@   @@@@@   @@@@@   @@@@@
@...@   ..@..   ....@   ....@   @...@   @....   @....   ....@   @...@   @...@
@...@   ..@..   @@@@@   @@@@@   @@@@@   @@@@@   @@@@@   ....@   @@@@@   @@@@@
@...@   ..@..   @....   ....@   ....@   ....@   @...@   ....@   @...@   ....@
@@@@@   ..@..   @@@@@   @@@@@   ....@   @@@@@   @@@@@   ....@   @@@@@   @@@@@
```

Our neural network wants an input to be a vector of numbers. So we'll transform each image to a vector of length 25, whose elements are either 1 ("this pixel is in the image") or 0 ("this pixel is not in the image").

For instance, the zero digit would be represented as:

```
zero_digit = [1,1,1,1,1,
              1,0,0,0,1,
              1,0,0,0,1,
              1,0,0,0,1,
              1,1,1,1,1]
```

We'll want our output to indicate which digit the neural network thinks it is, so we'll need 10 outputs. The correct output for digit 4, for instance, will be:

```
[0, 0, 0, 0, 1, 0, 0, 0, 0, 0]
```

Then, assuming our `inputs` are correctly ordered from 0 to 9, our targets will be:

```
targets = [[1 if i == j else 0 for i in range(10)]
           for j in range(10)]
```

so that (for example) `targets[4]` is the correct output for digit 4.

At which point we're ready to build our neural network:

```
random.seed(0)          # to get repeatable results
input_size = 25         # each input is a vector of length 25
num_hidden = 5          # we'll have 5 neurons in the hidden layer
output_size = 10        # we need 10 outputs for each input

# each hidden neuron has one weight per input, plus a bias weight
hidden_layer = [[random.random() for __ in range(input_size + 1)]
                for __ in range(num_hidden)]

# each output neuron has one weight per hidden neuron, plus a bias weight
output_layer = [[random.random() for __ in range(num_hidden + 1)]
                for __ in range(output_size)]

# the network starts out with random weights
network = [hidden_layer, output_layer]
```

And we can train it using the backpropagation algorithm:

```
# 10,000 iterations seems enough to converge
for __ in range(10000):
    for input_vector, target_vector in zip(inputs, targets):
        backpropagate(network, input_vector, target_vector)
```

It works well on the training set, obviously:

```
def predict(input):
    return feed_forward(network, input)[-1]

predict(inputs[7])
# [0.026, 0.0, 0.0, 0.018, 0.001, 0.0, 0.0, 0.967, 0.0, 0.0]
```

Which indicates that the digit 7 output neuron produces 0.97, while all the other output neurons produce very small numbers.

But we can also apply it to differently drawn digits, like my stylized 3:

```
predict([0,1,1,1,0,   # .@@@.
        0,0,0,1,1,   # ...@@
        0,0,1,1,0,   # ..@@.
        0,0,0,1,1,   # ...@@
        0,1,1,1,0]) # .@@@.

# [0.0, 0.0, 0.0, 0.92, 0.0, 0.0, 0.0, 0.01, 0.0, 0.12]
```

The network still thinks it looks like a 3, whereas my stylized 8 gets votes for being a 5, an 8, and a 9:

```
predict([0,1,1,1,0,   # .@@@.
        1,0,0,1,1,   # @..@@
        0,1,1,1,0,   # .@@@.
        1,0,0,1,1,   # @..@@
        0,1,1,1,0]) # .@@@.

# [0.0, 0.0, 0.0, 0.0, 0.0, 0.55, 0.0, 0.0, 0.93, 1.0]
```

Having a larger training set would probably help.

Although the network's operation is not exactly transparent, we can inspect the weights of the hidden layer to get a sense of what they're recognizing. In particular, we can plot the weights of each neuron as a 5 × 5 grid corresponding to the 5 × 5 inputs.

In real life you'd probably want to plot zero weights as white, with larger positive weights more and more (say) green and larger negative weights more and more (say) red. Unfortunately, that's hard to do in a black-and-white book.

Instead, we'll plot zero weights as white, with far-away-from-zero weights darker and darker. And we'll use crosshatching to indicate negative weights.

To do this we'll use pyplot.imshow, which we haven't seen before. With it we can plot images pixel by pixel. Normally this isn't all that useful for data science, but here it's a good choice:

```
import matplotlib
weights = network[0][0]              # first neuron in hidden layer
abs_weights = map(abs, weights)      # darkness only depends on absolute value
```

```
grid = [abs_weights[row:(row+5)]        # turn the weights into a 5x5 grid
        for row in range(0,25,5)]       # [weights[0:5], ..., weights[20:25]]

ax = plt.gca()                          # to use hatching, we'll need the axis

ax.imshow(grid,                         # here same as plt.imshow
          cmap=matplotlib.cm.binary,    # use white-black color scale
          interpolation='none')         # plot blocks as blocks

def patch(x, y, hatch, color):
    """return a matplotlib 'patch' object with the specified
    location, crosshatch pattern, and color"""
    return matplotlib.patches.Rectangle((x - 0.5, y - 0.5), 1, 1,
                                        hatch=hatch, fill=False, color=color)

# cross-hatch the negative weights
for i in range(5):                      # row
    for j in range(5):                  # column
        if weights[5*i + j] < 0:        # row i, column j = weights[5*i + j]
            # add black and white hatches, so visible whether dark or light
            ax.add_patch(patch(j, i, '/',  "white"))
            ax.add_patch(patch(j, i, '\\', "black"))

plt.show()
```

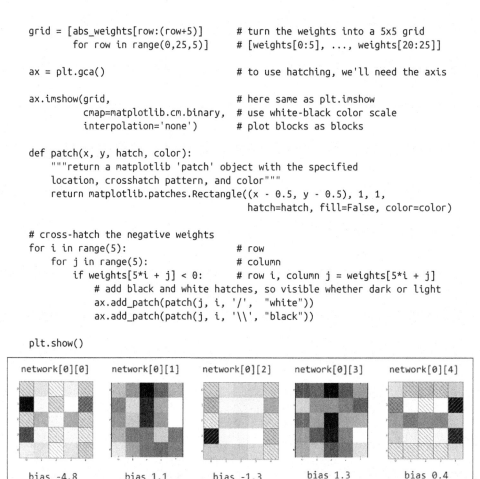

Figure 18-4. Weights for the hidden layer

In Figure 18-4 we see that the first hidden neuron has large positive weights in the left column and in the center of the middle row, while it has large negative weights in the right column. (And you can see that it has a pretty large negative bias, which means that it won't fire strongly unless it gets precisely the positive inputs it's "looking for.")

Indeed, on those inputs, it does what you'd expect:

```
left_column_only = [1, 0, 0, 0, 0] * 5
print feed_forward(network, left_column_only)[0][0]  # 1.0

center_middle_row = [0, 0, 0, 0, 0] * 2 + [0, 1, 1, 1, 0] + [0, 0, 0, 0, 0] * 2
print feed_forward(network, center_middle_row)[0][0]  # 0.95
```

```
right_column_only = [0, 0, 0, 0, 1] * 5
print feed_forward(network, right_column_only)[0][0]  # 0.0
```

Similarly, the middle hidden neuron seems to "like" horizontal lines but not side vertical lines, and the last hidden neuron seems to "like" the center row but not the right column. (The other two neurons are harder to interpret.)

What happens when we run my stylized 3 through the network?

```
my_three =  [0,1,1,1,0,  # .@@@.
             0,0,0,1,1,  # ...@@
             0,0,1,1,0,  # ..@@.
             0,0,0,1,1,  # ...@@
             0,1,1,1,0]  # .@@@.

hidden, output = feed_forward(network, my_three)
```

The hidden outputs are:

```
0.121080  # from network[0][0], probably dinged by (1, 4)
0.999979  # from network[0][1], big contributions from (0, 2) and (2, 2)
0.999999  # from network[0][2], positive everywhere except (3, 4)
0.999992  # from network[0][3], again big contributions from (0, 2) and (2, 2)
0.000000  # from network[0][4], negative or zero everywhere except center row
```

which enter into the "three" output neuron with weights network[-1][3]:

```
-11.61  # weight for hidden[0]
 -2.17  # weight for hidden[1]
  9.31  # weight for hidden[2]
 -1.38  # weight for hidden[3]
-11.47  # weight for hidden[4]
- 1.92  # weight for bias input
```

So that the neuron computes:

```
sigmoid(.121 * -11.61 + 1 * -2.17 + 1 * 9.31 - 1.38 * 1 - 0 * 11.47 - 1.92)
```

which is 0.92, as we saw. In essence, the hidden layer is computing five different partitions of 25-dimensional space, mapping each 25-dimensional input down to five numbers. And then each output neuron looks only at the results of those five partitions.

As we saw, my_three falls slightly on the "low" side of partition 0 (i.e., only slightly activates hidden neuron 0), far on the "high" side of partitions 1, 2, and 3, (i.e., strongly activates those hidden neurons), and far on the low side of partition 4 (i.e., doesn't active that neuron at all).

And then each of the 10 output neurons uses only those five activations to decide whether my_three is their digit or not.

For Further Exploration

- Coursera has a free course on Neural Networks for Machine Learning (*https://www.coursera.org/course/neuralnets*). As I write this it was last run in 2012, but the course materials are still available.

- Michael Nielsen is writing a free online book on Neural Networks and Deep Learning (*http://neuralnetworksanddeeplearning.com*). By the time you read this it might be finished.

- PyBrain (*http://pybrain.org*) is a pretty simple Python neural network library.

- Pylearn2 (*http://deeplearning.net/software/pylearn2/*) is a much more advanced (and much harder to use) neural network library.

## CHAPTER 19

Clustering

Where we such clusters had
As made us nobly wild, not mad
—Robert Herrick

Most of the algorithms in this book are what's known as supervised learning, in that they start with a set of *labeled* data and use that as the basis for making predictions about new, unlabeled data. Clustering, however, is an example of unsupervised learning, in which we work with completely unlabeled data (or in which our data has labels but we ignore them).

The Idea

Whenever you look at some source of data, it's likely that the data will somehow form *clusters*. A data set showing where millionaires live probably has clusters in places like Beverly Hills and Manhattan. A data set showing how many hours people work each week probably has a cluster around 40 (and if it's taken from a state with laws mandating special benefits for people who work at least 20 hours a week, it probably has another cluster right around 19). A data set of demographics of registered voters likely forms a variety of clusters (e.g., "soccer moms," "bored retirees," "unemployed millennials") that pollsters and political consultants likely consider relevant.

Unlike some of the problems we've looked at, there is generally no "correct" clustering. An alternative clustering scheme might group some of the "unemployed millennials" with "grad students," others with "parents' basement dwellers." Neither scheme is necessarily more correct—instead, each is likely more optimal with respect to its own "how good are the clusters?" metric.

Furthermore, the clusters won't label themselves. You'll have to do that by looking at the data underlying each one.

The Model

For us, each input will be a vector in d-dimensional space (which, as usual, we will represent as a list of numbers). Our goal will be to identify clusters of similar inputs and (sometimes) to find a representative value for each cluster.

For example, each input could be (a numeric vector that somehow represents) the title of a blog post, in which case the goal might be to find clusters of similar posts, perhaps in order to understand what our users are blogging about. Or imagine that we have a picture containing thousands of (red, green, blue) colors and that we need to screen-print a 10-color version of it. Clustering can help us choose 10 colors that will minimize the total "color error."

One of the simplest clustering methods is *k-means*, in which the number of clusters k is chosen in advance, after which the goal is to partition the inputs into sets $S_1, ..., S_k$ in a way that minimizes the total sum of squared distances from each point to the mean of its assigned cluster.

There are a lot of ways to assign n points to k clusters, which means that finding an optimal clustering is a very hard problem. We'll settle for an iterative algorithm that usually finds a good clustering:

1. Start with a set of *k-means*, which are points in d-dimensional space.

2. Assign each point to the mean to which it is closest.

3. If no point's assignment has changed, stop and keep the clusters.

4. If some point's assignment has changed, recompute the means and return to step 2.

Using the vector_mean function from Chapter 4, it's pretty simple to create a class that does this:

```
class KMeans:
    """performs k-means clustering"""

    def __init__(self, k):
        self.k = k            # number of clusters
        self.means = None     # means of clusters

    def classify(self, input):
        """return the index of the cluster closest to the input"""
        return min(range(self.k),
                   key=lambda i: squared_distance(input, self.means[i]))

    def train(self, inputs):
        # choose k random points as the initial means
        self.means = random.sample(inputs, self.k)
        assignments = None
```

```
        while True:
            # Find new assignments
            new_assignments = map(self.classify, inputs)

            # If no assignments have changed, we're done.
            if assignments == new_assignments:
                return

            # Otherwise keep the new assignments,
            assignments = new_assignments

            # And compute new means based on the new assignments
            for i in range(self.k):
                # find all the points assigned to cluster i
                i_points = [p for p, a in zip(inputs, assignments) if a == i]

                # make sure i_points is not empty so don't divide by 0
                if i_points:
                    self.means[i] = vector_mean(i_points)
```

Let's take a look at how this works.

Example: Meetups

To celebrate DataSciencester's growth, your VP of User Rewards wants to organize several in-person meetups for your hometown users, complete with beer, pizza, and DataSciencester t-shirts. You know the locations of all your local users (Figure 19-1), and she'd like you to choose meetup locations that make it convenient for everyone to attend.

Depending on how you look at it, you probably see two or three clusters. (It's easy to do visually because the data is only two-dimensional. With more dimensions, it would be a lot harder to eyeball.)

Imagine first that she has enough budget for three meetups. You go to your computer and try this:

```
random.seed(0)         # so you get the same results as me
clusterer = KMeans(3)
clusterer.train(inputs)
print clusterer.means
```

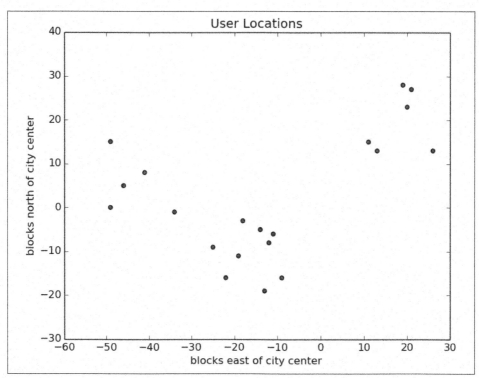

Figure 19-1. The locations of your hometown users

You find three clusters centered at [-44,5], [-16,-10], and [18, 20], and you look for meetup venues near those locations (Figure 19-2).

You show it to the VP, who informs you that now she only has enough budget for *two* meetups.

"No problem," you say:

```
random.seed(0)
clusterer = KMeans(2)
clusterer.train(inputs)
print clusterer.means
```

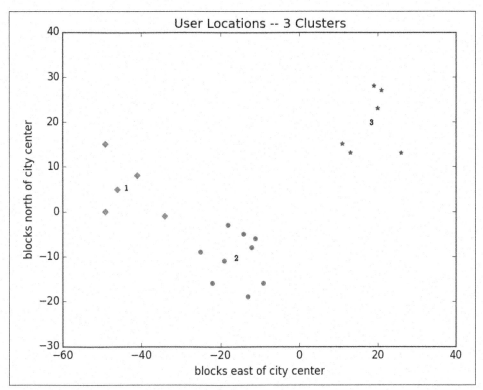

Figure 19-2. User locations grouped into three clusters

As shown in Figure 19-3, one meetup should still be near [18, 20], but now the other should be near [-26, -5].

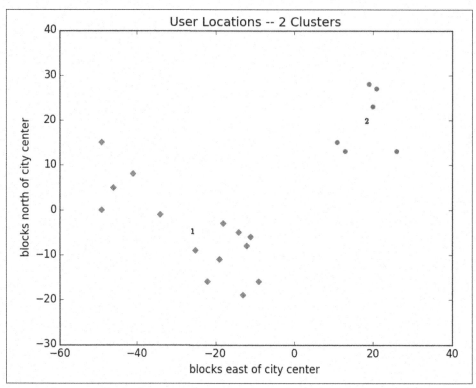

Figure 19-3. User locations grouped into two clusters

Choosing k

In the previous example, the choice of *k* was driven by factors outside of our control. In general, this won't be the case. There is a wide variety of ways to choose a *k*. One that's reasonably easy to understand involves plotting the sum of squared errors (between each point and the mean of its cluster) as a function of *k* and looking at where the graph "bends":

```
def squared_clustering_errors(inputs, k):
    """finds the total squared error from k-means clustering the inputs"""
    clusterer = KMeans(k)
    clusterer.train(inputs)
    means = clusterer.means
    assignments = map(clusterer.classify, inputs)

    return sum(squared_distance(input, means[cluster])
               for input, cluster in zip(inputs, assignments))

# now plot from 1 up to len(inputs) clusters

ks = range(1, len(inputs) + 1)
```

```
errors = [squared_clustering_errors(inputs, k) for k in ks]

plt.plot(ks, errors)
plt.xticks(ks)
plt.xlabel("k")
plt.ylabel("total squared error")
plt.title("Total Error vs. # of Clusters")
plt.show()
```

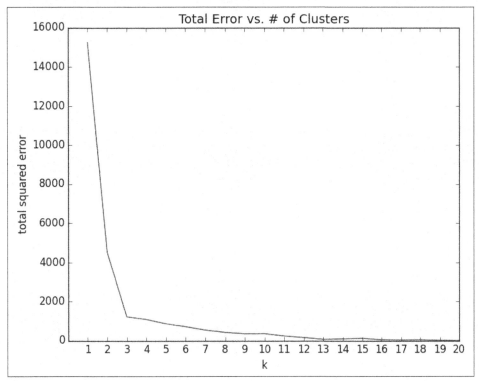

Figure 19-4. Choosing a k

Looking at Figure 19-4, this method agrees with our original eyeballing that 3 is the "right" number of clusters.

Example: Clustering Colors

The VP of Swag has designed attractive DataSciencester stickers that he'd like you to hand out at meetups. Unfortunately, your sticker printer can print at most five colors per sticker. And since the VP of Art is on sabbatical, the VP of Swag asks if there's some way you can take his design and modify it so that it only contains five colors.

Computer images can be represented as two-dimensional array of pixels, where each pixel is itself a three-dimensional vector (red, green, blue) indicating its color.

Creating a five-color version of the image then entails:

1. Choosing five colors
2. Assigning one of those colors to each pixel

It turns out this is a great task for k-means clustering, which can partition the pixels into five clusters in red-green-blue space. If we then recolor the pixels in each cluster to the mean color, we're done.

To start with, we'll need a way to load an image into Python. It turns out we can do this with `matplotlib`:

```
path_to_png_file = r"C:\images\image.png"    # wherever your image is
import matplotlib.image as mpimg
img = mpimg.imread(path_to_png_file)
```

Behind the scenes img is a NumPy array, but for our purposes, we can treat it as a list of lists of lists.

img[i][j] is the pixel in the *i*th row and *j*th column, and each pixel is a list [red, green, blue] of numbers between 0 and 1 indicating the color of that pixel (*http://en.wikipedia.org/wiki/RGB_color_model*):

```
top_row = img[0]
top_left_pixel = top_row[0]
red, green, blue = top_left_pixel
```

In particular, we can get a flattened list of all the pixels as:

```
pixels = [pixel for row in img for pixel in row]
```

and then feed them to our clusterer:

```
clusterer = KMeans(5)
clusterer.train(pixels)    # this might take a while
```

Once it finishes, we just construct a new image with the same format:

```
def recolor(pixel):
    cluster = clusterer.classify(pixel)        # index of the closest cluster
    return clusterer.means[cluster]            # mean of the closest cluster

new_img = [[recolor(pixel) for pixel in row]   # recolor this row of pixels
           for row in img]                     # for each row in the image
```

and display it, using `plt.imshow()`:

```
plt.imshow(new_img)
plt.axis('off')
plt.show()
```

It is difficult to show color results in a black-and-white book, but Figure 19-5 shows grayscale versions of a full-color picture and the output of using this process to reduce it to five colors:

Figure 19-5. Original picture and its 5-means decoloring

Bottom-up Hierarchical Clustering

An alternative approach to clustering is to "grow" clusters from the bottom up. We can do this in the following way:

1. Make each input its own cluster of one.
2. As long as there are multiple clusters remaining, find the two closest clusters and merge them.

At the end, we'll have one giant cluster containing all the inputs. If we keep track of the merge order, we can recreate any number of clusters by unmerging. For example, if we want three clusters, we can just undo the last two merges.

We'll use a really simple representation of clusters. Our values will live in *leaf* clusters, which we will represent as 1-tuples:

```
leaf1 = ([10, 20],)   # to make a 1-tuple you need the trailing comma
leaf2 = ([30, -15],)  # otherwise Python treats the parentheses as parentheses
```

We'll use these to grow *merged* clusters, which we will represent as 2-tuples (merge order, children):

```
merged = (1, [leaf1, leaf2])
```

We'll talk about merge order in a bit, but first let's create a few helper functions:

```
def is_leaf(cluster):
    """a cluster is a leaf if it has length 1"""
    return len(cluster) == 1

def get_children(cluster):
    """returns the two children of this cluster if it's a merged cluster;
    raises an exception if this is a leaf cluster"""
    if is_leaf(cluster):
        raise TypeError("a leaf cluster has no children")
    else:
        return cluster[1]

def get_values(cluster):
    """returns the value in this cluster (if it's a leaf cluster)
    or all the values in the leaf clusters below it (if it's not)"""
    if is_leaf(cluster):
        return cluster       # is already a 1-tuple containing value
    else:
        return [value
                for child in get_children(cluster)
                for value in get_values(child)]
```

In order to merge the closest clusters, we need some notion of the distance between clusters. We'll use the *minimum* distance between elements of the two clusters, which merges the two clusters that are closest to touching (but will sometimes produce large chain-like clusters that aren't very tight). If we wanted tight spherical clusters, we might use the *maximum* distance instead, as it merges the two clusters that fit in the smallest ball. Both are common choices, as is the *average* distance:

```
def cluster_distance(cluster1, cluster2, distance_agg=min):
    """compute all the pairwise distances between cluster1 and cluster2
    and apply _distance_agg_ to the resulting list"""
    return distance_agg([distance(input1, input2)
                         for input1 in get_values(cluster1)
                         for input2 in get_values(cluster2)])
```

We'll use the merge order slot to track the order in which we did the merging. Smaller numbers will represent *later* merges. This means when we want to unmerge clusters, we do so from lowest merge order to highest. Since leaf clusters were never merged (which means we never want to unmerge them), we'll assign them infinity:

```
def get_merge_order(cluster):
    if is_leaf(cluster):
        return float('inf')
    else:
        return cluster[0]  # merge_order is first element of 2-tuple
```

Now we're ready to create the clustering algorithm:

```
def bottom_up_cluster(inputs, distance_agg=min):
    # start with every input a leaf cluster / 1-tuple
    clusters = [(input,) for input in inputs]
```

```
# as long as we have more than one cluster left...
while len(clusters) > 1:
    # find the two closest clusters
    c1, c2 = min([(cluster1, cluster2)
                  for i, cluster1 in enumerate(clusters)
                  for cluster2 in clusters[:i]],
                 key=lambda (x, y): cluster_distance(x, y, distance_agg))

    # remove them from the list of clusters
    clusters = [c for c in clusters if c != c1 and c != c2]

    # merge them, using merge_order = # of clusters left
    merged_cluster = (len(clusters), [c1, c2])

    # and add their merge
    clusters.append(merged_cluster)

# when there's only one cluster left, return it
return clusters[0]
```

Its use is very simple:

```
base_cluster = bottom_up_cluster(inputs)
```

This produces a cluster whose ugly representation is:

```
(0, [(1, [(3, [(14, [(18, [([19, 28],),
                           ([21, 27],)]),
                     ([20, 23],)]),
               ([26, 13],)]),
          (16, [([11, 15],),
                ([13, 13],)])]),
     (2, [(4, [(5, [(9, [(11, [([-49, 0],),
                               ([-46, 5],)]),
                         ([-41, 8],)]),
                    ([-49, 15],)]),
               ([-34, -1],)]),
          (6, [(7, [(8, [(10, [([-22, -16],),
                               ([-19, -11],)]),
                         ([-25, -9],)]),
                    (13, [(15, [(17, [([-11, -6],),
                                      ([-12, -8],)]),
                                ([-14, -5],)]),
                          ([-18, -3],)])]),
               (12, [([-13, -19],),
                     ([-9, -16],)])])])])
```

For every merged cluster, I lined up its children vertically. If we say "cluster 0" for the cluster with merge order 0, you can interpret this as:

- Cluster 0 is the merger of cluster 1 and cluster 2.
- Cluster 1 is the merger of cluster 3 and cluster 16.

- Cluster 16 is the merger of the leaf [11, 15] and the leaf [13, 13].
- And so on...

Since we had 20 inputs, it took 19 merges to get to this one cluster. The first merge created cluster 18 by combining the leaves [19, 28] and [21, 27]. And the last merge created cluster 0.

Generally, though, we don't want to be squinting at nasty text representations like this. (Although it could be an interesting exercise to create a user-friendlier visualization of the cluster hierarchy.) Instead let's write a function that generates any number of clusters by performing the appropriate number of unmerges:

```
def generate_clusters(base_cluster, num_clusters):
    # start with a list with just the base cluster
    clusters = [base_cluster]

    # as long as we don't have enough clusters yet...
    while len(clusters) < num_clusters:
        # choose the last-merged of our clusters
        next_cluster = min(clusters, key=get_merge_order)
        # remove it from the list
        clusters = [c for c in clusters if c != next_cluster]
        # and add its children to the list (i.e., unmerge it)
        clusters.extend(get_children(next_cluster))

    # once we have enough clusters...
    return clusters
```

So, for example, if we want to generate three clusters, we can just do:

```
three_clusters = [get_values(cluster)
                  for cluster in generate_clusters(base_cluster, 3)]
```

which we can easily plot:

```
for i, cluster, marker, color in zip([1, 2, 3],
                                     three_clusters,
                                     ['D','o','*'],
                                     ['r','g','b']):
    xs, ys = zip(*cluster)  # magic unzipping trick
    plt.scatter(xs, ys, color=color, marker=marker)

    # put a number at the mean of the cluster
    x, y = vector_mean(cluster)
    plt.plot(x, y, marker='$' + str(i) + '$', color='black')

plt.title("User Locations -- 3 Bottom-Up Clusters, Min")
plt.xlabel("blocks east of city center")
plt.ylabel("blocks north of city center")
plt.show()
```

This gives very different results than k-means did, as shown in Figure 19-6.

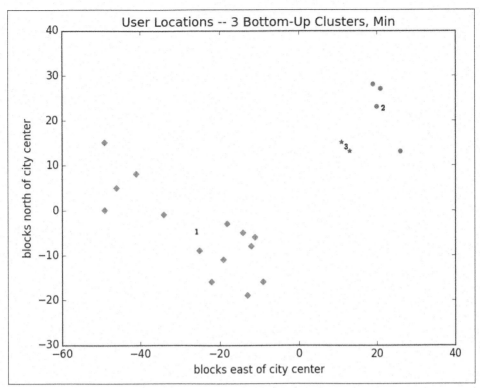

Figure 19-6. Three bottom-up clusters using min distance

As we mentioned above, this is because using `min` in `cluster_distance` tends to give chain-like clusters. If we instead use `max` (which gives tight clusters) it looks the same as the 3-means result (Figure 19-7).

The `bottom_up_clustering` implementation above is relatively simple, but it's also shockingly inefficient. In particular, it recomputes the distance between each pair of inputs at every step. A more efficient implementation might precompute the distances between each pair of inputs and then perform a lookup inside cluster_distance. A *really* efficient implementation would likely also remember the `cluster_distances` from the previous step.

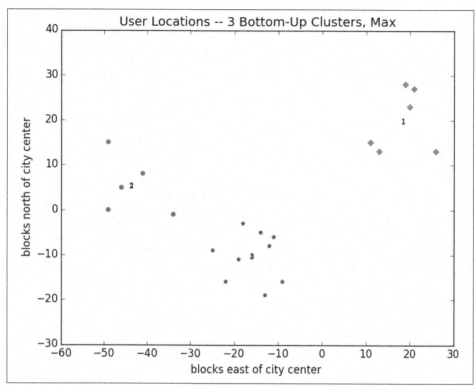

Figure 19-7. Three bottom-up clusters using max distance

For Further Exploration

- scikit-learn has an entire module sklearn.cluster (*http://scikit-learn.org/ stable/modules/clustering.html*) that contains several clustering algorithms including KMeans and the Ward hierarchical clustering algorithm (which uses a different criterion for merging clusters than ours did).

- SciPy (*http://www.scipy.org/*) has two clustering models scipy.cluster.vq (which does k-means) and scipy.cluster.hierarchy (which has a variety of hierarchical clustering algorithms).

## CHAPTER 20

Natural Language Processing

They have been at a great feast of languages, and stolen the scraps.
—William Shakespeare

Natural language processing (NLP) refers to computational techniques involving language. It's a broad field, but we'll look at a few techniques both simple and not simple.

Word Clouds

In Chapter 1, we computed word counts of users' interests. One approach to visualizing words and counts is word clouds, which artistically lay out the words with sizes proportional to their counts.

Generally, though, data scientists don't think much of word clouds, in large part because the placement of the words doesn't mean anything other than "here's some space where I was able to fit a word."

If you ever are forced to create a word cloud, think about whether you can make the axes convey something. For example, imagine that, for each of some collection of data science–related buzzwords, you have two numbers between 0 and 100—the first representing how frequently it appears in job postings, the second how frequently it appears on resumes:

```
data = [ ("big data", 100, 15), ("Hadoop", 95, 25), ("Python", 75, 50),
         ("R", 50, 40), ("machine learning", 80, 20), ("statistics", 20, 60),
         ("data science", 60, 70), ("analytics", 90, 3),
         ("team player", 85, 85), ("dynamic", 2, 90), ("synergies", 70, 0),
         ("actionable insights", 40, 30), ("think out of the box", 45, 10),
         ("self-starter", 30, 50), ("customer focus", 65, 15),
         ("thought leadership", 35, 35)]
```

The word cloud approach is just to arrange the words on a page in a cool-looking font (Figure 20-1).

Figure 20-1. Buzzword cloud

This looks neat but doesn't really tell us anything. A more interesting approach might be to scatter them so that horizontal position indicates posting popularity and vertical position indicates resume popularity, which produces a visualization that conveys a few insights (Figure 20-2):

```
def text_size(total):
    """equals 8 if total is 0, 28 if total is 200"""
    return 8 + total / 200 * 20

for word, job_popularity, resume_popularity in data:
    plt.text(job_popularity, resume_popularity, word,
             ha='center', va='center',
             size=text_size(job_popularity + resume_popularity))
plt.xlabel("Popularity on Job Postings")
plt.ylabel("Popularity on Resumes")
plt.axis([0, 100, 0, 100])
plt.xticks([])
plt.yticks([])
plt.show()
```

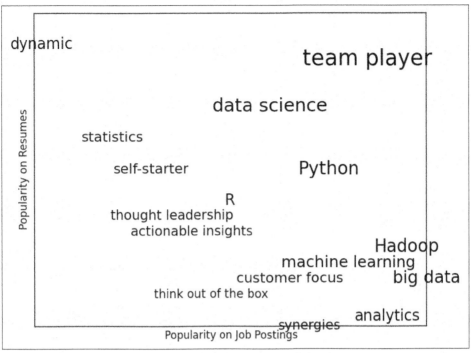

Figure 20-2. A more meaningful (if less attractive) word cloud

n-gram Models

The DataSciencester VP of Search Engine Marketing wants to create thousands of web pages about data science so that your site will rank higher in search results for data science–related terms. (You attempt to explain to her that search engine algorithms are clever enough that this won't actually work, but she refuses to listen.)

Of course, she doesn't want to write thousands of web pages, nor does she want to pay a horde of "content strategists" to do so. Instead she asks you whether you can somehow programatically generate these web pages. To do this, we'll need some way of modeling language.

One approach is to start with a corpus of documents and learn a statistical model of language. In our case, we'll start with Mike Loukides's essay "What is data science?" (*http://oreil.ly/1Cd6ykN*).

As in Chapter 9, we'll use `requests` and `BeautifulSoup` to retrieve the data. There are a couple of issues worth calling attention to.

The first is that the apostrophes in the text are actually the Unicode character u"\u2019". We'll create a helper function to replace them with normal apostrophes:

```
def fix_unicode(text):
    return text.replace(u"\u2019", "'")
```

The second issue is that once we get the text of the web page, we'll want to split it into a sequence of words and periods (so that we can tell where sentences end). We can do this using re.findall():

```
from bs4 import BeautifulSoup
import requests
url = "http://radar.oreilly.com/2010/06/what-is-data-science.html"
html = requests.get(url).text
soup = BeautifulSoup(html, 'html5lib')

content = soup.find("div", "entry-content")   # find entry-content div
regex = r"[\w']+|[\.]"                         # matches a word or a period

document = []

for paragraph in content("p"):
    words = re.findall(regex, fix_unicode(paragraph.text))
    document.extend(words)
```

We certainly could (and likely should) clean this data further. There is still some amount of extraneous text in the document (for example, the first word is "Section"), and we've split on midsentence periods (for example, in "Web 2.0"), and there are a handful of captions and lists sprinkled throughout. Having said that, we'll work with the document as it is.

Now that we have the text as a sequence of words, we can model language in the following way: given some starting word (say "book") we look at all the words that follow it in the source documents (here "isn't," "a," "shows," "demonstrates," and "teaches"). We randomly choose one of these to be the next word, and we repeat the process until we get to a period, which signifies the end of the sentence. We call this a *bigram model*, as it is determined completely by the frequencies of the bigrams (word pairs) in the original data.

What about a starting word? We can just pick randomly from words that *follow* a period. To start, let's precompute the possible word transitions. Recall that zip stops when any of its inputs is done, so that zip(document, document[1:]) gives us precisely the pairs of consecutive elements of document:

```
bigrams = zip(document, document[1:])
transitions = defaultdict(list)
for prev, current in bigrams:
    transitions[prev].append(current)
```

Now we're ready to generate sentences:

```
def generate_using_bigrams():
    current = "."    # this means the next word will start a sentence
    result = []
```

```
    while True:
        next_word_candidates = transitions[current]      # bigrams (current, _)
        current = random.choice(next_word_candidates)    # choose one at random
        result.append(current)                           # append it to results
        if current == ".": return " ".join(result)       # if "." we're done
```

The sentences it produces are gibberish, but they're the kind of gibberish you might put on your website if you were trying to sound data-sciencey. For example:

> If you may know which are you want to data sort the data feeds web friend someone on trending topics as the data in Hadoop is the data science requires a book demonstrates why visualizations are but we do massive correlations across many commercial disk drives in Python language and creates more tractable form making connections then use and uses it to solve a data.

—Bigram Model

We can make the sentences less gibberishy by looking at *trigrams*, triplets of consecutive words. (More generally, you might look at *n-grams* consisting of *n* consecutive words, but three will be plenty for us.) Now the transitions will depend on the previous *two* words:

```
trigrams = zip(document, document[1:], document[2:])
trigram_transitions = defaultdict(list)
starts = []

for prev, current, next in trigrams:

    if prev == ".":                 # if the previous "word" was a period
        starts.append(current)      # then this is a start word

    trigram_transitions[(prev, current)].append(next)
```

Notice that now we have to track the starting words separately. We can generate sentences in pretty much the same way:

```
def generate_using_trigrams():
    current = random.choice(starts)    # choose a random starting word
    prev = "."                         # and precede it with a '.'
    result = [current]
    while True:
        next_word_candidates = trigram_transitions[(prev, current)]
        next_word = random.choice(next_word_candidates)

        prev, current = current, next_word
        result.append(current)

        if current == ".":
            return " ".join(result)
```

This produces better sentences like:

In hindsight MapReduce seems like an epidemic and if so does that give us new insights into how economies work That's not a question we could even have asked a few years there has been instrumented.

—Trigram Model

Of course, they sound better because at each step the generation process has fewer choices, and at many steps only a single choice. This means that you frequently generate sentences (or at least long phrases) that were seen verbatim in the original data. Having more data would help; it would also work better if you collected *n*-grams from multiple essays about data science.

Grammars

A different approach to modeling language is with *grammars*, rules for generating acceptable sentences. In elementary school, you probably learned about parts of speech and how to combine them. For example, if you had a really bad English teacher, you might say that a sentence necessarily consists of a *noun* followed by a *verb*. If you then have a list of nouns and verbs, you can generate sentences according to the rule.

We'll define a slightly more complicated grammar:

```
grammar = {
    "_S"  : ["_NP _VP"],
    "_NP" : ["_N",
             "_A _NP _P _A _N"],
    "_VP" : ["_V",
             "_V _NP"],
    "_N"  : ["data science", "Python", "regression"],
    "_A"  : ["big", "linear", "logistic"],
    "_P"  : ["about", "near"],
    "_V"  : ["learns", "trains", "tests", "is"]
}
```

I made up the convention that names starting with underscores refer to *rules* that need further expanding, and that other names are *terminals* that don't need further processing.

So, for example, "_S" is the "sentence" rule, which produces a "_NP" ("noun phrase") rule followed by a "_VP" ("verb phrase") rule.

The verb phrase rule can produce either the "_V" ("verb") rule, or the verb rule followed by the noun phrase rule.

Notice that the "_NP" rule contains itself in one of its productions. Grammars can be recursive, which allows even finite grammars like this to generate infinitely many different sentences.

How do we generate sentences from this grammar? We'll start with a list containing the sentence rule ["_S"]. And then we'll repeatedly expand each rule by replacing it with a randomly chosen one of its productions. We stop when we have a list consisting solely of terminals.

For example, one such progression might look like:

```
['_S']
['_NP','_VP']
['_N','_VP']
['Python','_VP']
['Python','_V','_NP']
['Python','trains','_NP']
['Python','trains','_A','_NP','_P','_A','_N']
['Python','trains','logistic','_NP','_P','_A','_N']
['Python','trains','logistic','_N','_P','_A','_N']
['Python','trains','logistic','data science','_P','_A','_N']
['Python','trains','logistic','data science','about','_A', '_N']
['Python','trains','logistic','data science','about','logistic','_N']
['Python','trains','logistic','data science','about','logistic','Python']
```

How do we implement this? Well, to start, we'll create a simple helper function to identify terminals:

```
def is_terminal(token):
    return token[0] != "_"
```

Next we need to write a function to turn a list of tokens into a sentence. We'll look for the first nonterminal token. If we can't find one, that means we have a completed sentence and we're done.

If we do find a nonterminal, then we randomly choose one of its productions. If that production is a terminal (i.e., a word), we simply replace the token with it. Otherwise it's a sequence of space-separated nonterminal tokens that we need to split and then splice into the current tokens. Either way, we repeat the process on the new set of tokens.

Putting it all together we get:

```
def expand(grammar, tokens):
    for i, token in enumerate(tokens):

        # skip over terminals
        if is_terminal(token): continue

        # if we get here, we found a non-terminal token
        # so we need to choose a replacement at random
        replacement = random.choice(grammar[token])

        if is_terminal(replacement):
            tokens[i] = replacement
        else:
```

```
        tokens = tokens[:i] + replacement.split() + tokens[(i+1):]

        # now call expand on the new list of tokens
        return expand(grammar, tokens)

    # if we get here we had all terminals and are done
    return tokens
```

And now we can start generating sentences:

```
def generate_sentence(grammar):
    return expand(grammar, ["_S"])
```

Try changing the grammar—add more words, add more rules, add your own parts of speech—until you're ready to generate as many web pages as your company needs.

Grammars are actually more interesting when they're used in the other direction. Given a sentence we can use a grammar to *parse* the sentence. This then allows us to identify subjects and verbs and helps us make sense of the sentence.

Using data science to generate text is a neat trick; using it to *understand* text is more magical. (See "For Further Investigation" on page 200 for libraries that you could use for this.)

An Aside: Gibbs Sampling

Generating samples from some distributions is easy. We can get uniform random variables with:

```
random.random()
```

and normal random variables with:

```
inverse_normal_cdf(random.random())
```

But some distributions are harder to sample from. *Gibbs sampling* is a technique for generating samples from multidimensional distributions when we only know some of the conditional distributions.

For example, imagine rolling two dice. Let x be the value of the first die and y be the sum of the dice, and imagine you wanted to generate lots of (x, y) pairs. In this case it's easy to generate the samples directly:

```
def roll_a_die():
    return random.choice([1,2,3,4,5,6])

def direct_sample():
    d1 = roll_a_die()
    d2 = roll_a_die()
    return d1, d1 + d2
```

But imagine that you only knew the conditional distributions. The distribution of y conditional on x is easy—if you know the value of x, y is equally likely to be $x + 1$, $x + 2$, $x + 3$, $x + 4$, $x + 5$, or $x + 6$:

```python
def random_y_given_x(x):
    """equally likely to be x + 1, x + 2, ... , x + 6"""
    return x + roll_a_die()
```

The other direction is more complicated. For example, if you know that y is 2, then necessarily x is 1 (since the only way two dice can sum to 2 is if both of them are 1). If you know y is 3, then x is equally likely to be 1 or 2. Similarly, if y is 11, then x has to be either 5 or 6:

```python
def random_x_given_y(y):
    if y <= 7:
        # if the total is 7 or less, the first die is equally likely to be
        # 1, 2, ..., (total - 1)
        return random.randrange(1, y)
    else:
        # if the total is 7 or more, the first die is equally likely to be
        # (total - 6), (total - 5), ..., 6
        return random.randrange(y - 6, 7)
```

The way Gibbs sampling works is that we start with any (valid) value for x and y and then repeatedly alternate replacing x with a random value picked conditional on y and replacing y with a random value picked conditional on x. After a number of iterations, the resulting values of x and y will represent a sample from the unconditional joint distribution:

```python
def gibbs_sample(num_iters=100):
    x, y = 1, 2 # doesn't really matter
    for _ in range(num_iters):
        x = random_x_given_y(y)
        y = random_y_given_x(x)
    return x, y
```

You can check that this gives similar results to the direct sample:

```python
def compare_distributions(num_samples=1000):
    counts = defaultdict(lambda: [0, 0])
    for _ in range(num_samples):
        counts[gibbs_sample()][0] += 1
        counts[direct_sample()][1] += 1
    return counts
```

We'll use this technique in the next section.

Topic Modeling

When we built our Data Scientists You Should Know recommender in Chapter 1, we simply looked for exact matches in people's stated interests.

A more sophisticated approach to understanding our users' interests might try to identify the *topics* that underlie those interests. A technique called *Latent Dirichlet Analysis* (LDA) is commonly used to identify common topics in a set of documents. We'll apply it to documents that consist of each user's interests.

LDA has some similarities to the Naive Bayes Classifier we built in Chapter 13, in that it assumes a probabilistic model for documents. We'll gloss over the hairier mathematical details, but for our purposes the model assumes that:

- There is some fixed number K of topics.
- There is a random variable that assigns each topic an associated probability distribution over words. You should think of this distribution as the probability of seeing word w given topic k.
- There is another random variable that assigns each document a probability distribution over topics. You should think of this distribution as the mixture of topics in document d.
- Each word in a document was generated by first randomly picking a topic (from the document's distribution of topics) and then randomly picking a word (from the topic's distribution of words).

In particular, we have a collection of `documents` each of which is a `list` of words. And we have a corresponding collection of `document_topics` that assigns a topic (here a number between 0 and $K - 1$) to each word in each document.

So that the fifth word in the fourth document is:

```
documents[3][4]
```

and the topic from which that word was chosen is:

```
document_topics[3][4]
```

This very explicitly defines each document's distribution over topics, and it implicitly defines each topic's distribution over words.

We can estimate the likelihood that topic 1 produces a certain word by comparing how many times topic 1 produces that word with how many times topic 1 produces *any* word. (Similarly, when we built a spam filter in Chapter 13, we compared how many times each word appeared in spams with the total number of words appearing in spams.)

Although these topics are just numbers, we can give them descriptive names by looking at the words on which they put the heaviest weight. We just have to somehow generate the `document_topics`. This is where Gibbs sampling comes into play.

We start by assigning every word in every document a topic completely at random. Now we go through each document one word at a time. For that word and document, we construct weights for each topic that depend on the (current) distribution of topics in that document and the (current) distribution of words for that topic. We then use those weights to sample a new topic for that word. If we iterate this process many times, we will end up with a joint sample from the topic-word distribution and the document-topic distribution.

To start with, we'll need a function to randomly choose an index based on an arbitrary set of weights:

```
def sample_from(weights):
    """returns i with probability weights[i] / sum(weights)"""
    total = sum(weights)
    rnd = total * random.random()      # uniform between 0 and total
    for i, w in enumerate(weights):
        rnd -= w                       # return the smallest i such that
        if rnd <= 0: return i          # weights[0] + ... + weights[i] >= rnd
```

For instance, if you give it weights [1, 1, 3] then one-fifth of the time it will return 0, one-fifth of the time it will return 1, and three-fifths of the time it will return 2.

Our documents are our users' interests, which look like:

```
documents = [
    ["Hadoop", "Big Data", "HBase", "Java", "Spark", "Storm", "Cassandra"],
    ["NoSQL", "MongoDB", "Cassandra", "HBase", "Postgres"],
    ["Python", "scikit-learn", "scipy", "numpy", "statsmodels", "pandas"],
    ["R", "Python", "statistics", "regression", "probability"],
    ["machine learning", "regression", "decision trees", "libsvm"],
    ["Python", "R", "Java", "C++", "Haskell", "programming languages"],
    ["statistics", "probability", "mathematics", "theory"],
    ["machine learning", "scikit-learn", "Mahout", "neural networks"],
    ["neural networks", "deep learning", "Big Data", "artificial intelligence"],
    ["Hadoop", "Java", "MapReduce", "Big Data"],
    ["statistics", "R", "statsmodels"],
    ["C++", "deep learning", "artificial intelligence", "probability"],
    ["pandas", "R", "Python"],
    ["databases", "HBase", "Postgres", "MySQL", "MongoDB"],
    ["libsvm", "regression", "support vector machines"]
]
```

And we'll try to find K = 4 topics.

In order to calculate the sampling weights, we'll need to keep track of several counts. Let's first create the data structures for them.

How many times each topic is assigned to each document:

```
# a list of Counters, one for each document
document_topic_counts = [Counter() for _ in documents]
```

How many times each word is assigned to each topic:

```
# a list of Counters, one for each topic
topic_word_counts = [Counter() for _ in range(K)]
```

The total number of words assigned to each topic:

```
# a list of numbers, one for each topic
topic_counts = [0 for _ in range(K)]
```

The total number of words contained in each document:

```
# a list of numbers, one for each document
document_lengths = map(len, documents)
```

The number of distinct words:

```
distinct_words = set(word for document in documents for word in document)
W = len(distinct_words)
```

And the number of documents:

```
D = len(documents)
```

For example, once we populate these, we can find, for example, the number of words in documents[3] associated with topic 1 as:

```
document_topic_counts[3][1]
```

And we can find the number of times *nlp* is associated with topic 2 as:

```
topic_word_counts[2]["nlp"]
```

Now we're ready to define our conditional probability functions. As in Chapter 13, each has a smoothing term that ensures every topic has a nonzero chance of being chosen in any document and that every word has a nonzero chance of being chosen for any topic:

```
def p_topic_given_document(topic, d, alpha=0.1):
    """the fraction of words in document _d_
    that are assigned to _topic_ (plus some smoothing)"""

    return ((document_topic_counts[d][topic] + alpha) /
            (document_lengths[d] + K * alpha))

def p_word_given_topic(word, topic, beta=0.1):
    """the fraction of words assigned to _topic_
    that equal _word_ (plus some smoothing)"""

    return ((topic_word_counts[topic][word] + beta) /
            (topic_counts[topic] + W * beta))
```

We'll use these to create the weights for updating topics:

```
def topic_weight(d, word, k):
    """given a document and a word in that document,
    return the weight for the kth topic"""
```

```
        return p_word_given_topic(word, k) * p_topic_given_document(k, d)

def choose_new_topic(d, word):
    return sample_from([topic_weight(d, word, k)
                        for k in range(K)])
```

There are solid mathematical reasons why `topic_weight` is defined the way it is, but
their details would lead us too far afield. Hopefully it makes at least intuitive sense
that—given a word and its document—the likelihood of any topic choice depends on
both how likely that topic is for the document and how likely that word is for the
topic.

This is all the machinery we need. We start by assigning every word to a random
topic, and populating our counters appropriately:

```
random.seed(0)
document_topics = [[random.randrange(K) for word in document]
                   for document in documents]

for d in range(D):
    for word, topic in zip(documents[d], document_topics[d]):
        document_topic_counts[d][topic] += 1
        topic_word_counts[topic][word] += 1
        topic_counts[topic] += 1
```

Our goal is to get a joint sample of the topics-words distribution and the documents-
topics distribution. We do this using a form of Gibbs sampling that uses the conditional probabilities defined previously:

```
for iter in range(1000):
    for d in range(D):
        for i, (word, topic) in enumerate(zip(documents[d],
                                               document_topics[d])):

            # remove this word / topic from the counts
            # so that it doesn't influence the weights
            document_topic_counts[d][topic] -= 1
            topic_word_counts[topic][word] -= 1
            topic_counts[topic] -= 1
            document_lengths[d] -= 1

            # choose a new topic based on the weights
            new_topic = choose_new_topic(d, word)
            document_topics[d][i] = new_topic

            # and now add it back to the counts
            document_topic_counts[d][new_topic] += 1
            topic_word_counts[new_topic][word] += 1
            topic_counts[new_topic] += 1
            document_lengths[d] += 1
```

What are the topics? They're just numbers 0, 1, 2, and 3. If we want names for them we have to do that ourselves. Let's look at the five most heavily weighted words for each (Table 20-1):

```
for k, word_counts in enumerate(topic_word_counts):
    for word, count in word_counts.most_common():
        if count > 0: print k, word, count
```

Table 20-1. Most common words per topic

Topic 0	Topic 1	Topic 2	Topic 3
Java	R	HBase	regression
Big Data	statistics	Postgres	libsvm
Hadoop	Python	MongoDB	scikit-learn
deep learning	probability	Cassandra	machine learning
artificial intelligence	pandas	NoSQL	neural networks

Based on these I'd probably assign topic names:

```
topic_names = ["Big Data and programming languages",
               "Python and statistics",
               "databases",
               "machine learning"]
```

at which point we can see how the model assigns topics to each user's interests:

```
for document, topic_counts in zip(documents, document_topic_counts):
    print document
    for topic, count in topic_counts.most_common():
        if count > 0:
            print topic_names[topic], count,
    print
```

which gives:

```
['Hadoop', 'Big Data', 'HBase', 'Java', 'Spark', 'Storm', 'Cassandra']
Big Data and programming languages 4 databases 3
['NoSQL', 'MongoDB', 'Cassandra', 'HBase', 'Postgres']
databases 5
['Python', 'scikit-learn', 'scipy', 'numpy', 'statsmodels', 'pandas']
Python and statistics 5 machine learning 1
```

and so on. Given the "ands" we needed in some of our topic names, it's possible we should use more topics, although most likely we don't have enough data to success-fully learn them.

For Further Exploration

- Natural Language Toolkit (*http://www.nltk.org/*) is a popular (and pretty comprehensive) library of NLP tools for Python. It has its own entire book (*http://www.nltk.org/book/*), which is available to read online.

- gensim (*http://radimrehurek.com/gensim/*) is a Python library for topic modeling, which is a better bet than our from-scratch model.

## CHAPTER 21

Network Analysis

Your connections to all the things around you literally define who you are.
—Aaron O'Connell

Many interesting data problems can be fruitfully thought of in terms of *networks*, consisting of *nodes* of some type and the *edges* that join them.

For instance, your Facebook friends form the nodes of a network whose edges are friendship relations. A less obvious example is the World Wide Web itself, with each web page a node, and each hyperlink from one page to another an edge.

Facebook friendship is mutual—if I am Facebook friends with you than necessarily you are friends with me. In this case, we say that the edges are *undirected*. Hyperlinks are not—my website links to whitehouse.gov, but (for reasons inexplicable to me) whitehouse.gov refuses to link to my website. We call these types of edges *directed*. We'll look at both kinds of networks.

Betweenness Centrality

In Chapter 1, we computed the key connectors in the DataSciencester network by counting the number of friends each user had. Now we have enough machinery to look at other approaches. Recall that the network (Figure 21-1) comprised users:

```
users = [
    { "id": 0, "name": "Hero" },
    { "id": 1, "name": "Dunn" },
    { "id": 2, "name": "Sue" },
    { "id": 3, "name": "Chi" },
    { "id": 4, "name": "Thor" },
    { "id": 5, "name": "Clive" },
    { "id": 6, "name": "Hicks" },
    { "id": 7, "name": "Devin" },
```

```
        { "id": 8, "name": "Kate" },
        { "id": 9, "name": "Klein" }
    ]
```

and friendships:

```
friendships = [(0, 1), (0, 2), (1, 2), (1, 3), (2, 3), (3, 4),
               (4, 5), (5, 6), (5, 7), (6, 8), (7, 8), (8, 9)]
```

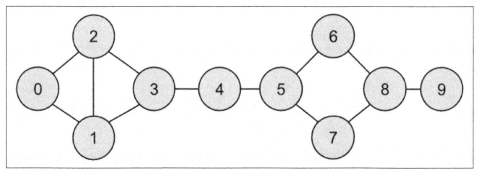

Figure 21-1. The DataSciencester network

We also added friend lists to each user `dict`:

```
for user in users:
    user["friends"] = []

for i, j in friendships:
    # this works because users[i] is the user whose id is i
    users[i]["friends"].append(users[j]) # add i as a friend of j
    users[j]["friends"].append(users[i]) # add j as a friend of i
```

When we left off we were dissatisfied with our notion of *degree centrality*, which didn't really agree with our intuition about who were the key connectors of the network.

An alternative metric is *betweenness centrality*, which identifies people who frequently are on the shortest paths between pairs of other people. In particular, the betweenness centrality of node i is computed by adding up, for every other pair of nodes j and k, the proportion of shortest paths between node j and node k that pass through i.

That is, to figure out Thor's betweenness centrality, we'll need to compute all the shortest paths between all pairs of people who aren't Thor. And then we'll need to count how many of those shortest paths pass through Thor. For instance, the only shortest path between Chi (`id` 3) and Clive (`id` 5) passes through Thor, while neither of the two shortest paths between Hero (`id` 0) and Chi (`id` 3) does.

So, as a first step, we'll need to figure out the shortest paths between all pairs of people. There are some pretty sophisticated algorithms for doing so efficiently, but (as is almost always the case) we will use a less efficient, easier-to-understand algorithm.

This algorithm (an implementation of breadth-first search) is one of the more complicated ones in the book, so let's talk through it carefully:

1. Our goal is a function that takes a `from_user` and finds *all* shortest paths to every other user.

2. We'll represent a path as `list` of user IDs. Since every path starts at `from_user`, we won't include her ID in the list. This means that the length of the list representing the path will be the length of the path itself.

3. We'll maintain a dictionary `shortest_paths_to` where the keys are user IDs and the values are lists of paths that end at the user with the specified ID. If there is a unique shortest path, the list will just contain that one path. If there are multiple shortest paths, the list will contain all of them.

4. We'll also maintain a queue `frontier` that contains the users we want to explore in the order we want to explore them. We'll store them as pairs (`prev_user`, `user`) so that we know how we got to each one. We initialize the queue with all the neighbors of `from_user`. (We haven't ever talked about queues, which are data structures optimized for "add to the end" and "remove from the front" operations. In Python, they are implemented as `collections.deque` which is actually a double-ended queue.)

5. As we explore the graph, whenever we find new neighbors that we don't already know shortest paths to, we add them to the end of the queue to explore later, with the current user as `prev_user`.

6. When we take a user off the queue, and we've never encountered that user before, we've definitely found one or more shortest paths to him—each of the shortest paths to `prev_user` with one extra step added.

7. When we take a user off the queue and we *have* encountered that user before, then either we've found another shortest path (in which case we should add it) or we've found a longer path (in which case we shouldn't).

8. When no more users are left on the queue, we've explored the whole graph (or, at least, the parts of it that are reachable from the starting user) and we're done.

We can put this all together into a (large) function:

```
from collections import deque

def shortest_paths_from(from_user):

    # a dictionary from "user_id" to *all* shortest paths to that user
    shortest_paths_to = { from_user["id"] : [[]] }

    # a queue of (previous user, next user) that we need to check.
    # starts out with all pairs (from_user, friend_of_from_user)
```

```
        frontier = deque((from_user, friend)
                          for friend in from_user["friends"])

        # keep going until we empty the queue
        while frontier:

            prev_user, user = frontier.popleft()    # remove the user who's
            user_id = user["id"]                     # first in the queue

            # because of the way we're adding to the queue,
            # necessarily we already know some shortest paths to prev_user
            paths_to_prev_user = shortest_paths_to[prev_user["id"]]
            new_paths_to_user = [path + [user_id] for path in paths_to_prev_user]

            # it's possible we already know a shortest path
            old_paths_to_user = shortest_paths_to.get(user_id, [])

            # what's the shortest path to here that we've seen so far?
            if old_paths_to_user:
                min_path_length = len(old_paths_to_user[0])
            else:
                min_path_length = float('inf')

            # only keep paths that aren't too long and are actually new
            new_paths_to_user = [path
                                 for path in new_paths_to_user
                                 if len(path) <= min_path_length
                                 and path not in old_paths_to_user]

            shortest_paths_to[user_id] = old_paths_to_user + new_paths_to_user

            # add never-seen neighbors to the frontier
            frontier.extend((user, friend)
                            for friend in user["friends"]
                            if friend["id"] not in shortest_paths_to)

    return shortest_paths_to
```

Now we can store these dicts with each node:

```
for user in users:
    user["shortest_paths"] = shortest_paths_from(user)
```

And we're finally ready to compute betweenness centrality. For every pair of nodes i and j, we know the n shortest paths from i to j. Then, for each of those paths, we just add $1/n$ to the centrality of each node on that path:

```
for user in users:
    user["betweenness_centrality"] = 0.0

for source in users:
    source_id = source["id"]
    for target_id, paths in source["shortest_paths"].iteritems():
```

```
if source_id < target_id:        # don't double count
    num_paths = len(paths)       # how many shortest paths?
    contrib = 1 / num_paths      # contribution to centrality
    for path in paths:
        for id in path:
            if id not in [source_id, target_id]:
                users[id]["betweenness_centrality"] += contrib
```

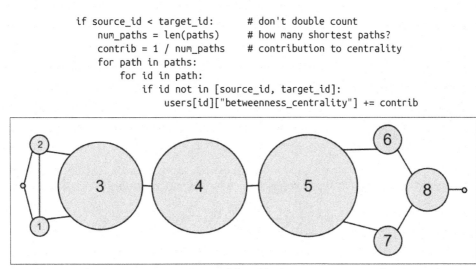

Figure 21-2. The DataSciencester network sized by betweenness centrality

As shown in Figure 21-2, users 0 and 9 have centrality 0 (as neither is on any shortest path between other users), whereas 3, 4, and 5 all have high centralities (as all three lie on many shortest paths).

 Generally the centrality numbers aren't that meaningful themselves. What we care about is how the numbers for each node compare to the numbers for other nodes.

Another measure we can look at is *closeness centrality*. First, for each user we compute her *farness*, which is the sum of the lengths of her shortest paths to each other user. Since we've already computed the shortest paths between each pair of nodes, it's easy to add their lengths. (If there are multiple shortest paths, they all have the same length, so we can just look at the first one.)

```
def farness(user):
    """the sum of the lengths of the shortest paths to each other user"""
    return sum(len(paths[0])
               for paths in user["shortest_paths"].values())
```

after which it's very little work to compute closeness centrality (Figure 21-3):

```
for user in users:
    user["closeness_centrality"] = 1 / farness(user)
```

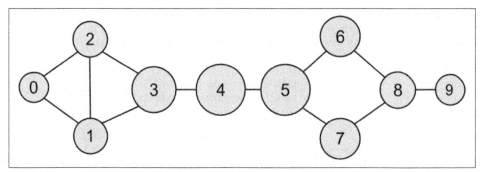

Figure 21-3. The DataSciencester network sized by closeness centrality

There is much less variation here—even the very central nodes are still pretty far from the nodes out on the periphery.

As we saw, computing shortest paths is kind of a pain. For this reason, betweenness and closeness centrality aren't often used on large networks. The less intuitive (but generally easier to compute) *eigenvector centrality* is more frequently used.

Eigenvector Centrality

In order to talk about eigenvector centrality, we have to talk about eigenvectors, and in order to talk about eigenvectors, we have to talk about matrix multiplication.

Matrix Multiplication

If A is a $n_1 \times k_1$ matrix and B is a $n_2 \times k_2$ matrix, and if $k_1 = n_2$, then their product AB is the $n_1 \times k_2$ matrix whose (i,j)th entry is:

$$A_{i1}B_{1j} + A_{i2}B_{2j} + \cdots + A_{ik}B_{kj}$$

Which is just the dot product of the *i*th row of A (thought of as a vector) with the *j*th column of B (also thought of as a vector):

```
def matrix_product_entry(A, B, i, j):
    return dot(get_row(A, i), get_column(B, j))
```

after which we have:

```
def matrix_multiply(A, B):
    n1, k1 = shape(A)
    n2, k2 = shape(B)
    if k1 != n2:
        raise ArithmeticError("incompatible shapes!")

    return make_matrix(n1, k2, partial(matrix_product_entry, A, B))
```

Notice that if A is a $n \times k$ matrix and B is a $k \times 1$ matrix, then AB is a $n \times 1$ matrix. If we treat a vector as a one-column matrix, we can think of A as a function that maps k-dimensional vectors to n-dimensional vectors, where the function is just matrix multiplication.

Previously we represented vectors simply as lists, which isn't quite the same:

```
v = [1, 2, 3]
v_as_matrix = [[1],
               [2],
               [3]]
```

So we'll need some helper functions to convert back and forth between the two representations:

```
def vector_as_matrix(v):
    """returns the vector v (represented as a list) as a n x 1 matrix"""
    return [[v_i] for v_i in v]

def vector_from_matrix(v_as_matrix):
    """returns the n x 1 matrix as a list of values"""
    return [row[0] for row in v_as_matrix]
```

after which we can define the matrix operation using `matrix_multiply`:

```
def matrix_operate(A, v):
    v_as_matrix = vector_as_matrix(v)
    product = matrix_multiply(A, v_as_matrix)
    return vector_from_matrix(product)
```

When A is a *square* matrix, this operation maps n-dimensional vectors to other n-dimensional vectors. It's possible that, for some matrix A and vector v, when A operates on v we get back a scalar multiple of v. That is, that the result is a vector that points in the same direction as v. When this happens (and when, in addition, v is not a vector of all zeroes), we call v an *eigenvector* of A. And we call the multiplier an *eigenvalue*.

One possible way to find an eigenvector of A is by picking a starting vector v, applying `matrix_operate`, rescaling the result to have magnitude 1, and repeating until the process converges:

```
def find_eigenvector(A, tolerance=0.00001):
    guess = [random.random() for __ in A]

    while True:
        result = matrix_operate(A, guess)
        length = magnitude(result)
        next_guess = scalar_multiply(1/length, result)

        if distance(guess, next_guess) < tolerance:
            return next_guess, length    # eigenvector, eigenvalue
```

```
        guess = next_guess
```

By construction, the returned `guess` is a vector such that, when you apply `matrix_operate` to it and rescale it to have length 1, you get back (a vector very close to) itself. Which means it's an eigenvector.

Not all matrices of real numbers have eigenvectors and eigenvalues. For example the matrix:

```
rotate = [[ 0, 1],
          [-1, 0]]
```

rotates vectors 90 degrees clockwise, which means that the only vector it maps to a scalar multiple of itself is a vector of zeroes. If you tried `find_eigenvector(rotate)` it would run forever. Even matrices that have eigenvectors can sometimes get stuck in cycles. Consider the matrix:

```
flip = [[0, 1],
        [1, 0]]
```

This matrix maps any vector [x, y] to [y, x]. This means that, for example, [1, 1] is an eigenvector with eigenvalue 1. However, if you start with a random vector with unequal coordinates, `find_eigenvector` will just repeatedly swap the coordinates forever. (Not-from-scratch libraries like NumPy use different methods that would work in this case.) Nonetheless, when `find_eigenvector` does return a result, that result is indeed an eigenvector.

Centrality

How does this help us understand the DataSciencester network?

To start with, we'll need to represent the connections in our network as an `adja cency_matrix`, whose (i,j)th entry is either 1 (if user *i* and user *j* are friends) or 0 (if they're not):

```
def entry_fn(i, j):
    return 1 if (i, j) in friendships or (j, i) in friendships else 0

n = len(users)
adjacency_matrix = make_matrix(n, n, entry_fn)
```

The eigenvector centrality for each user is then the entry corresponding to that user in the eigenvector returned by `find_eigenvector` (Figure 21-4):

For technical reasons that are way beyond the scope of this book, any nonzero adjacency matrix necessarily has an eigenvector all of whose values are non-negative. And fortunately for us, for this `adjacency_matrix` our `find_eigenvector` function finds it.

```
eigenvector_centralities, _ = find_eigenvector(adjacency_matrix)
```

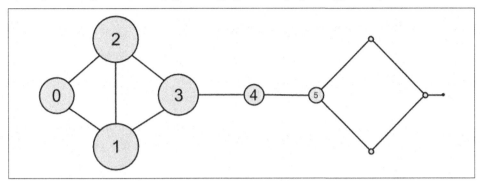

Figure 21-4. The DataSciencester network sized by eigenvector centrality

Users with high eigenvector centrality should be those who have a lot of connections and connections to people who themselves have high centrality.

Here users 1 and 2 are the most central, as they both have three connections to people who are themselves highly central. As we move away from them, people's centralities steadily drop off.

On a network this small, eigenvector centrality behaves somewhat erratically. If you try adding or subtracting links, you'll find that small changes in the network can dramatically change the centrality numbers. In a much larger network this would not particularly be the case.

We still haven't motivated why an eigenvector might lead to a reasonable notion of centrality. Being an eigenvector means that if you compute:

```
matrix_operate(adjacency_matrix, eigenvector_centralities)
```

the result is a scalar multiple of `eigenvector_centralities`.

If you look at how matrix multiplication works, `matrix_operate` produces a vector whose *i*th element is:

```
dot(get_row(adjacency_matrix, i), eigenvector_centralities)
```

which is precisely the sum of the eigenvector centralities of the users connected to user *i*.

In other words, eigenvector centralities are numbers, one per user, such that each user's value is a constant multiple of the sum of his neighbors' values. In this case centrality means being connected to people who themselves are central. The more centrality you are directly connected to, the more central you are. This is of course a circular definition—eigenvectors are the way of breaking out of the circularity.

Another way of understanding this is by thinking about what `find_eigenvector` is doing here. It starts by assigning each node a random centrality. It then repeats the following two steps until the process converges:

1. Give each node a new centrality score that equals the sum of its neighbors' (old) centrality scores.
2. Rescale the vector of centralities to have magnitude 1.

Although the mathematics behind it may seem somewhat opaque at first, the calculation itself is relatively straightforward (unlike, say, betweenness centrality) and is pretty easy to perform on even very large graphs.

Directed Graphs and PageRank

DataSciencester isn't getting much traction, so the VP of Revenue considers pivoting from a friendship model to an endorsement model. It turns out that no one particularly cares which data scientists are *friends* with one another, but tech recruiters care very much which data scientists are respected by other data scientists.

In this new model, we'll track endorsements (`source`, `target`) that no longer represent a reciprocal relationship, but rather that `source` endorses `target` as an awesome data scientist (Figure 21-5). We'll need to account for this asymmetry:

```
endorsements = [(0, 1), (1, 0), (0, 2), (2, 0), (1, 2),
                (2, 1), (1, 3), (2, 3), (3, 4), (5, 4),
                (5, 6), (7, 5), (6, 8), (8, 7), (8, 9)]

for user in users:
    user["endorses"] = []       # add one list to track outgoing endorsements
    user["endorsed_by"] = []    # and another to track endorsements

for source_id, target_id in endorsements:
    users[source_id]["endorses"].append(users[target_id])
    users[target_id]["endorsed_by"].append(users[source_id])
```

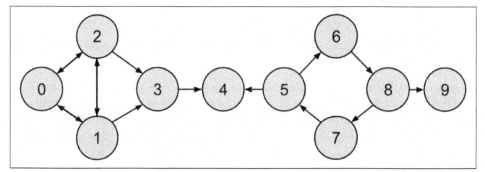

Figure 21-5. The DataSciencester network of endorsements

after which we can easily find the most_endorsed data scientists and sell that information to recruiters:

```
endorsements_by_id = [(user["id"], len(user["endorsed_by"]))
                      for user in users]

sorted(endorsements_by_id,
       key=lambda (user_id, num_endorsements): num_endorsements,
       reverse=True)
```

However, "number of endorsements" is an easy metric to game. All you need to do is create phony accounts and have them endorse you. Or arrange with your friends to endorse each other. (As users 0, 1, and 2 seem to have done.)

A better metric would take into account *who* endorses you. Endorsements from people who have a lot of endorsements should somehow count more than endorsements from people with few endorsements. This is the essence of the PageRank algorithm, used by Google to rank websites based on which other websites link to them, which other websites link to those, and so on.

(If this sort of reminds you of the idea behind eigenvector centrality, it should.)

A simplified version looks like this:

1. There is a total of 1.0 (or 100%) PageRank in the network.
2. Initially this PageRank is equally distributed among nodes.
3. At each step, a large fraction of each node's PageRank is distributed evenly among its outgoing links.
4. At each step, the remainder of each node's PageRank is distributed evenly among all nodes.

```
def page_rank(users, damping = 0.85, num_iters = 100):

    # initially distribute PageRank evenly
    num_users = len(users)
    pr = { user["id"] : 1 / num_users for user in users }

    # this is the small fraction of PageRank
    # that each node gets each iteration
    base_pr = (1 - damping) / num_users

    for __ in range(num_iters):
        next_pr = { user["id"] : base_pr for user in users }
        for user in users:
            # distribute PageRank to outgoing links
            links_pr = pr[user["id"]] * damping
            for endorsee in user["endorses"]:
                next_pr[endorsee["id"]] += links_pr / len(user["endorses"])
```

```
        pr = next_pr

    return pr
```

PageRank (Figure 21-6) identifies user 4 (Thor) as the highest ranked data scientist.

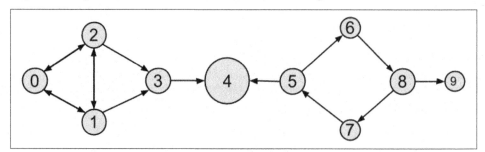

Figure 21-6. The DataSciencester network sized by PageRank

Even though he has fewer endorsements (2) than users 0, 1, and 2, his endorsements carry with them rank from their endorsements. Additionally, both of his endorsers endorsed only him, which means that he doesn't have to divide their rank with anyone else.

For Further Exploration

- There are many other notions of centrality (*http://en.wikipedia.org/wiki/Central ity*) besides the ones we used (although the ones we used are pretty much the most popular ones).

- NetworkX (*http://networkx.github.io/*) is a Python library for network analysis. It has functions for computing centralities and for visualizing graphs.

- Gephi (*http://gephi.github.io/*) is a love-it/hate-it GUI-based network-visualization tool.

## CHAPTER 22

Recommender Systems

O nature, nature, why art thou so dishonest, as ever to send men with these false recommendations into the world!

—Henry Fielding

Another common data problem is producing *recommendations* of some sort. Netflix recommends movies you might want to watch. Amazon recommends products you might want to buy. Twitter recommends users you might want to follow. In this chapter, we'll look at several ways to use data to make recommendations.

In particular, we'll look at the data set of `users_interests` that we've used before:

```
users_interests = [
    ["Hadoop", "Big Data", "HBase", "Java", "Spark", "Storm", "Cassandra"],
    ["NoSQL", "MongoDB", "Cassandra", "HBase", "Postgres"],
    ["Python", "scikit-learn", "scipy", "numpy", "statsmodels", "pandas"],
    ["R", "Python", "statistics", "regression", "probability"],
    ["machine learning", "regression", "decision trees", "libsvm"],
    ["Python", "R", "Java", "C++", "Haskell", "programming languages"],
    ["statistics", "probability", "mathematics", "theory"],
    ["machine learning", "scikit-learn", "Mahout", "neural networks"],
    ["neural networks", "deep learning", "Big Data", "artificial intelligence"],
    ["Hadoop", "Java", "MapReduce", "Big Data"],
    ["statistics", "R", "statsmodels"],
    ["C++", "deep learning", "artificial intelligence", "probability"],
    ["pandas", "R", "Python"],
    ["databases", "HBase", "Postgres", "MySQL", "MongoDB"],
    ["libsvm", "regression", "support vector machines"]
]
```

And we'll think about the problem of recommending new interests to a user based on her currently specified interests.

Manual Curation

Before the Internet, when you needed book recommendations you would go to the library, where a librarian was available to suggest books that were relevant to your interests or similar to books you liked.

Given DataSciencester's limited number of users and interests, it would be easy for you to spend an afternoon manually recommending interests for each user. But this method doesn't scale particularly well, and it's limited by your personal knowledge and imagination. (Not that I'm suggesting that your personal knowledge and imagination are limited.) So let's think about what we can do with *data*.

Recommending What's Popular

One easy approach is to simply recommend what's popular:

```python
popular_interests = Counter(interest
                            for user_interests in users_interests
                            for interest in user_interests).most_common()
```

which looks like:

```python
[('Python', 4),
 ('R', 4),
 ('Java', 3),
 ('regression', 3),
 ('statistics', 3),
 ('probability', 3),
 # ...
]
```

Having computed this, we can just suggest to a user the most popular interests that he's not already interested in:

```python
def most_popular_new_interests(user_interests, max_results=5):
    suggestions = [(interest, frequency)
                   for interest, frequency in popular_interests
                   if interest not in user_interests]
    return suggestions[:max_results]
```

So, if you are user 1, with interests:

```python
["NoSQL", "MongoDB", "Cassandra", "HBase", "Postgres"]
```

then we'd recommend you:

```python
most_popular_new_interests(users_interests[1], 5)

# [('Python', 4), ('R', 4), ('Java', 3), ('regression', 3), ('statistics', 3)]
```

If you are user 3, who's already interested in many of those things, you'd instead get:

```
[('Java', 3),
 ('HBase', 3),
 ('Big Data', 3),
 ('neural networks', 2),
 ('Hadoop', 2)]
```

Of course, "lots of people are interested in Python so maybe you should be too" is not the most compelling sales pitch. If someone is brand new to our site and we don't know anything about them, that's possibly the best we can do. Let's see how we can do better by basing each user's recommendations on her interests.

User-Based Collaborative Filtering

One way of taking a user's interests into account is to look for users who are somehow *similar* to him, and then suggest the things that those users are interested in.

In order to do that, we'll need a way to measure how similar two users are. Here we'll use a metric called *cosine similarity*. Given two vectors, v and w, it's defined as:

```
def cosine_similarity(v, w):
    return dot(v, w) / math.sqrt(dot(v, v) * dot(w, w))
```

It measures the "angle" between v and w. If v and w point in the same direction, then the numerator and denominator are equal, and their cosine similarity equals 1. If v and w point in opposite directions, then their cosine similarity equals -1. And if v is 0 whenever w is not (and vice versa) then dot(v, w) is 0 and so the cosine similarity will be 0.

We'll apply this to vectors of 0s and 1s, each vector v representing one user's interests. v[i] will be 1 if the user is specified the ith interest, 0 otherwise. Accordingly, "similar users" will mean "users whose interest vectors most nearly point in the same direction." Users with identical interests will have similarity 1. Users with no identical interests will have similarity 0. Otherwise the similarity will fall in between, with numbers closer to 1 indicating "very similar" and numbers closer to 0 indicating "not very similar."

A good place to start is collecting the known interests and (implicitly) assigning indices to them. We can do this by using a set comprehension to find the unique interests, putting them in a list, and then sorting them. The first interest in the resulting list will be interest 0, and so on:

```
unique_interests = sorted(list({ interest
                                 for user_interests in users_interests
                                 for interest in user_interests }))
```

This gives us a list that starts:

```
['Big Data',
 'C++',
```

```
    'Cassandra',
    'HBase',
    'Hadoop',
    'Haskell',
    # ...
]
```

Next we want to produce an "interest" vector of 0s and 1s for each user. We just need to iterate over the unique_interests list, substituting a 1 if the user has each interest, a 0 if not:

```
def make_user_interest_vector(user_interests):
    """given a list of interests, produce a vector whose ith element is 1
    if unique_interests[i] is in the list, 0 otherwise"""
    return [1 if interest in user_interests else 0
            for interest in unique_interests]
```

after which, we can create a matrix of user interests simply by map-ping this function against the list of lists of interests:

```
user_interest_matrix = map(make_user_interest_vector, users_interests)
```

Now user_interest_matrix[i][j] equals 1 if user i specified interest j, 0 otherwise.

Because we have a small data set, it's no problem to compute the pairwise similarities between all of our users:

```
user_similarities = [[cosine_similarity(interest_vector_i, interest_vector_j)
                      for interest_vector_j in user_interest_matrix]
                     for interest_vector_i in user_interest_matrix]
```

after which, user_similarities[i][j] gives us the similarity between users *i* and *j*.

For instance, user_similarities[0][9] is 0.57, as those two users share interests in Hadoop, Java, and Big Data. On the other hand, user_similarities[0][8] is only 0.19, as users 0 and 8 share only one interest, Big Data.

In particular, user_similarities[i] is the vector of user *i*'s similarities to every other user. We can use this to write a function that finds the most similar users to a given user. We'll make sure not to include the user herself, nor any users with zero similarity. And we'll sort the results from most similar to least similar:

```
def most_similar_users_to(user_id):
    pairs = [(other_user_id, similarity)              # find other
             for other_user_id, similarity in         # users with
               enumerate(user_similarities[user_id])  # nonzero
             if user_id != other_user_id and similarity > 0]  # similarity

    return sorted(pairs,                              # sort them
                  key=lambda (_, similarity): similarity,  # most similar
                  reverse=True)                       # first
```

For instance, if we call `most_similar_users_to(0)` we get:

```
[(9, 0.5669467095138409),
 (1, 0.3380617018914066),
 (8, 0.1889822365046136),
 (13, 0.1690308509457033),
 (5, 0.1543033499620919)]
```

How do we use this to suggest new interests to a user? For each interest, we can just add up the user-similarities of the other users interested in it:

```python
def user_based_suggestions(user_id, include_current_interests=False):
    # sum up the similarities
    suggestions = defaultdict(float)
    for other_user_id, similarity in most_similar_users_to(user_id):
        for interest in users_interests[other_user_id]:
            suggestions[interest] += similarity

    # convert them to a sorted list
    suggestions = sorted(suggestions.items(),
                         key=lambda (_, weight): weight,
                         reverse=True)

    # and (maybe) exclude already-interests
    if include_current_interests:
        return suggestions
    else:
        return [(suggestion, weight)
                for suggestion, weight in suggestions
                if suggestion not in users_interests[user_id]]
```

If we call `user_based_suggestions(0)`, the first several suggested interests are:

```
[('MapReduce', 0.5669467095138409),
 ('MongoDB', 0.50709255283711),
 ('Postgres', 0.50709255283711),
 ('NoSQL', 0.3380617018914066),
 ('neural networks', 0.1889822365046136),
 ('deep learning', 0.1889822365046136),
 ('artificial intelligence', 0.1889822365046136),
 #...
]
```

These seem like pretty decent suggestions for someone whose stated interests are "Big Data" and database-related. (The weights aren't intrinsically meaningful; we just use them for ordering.)

This approach doesn't work as well when the number of items gets very large. Recall the curse of dimensionality from Chapter 12—in large-dimensional vector spaces most vectors are very far apart (and therefore point in very different directions). That is, when there are a large number of interests the "most similar users" to a given user might not be similar at all.

Imagine a site like Amazon.com, from which I've bought thousands of items over the last couple of decades. You could attempt to identify similar users to me based on buying patterns, but most likely in all the world there's no one whose purchase history looks even remotely like mine. Whoever my "most similar" shopper is, he's probably not similar to me at all, and his purchases would almost certainly make for lousy recommendations.

Item-Based Collaborative Filtering

An alternative approach is to compute similarities between interests directly. We can then generate suggestions for each user by aggregating interests that are similar to her current interests.

To start with, we'll want to *transpose* our user-interest matrix so that rows correspond to interests and columns correspond to users:

```
interest_user_matrix = [[user_interest_vector[j]
                         for user_interest_vector in user_interest_matrix]
                        for j, _ in enumerate(unique_interests)]
```

What does this look like? Row j of `interest_user_matrix` is column j of `user_interest_matrix`. That is, it has 1 for each user with that interest and 0 for each user without that interest.

For example, `unique_interests[0]` is Big Data, and so `interest_user_matrix[0]` is:

```
[1, 0, 0, 0, 0, 0, 0, 0, 1, 1, 0, 0, 0, 0, 0]
```

because users 0, 8, and 9 indicated interest in Big Data.

We can now use cosine similarity again. If precisely the same users are interested in two topics, their similarity will be 1. If no two users are interested in both topics, their similarity will be 0:

```
interest_similarities = [[cosine_similarity(user_vector_i, user_vector_j)
                          for user_vector_j in interest_user_matrix]
                         for user_vector_i in interest_user_matrix]
```

For example, we can find the interests most similar to Big Data (interest 0) using:

```
def most_similar_interests_to(interest_id):
    similarities = interest_similarities[interest_id]
    pairs = [(unique_interests[other_interest_id], similarity)
             for other_interest_id, similarity in enumerate(similarities)
             if interest_id != other_interest_id and similarity > 0]
    return sorted(pairs,
                  key=lambda (_, similarity): similarity,
                  reverse=True)
```

which suggests the following similar interests:

```
[('Hadoop', 0.8164965809277261),
 ('Java', 0.6666666666666666),
 ('MapReduce', 0.5773502691896258),
 ('Spark', 0.5773502691896258),
 ('Storm', 0.5773502691896258),
 ('Cassandra', 0.4082482904638631),
 ('artificial intelligence', 0.4082482904638631),
 ('deep learning', 0.4082482904638631),
 ('neural networks', 0.4082482904638631),
 ('HBase', 0.3333333333333333)]
```

Now we can create recommendations for a user by summing up the similarities of the interests similar to his:

```
def item_based_suggestions(user_id, include_current_interests=False):
    # add up the similar interests
    suggestions = defaultdict(float)
    user_interest_vector = user_interest_matrix[user_id]
    for interest_id, is_interested in enumerate(user_interest_vector):
        if is_interested == 1:
            similar_interests = most_similar_interests_to(interest_id)
            for interest, similarity in similar_interests:
                suggestions[interest] += similarity

    # sort them by weight
    suggestions = sorted(suggestions.items(),
                         key=lambda (_, similarity): similarity,
                         reverse=True)

    if include_current_interests:
        return suggestions
    else:
        return [(suggestion, weight)
                for suggestion, weight in suggestions
                if suggestion not in users_interests[user_id]]
```

For user 0, this generates the following (seemingly reasonable) recommendations:

```
[('MapReduce', 1.861807319565799),
 ('Postgres', 1.3164965809277263),
 ('MongoDB', 1.3164965809277263),
 ('NoSQL', 1.2844570503761732),
 ('programming languages', 0.5773502691896258),
 ('MySQL', 0.5773502691896258),
 ('Haskell', 0.5773502691896258),
 ('databases', 0.5773502691896258),
 ('neural networks', 0.4082482904638631),
 ('deep learning', 0.4082482904638631),
 ('C++', 0.4082482904638631),
 ('artificial intelligence', 0.4082482904638631),
 ('Python', 0.2886751345948129),
 ('R', 0.2886751345948129)]
```

For Further Exploration

- Crab (*http://muricoca.github.io/crab/*) is a framework for building recommender systems in Python.
- Graphlab also has a recommender toolkit (*http://bit.ly/1MF9Tsy*).
- The Netflix Prize (*http://www.netflixprize.com*) was a somewhat famous competition to build a better system to recommend movies to Netflix users.

## CHAPTER 23

Databases and SQL

Memory is man's greatest friend and worst enemy.
—Gilbert Parker

The data you need will often live in *databases*, systems designed for efficiently storing and querying data. The bulk of these are *relational* databases, such as Oracle, MySQL, and SQL Server, which store data in *tables* and are typically queried using Structured Query Language (SQL), a declarative language for manipulating data.

SQL is a pretty essential part of the data scientist's toolkit. In this chapter, we'll create NotQuiteABase, a Python implementation of something that's not quite a database. We'll also cover the basics of SQL while showing how they work in our not-quite database, which is the most "from scratch" way I could think of to help you understand what they're doing. My hope is that solving problems in NotQuiteABase will give you a good sense of how you might solve the same problems using SQL.

CREATE TABLE and INSERT

A relational database is a collection of tables (and of relationships among them). A table is simply a collection of rows, not unlike the matrices we've been working with. However, a table also has associated with it a fixed *schema* consisting of column names and column types.

For example, imagine a `users` data set containing for each user her `user_id`, `name`, and `num_friends`:

```
users = [[0, "Hero", 0],
         [1, "Dunn", 2],
         [2, "Sue", 3],
         [3, "Chi", 3]]
```

In SQL, we might create this table with:

```
CREATE TABLE users (
    user_id INT NOT NULL,
    name VARCHAR(200),
    num_friends INT);
```

Notice that we specified that the user_id and num_friends must be integers (and that user_id isn't allowed to be NULL, which indicates a missing value and is sort of like our None) and that the name should be a string of length 200 or less. NotQuiteABase won't take types into account, but we'll behave as if it did.

 SQL is almost completely case and indentation insensitive. The capitalization and indentation style here is my preferred style. If you start learning SQL, you will surely encounter other examples styled differently.

You can insert the rows with INSERT statements:

```
INSERT INTO users (user_id, name, num_friends) VALUES (0, 'Hero', 0);
```

Notice also that SQL statements need to end with semicolons, and that SQL requires single quotes for its strings.

In NotQuiteABase, you'll create a Table simply by specifying the names of its columns. And to insert a row, you'll use the table's insert() method, which takes a list of row values that need to be in the same order as the table's column names.

Behind the scenes, we'll store each row as a dict from column names to values. A real database would never use such a space-wasting representation, but doing so will make NotQuiteABase much easier to work with:

```
class Table:
    def __init__(self, columns):
        self.columns = columns
        self.rows = []

    def __repr__(self):
        """pretty representation of the table: columns then rows"""
        return str(self.columns) + "\n" + "\n".join(map(str, self.rows))

    def insert(self, row_values):
        if len(row_values) != len(self.columns):
            raise TypeError("wrong number of elements")
        row_dict = dict(zip(self.columns, row_values))
        self.rows.append(row_dict)
```

For example, we could set up:

```
users = Table(["user_id", "name", "num_friends"])
users.insert([0, "Hero", 0])
users.insert([1, "Dunn", 2])
users.insert([2, "Sue", 3])
users.insert([3, "Chi", 3])
users.insert([4, "Thor", 3])
users.insert([5, "Clive", 2])
users.insert([6, "Hicks", 3])
users.insert([7, "Devin", 2])
users.insert([8, "Kate", 2])
users.insert([9, "Klein", 3])
users.insert([10, "Jen", 1])
```

If you now print users, you'll see:

```
['user_id', 'name', 'num_friends']
{'user_id': 0, 'name': 'Hero', 'num_friends': 0}
{'user_id': 1, 'name': 'Dunn', 'num_friends': 2}
{'user_id': 2, 'name': 'Sue', 'num_friends': 3}
...
```

UPDATE

Sometimes you need to update the data that's already in the database. For instance, if Dunn acquires another friend, you might need to do this:

```
UPDATE users
SET num_friends = 3
WHERE user_id = 1;
```

The key features are:

- What table to update
- Which rows to update
- Which fields to update
- What their new values should be

We'll add a similar update method to NotQuiteABase. Its first argument will be a dict whose keys are the columns to update and whose values are the new values for those fields. And its second argument is a predicate that returns True for rows that should be updated, False otherwise:

```
def update(self, updates, predicate):
    for row in self.rows:
        if predicate(row):
            for column, new_value in updates.iteritems():
                row[column] = new_value
```

after which we can simply do this:

```
users.update({'num_friends' : 3},                # set num_friends = 3
              lambda row: row['user_id'] == 1)   # in rows where user_id == 1
```

DELETE

There are two ways to delete rows from a table in SQL. The dangerous way deletes every row from a table:

```
DELETE FROM users;
```

The less dangerous way adds a WHERE clause and only deletes rows that match a certain condition:

```
DELETE FROM users WHERE user_id = 1;
```

It's easy to add this functionality to our Table:

```
def delete(self, predicate=lambda row: True):
    """delete all rows matching predicate
    or all rows if no predicate supplied"""
    self.rows = [row for row in self.rows if not(predicate(row))]
```

If you supply a predicate function (i.e., a WHERE clause), this deletes only the rows that satisfy it. If you don't supply one, the default predicate always returns True, and you will delete every row.

For example:

```
users.delete(lambda row: row["user_id"] == 1)  # deletes rows with user_id == 1
users.delete()                                  # deletes every row
```

SELECT

Typically you don't inspect SQL tables directly. Instead you query them with a SELECT statement:

```
SELECT * FROM users;                           -- get the entire contents
SELECT * FROM users LIMIT 2;                    -- get the first two rows
SELECT user_id FROM users;                      -- only get specific columns
SELECT user_id FROM users WHERE name = 'Dunn';  -- only get specific rows
```

You can also use SELECT statements to calculate fields:

```
SELECT LENGTH(name) AS name_length FROM users;
```

We'll give our Table class a select() method that returns a new Table. The method accepts two optional arguments:

- keep_columns specifies the name of the columns you want to keep in the result. If you don't supply it, the result contains all the columns.

- additional_columns is a dictionary whose keys are new column names and whose values are functions specifying how to compute the values of the new columns.

If you were to supply neither of them, you'd simply get back a copy of the table:

```
def select(self, keep_columns=None, additional_columns=None):

    if keep_columns is None:         # if no columns specified,
        keep_columns = self.columns  # return all columns

    if additional_columns is None:
        additional_columns = {}

    # new table for results
    result_table = Table(keep_columns + additional_columns.keys())

    for row in self.rows:
        new_row = [row[column] for column in keep_columns]
        for column_name, calculation in additional_columns.iteritems():
            new_row.append(calculation(row))
        result_table.insert(new_row)

    return result_table
```

Our select() returns a new Table, while the typical SQL SELECT just produces some sort of transient result set (unless you explicitly insert the results into a table).

We'll also need where() and limit() methods. Both are pretty simple:

```
def where(self, predicate=lambda row: True):
    """return only the rows that satisfy the supplied predicate"""
    where_table = Table(self.columns)
    where_table.rows = filter(predicate, self.rows)
    return where_table

def limit(self, num_rows):
    """return only the first num_rows rows"""
    limit_table = Table(self.columns)
    limit_table.rows = self.rows[:num_rows]
    return limit_table
```

after which we can easily construct NotQuiteABase equivalents to the preceding SQL statements:

```
# SELECT * FROM users;
users.select()

# SELECT * FROM users LIMIT 2;
users.limit(2)

# SELECT user_id FROM users;
users.select(keep_columns=["user_id"])
```

```
# SELECT user_id FROM users WHERE name = 'Dunn';
users.where(lambda row: row["name"] == "Dunn") \
    .select(keep_columns=["user_id"])

# SELECT LENGTH(name) AS name_length FROM users;
def name_length(row): return len(row["name"])

users.select(keep_columns=[],
             additional_columns = { "name_length" : name_length })
```

Notice that—unlike in the rest of the book—here I use backslash \ to continue statements across multiple lines. I find it makes the chained-together NotQuiteABase queries more readable than any other way of writing them.

GROUP BY

Another common SQL operation is GROUP BY, which groups together rows with identical values in specified columns and produces aggregate values like MIN and MAX and COUNT and SUM. (This should remind you of the group_by function from "Manipulating Data" on page 129.)

For example, you might want to find the number of users and the smallest user_id for each possible name length:

```
SELECT LENGTH(name) as name_length,
 MIN(user_id) AS min_user_id,
 COUNT(*) AS num_users
FROM users
GROUP BY LENGTH(name);
```

Every field we SELECT needs to be either in the GROUP BY clause (which name_length is) or an aggregate computation (which min_user_id and num_users are).

SQL also supports a HAVING clause that behaves similarly to a WHERE clause except that its filter is applied to the aggregates (whereas a WHERE would filter out rows before aggregation even took place).

You might want to know the average number of friends for users whose names start with specific letters but only see the results for letters whose corresponding average is greater than 1. (Yes, some of these examples are contrived.)

```
SELECT SUBSTR(name, 1, 1) AS first_letter,
 AVG(num_friends) AS avg_num_friends
FROM users
GROUP BY SUBSTR(name, 1, 1)
HAVING AVG(num_friends) > 1;
```

(Functions for working with strings vary across SQL implementations; some databases might instead use SUBSTRING or something else.)

You can also compute overall aggregates. In that case, you leave off the GROUP BY:

```
SELECT SUM(user_id) as user_id_sum
FROM users
WHERE user_id > 1;
```

To add this functionality to NotQuiteABase Tables, we'll add a group_by() method. It takes the names of the columns you want to group by, a dictionary of the aggregation functions you want to run over each group, and an optional predicate having that operates on multiple rows.

Then it does the following steps:

1. Creates a defaultdict to map tuples (of the group-by-values) to rows (containing the group-by-values). Recall that you can't use lists as dict keys; you have to use tuples.

2. Iterates over the rows of the table, populating the defaultdict.

3. Creates a new table with the correct output columns.

4. Iterates over the defaultdict and populates the output table, applying the hav ing filter if any.

(An actual database would almost certainly do this in a more efficient manner.)

```
def group_by(self, group_by_columns, aggregates, having=None):

    grouped_rows = defaultdict(list)

    # populate groups
    for row in self.rows:
        key = tuple(row[column] for column in group_by_columns)
        grouped_rows[key].append(row)

    # result table consists of group_by columns and aggregates
    result_table = Table(group_by_columns + aggregates.keys())

    for key, rows in grouped_rows.iteritems():
        if having is None or having(rows):
            new_row = list(key)
            for aggregate_name, aggregate_fn in aggregates.iteritems():
                new_row.append(aggregate_fn(rows))
            result_table.insert(new_row)

    return result_table
```

Again, let's see how we would do the equivalent of the preceding SQL statements. The name_length metrics are:

```
def min_user_id(rows): return min(row["user_id"] for row in rows)
```

```
stats_by_length = users \
    .select(additional_columns={"name_length" : name_length}) \
    .group_by(group_by_columns=["name_length"],
              aggregates={ "min_user_id" : min_user_id,
                           "num_users" : len })
```

The `first_letter` metrics:

```
def first_letter_of_name(row):
    return row["name"][0] if row["name"] else ""

def average_num_friends(rows):
    return sum(row["num_friends"] for row in rows) / len(rows)

def enough_friends(rows):
    return average_num_friends(rows) > 1

avg_friends_by_letter = users \
    .select(additional_columns={'first_letter' : first_letter_of_name}) \
    .group_by(group_by_columns=['first_letter'],
              aggregates={ "avg_num_friends" : average_num_friends },
              having=enough_friends)
```

and the `user_id_sum` is:

```
def sum_user_ids(rows): return sum(row["user_id"] for row in rows)

user_id_sum = users \
    .where(lambda row: row["user_id"] > 1) \
    .group_by(group_by_columns=[],
              aggregates={ "user_id_sum" : sum_user_ids })
```

ORDER BY

Frequently, you'll want to sort your results. For example, you might want to know the (alphabetically) first two names of your users:

```
SELECT * FROM users
ORDER BY name
LIMIT 2;
```

This is easy to implement by giving our `Table` an `order_by()` method that takes an order function:

```
def order_by(self, order):
    new_table = self.select()      # make a copy
    new_table.rows.sort(key=order)
    return new_table
```

which we can then use as follows:

```
friendliest_letters = avg_friends_by_letter \
    .order_by(lambda row: -row["avg_num_friends"]) \
    .limit(4)
```

The SQL ORDER BY lets you specify ASC (ascending) or DESC (descending) for each sort field; here we'd have to bake that into our order function.

JOIN

Relational database tables are often *normalized*, which means that they're organized to minimize redundancy. For example, when we work with our users' interests in Python we can just give each user a list containing his interests.

SQL tables can't typically contain lists, so the typical solution is to create a second table user_interests containing the one-to-many relationship between user_ids and interests. In SQL you might do:

```
CREATE TABLE user_interests (
    user_id INT NOT NULL,
    interest VARCHAR(100) NOT NULL
);
```

whereas in NotQuiteABase you'd create the table:

```
user_interests = Table(["user_id", "interest"])
user_interests.insert([0, "SQL"])
user_interests.insert([0, "NoSQL"])
user_interests.insert([2, "SQL"])
user_interests.insert([2, "MySQL"])
```

 There's still plenty of redundancy—the interest "SQL" is stored in two different places. In a real database you might store user_id and interest_id in the user_interests table and then create a third table interests mapping interest_id to interest so you could store the interest names only once each. Here that would just make our examples more complicated than they need to be.

When our data lives across different tables, how do we analyze it? By JOINing the tables together. A JOIN combines rows in the left table with corresponding rows in the right table, where the meaning of "corresponding" is based on how we specify the join.

For example, to find the users interested in SQL you'd query:

```
SELECT users.name
FROM users
JOIN user_interests
ON users.user_id = user_interests.user_id
WHERE user_interests.interest = 'SQL'
```

The JOIN says that, for each row in users, we should look at the user_id and associate that row with every row in user_interests containing the same user_id.

Notice we had to specify which tables to JOIN and also which columns to join ON. This is an INNER JOIN, which returns the combinations of rows (and only the combinations of rows) that match according to the specified join criteria.

There is also a LEFT JOIN, which—in addition to the combinations of matching rows—returns a row for each left-table row with no matching rows (in which case, the fields that would have come from the right table are all NULL).

Using a LEFT JOIN, it's easy to count the number of interests each user has:

```
SELECT users.id, COUNT(user_interests.interest) AS num_interests
FROM users
LEFT JOIN user_interests
ON users.user_id = user_interests.user_id
```

The LEFT JOIN ensures that users with no interests will still have rows in the joined data set (with NULL values for the fields coming from user_interests), and COUNT only counts values that are non-NULL.

The NotQuiteABase join() implementation will be more restrictive—it simply joins two tables on whatever columns they have in common. Even so, it's not trivial to write:

```
def join(self, other_table, left_join=False):

    join_on_columns = [c for c in self.columns       # columns in
                         if c in other_table.columns]  # both tables

    additional_columns = [c for c in other_table.columns # columns only
                            if c not in join_on_columns]   # in right table

    # all columns from left table + additional_columns from right table
    join_table = Table(self.columns + additional_columns)

    for row in self.rows:
        def is_join(other_row):
            return all(other_row[c] == row[c] for c in join_on_columns)

        other_rows = other_table.where(is_join).rows

        # each other row that matches this one produces a result row
        for other_row in other_rows:
            join_table.insert([row[c] for c in self.columns] +
                                [other_row[c] for c in additional_columns])

        # if no rows match and it's a left join, output with Nones
        if left_join and not other_rows:
            join_table.insert([row[c] for c in self.columns] +
```

```
                    [None for c in additional_columns])

        return join_table
```

So, we could find users interested in SQL with:

```
sql_users = users \
    .join(user_interests) \
    .where(lambda row: row["interest"] == "SQL") \
    .select(keep_columns=["name"])
```

And we could get the interest counts with:

```
def count_interests(rows):
    """counts how many rows have non-None interests"""
    return len([row for row in rows if row["interest"] is not None])

user_interest_counts = users \
    .join(user_interests, left_join=True) \
    .group_by(group_by_columns=["user_id"],
              aggregates={"num_interests" : count_interests })
```

In SQL, there is also a RIGHT JOIN, which keeps rows from the right table that have
no matches, and a FULL OUTER JOIN, which keeps rows from both tables that have no
matches. We won't implement either of those.

Subqueries

In SQL, you can SELECT from (and JOIN) the results of queries as if they were tables.
So if you wanted to find the smallest user_id of anyone interested in SQL, you could
use a subquery. (Of course, you could do the same calculation using a JOIN, but that
wouldn't illustrate subqueries.)

```
SELECT MIN(user_id) AS min_user_id FROM
(SELECT user_id FROM user_interests WHERE interest = 'SQL') sql_interests;
```

Given the way we've designed NotQuiteABase, we get this for free. (Our query results
are actual tables.)

```
likes_sql_user_ids = user_interests \
    .where(lambda row: row["interest"] == "SQL") \
    .select(keep_columns=['user_id'])

likes_sql_user_ids.group_by(group_by_columns=[],
                            aggregates={ "min_user_id" : min_user_id })
```

Indexes

To find rows containing a specific value (say, where name is "Hero"), NotQuiteABase
has to inspect every row in the table. If the table has a lot of rows, this can take a very
long time.

Similarly, our `join` algorithm is extremely inefficient. For each row in the left table, it inspects every row in the right table to see if it's a match. With two large tables this could take approximately forever.

Also, you'd often like to apply constraints to some of your columns. For example, in your `users` table you probably don't want to allow two different users to have the same `user_id`.

Indexes solve all these problems. If the `user_interests` table had an index on `user_id`, a smart `join` algorithm could find matches directly rather than scanning the whole table. If the `users` table had a "unique" index on `user_id`, you'd get an error if you tried to insert a duplicate.

Each table in a database can have one or more indexes, which allow you to quickly look up rows by key columns, efficiently join tables together, and enforce unique constraints on columns or combinations of columns.

Designing and using indexes well is somewhat of a black art (which varies somewhat depending on the specific database), but if you end up doing a lot of database work it's worth learning about.

Query Optimization

Recall the query to find all users who are interested in SQL:

```
SELECT users.name
FROM users
JOIN user_interests
ON users.user_id = user_interests.user_id
WHERE user_interests.interest = 'SQL'
```

In NotQuiteABase there are (at least) two different ways to write this query. You could filter the `user_interests` table before performing the join:

```
user_interests \
    .where(lambda row: row["interest"] == "SQL") \
    .join(users) \
    .select(["name"])
```

Or you could filter the results of the join:

```
user_interests \
    .join(users) \
    .where(lambda row: row["interest"] == "SQL") \
    .select(["name"])
```

You'll end up with the same results either way, but filter-before-join is almost certainly more efficient, since in that case `join` has many fewer rows to operate on.

In SQL, you generally wouldn't worry about this. You "declare" the results you want and leave it up to the query engine to execute them (and use indexes efficiently).

NoSQL

A recent trend in databases is toward nonrelational "NoSQL" databases, which don't represent data in tables. For instance, MongoDB is a popular schema-less database whose elements are arbitrarily complex JSON documents rather than rows.

There are column databases that store data in columns instead of rows (good when data has many columns but queries need few of them), key-value stores that are optimized for retrieving single (complex) values by their keys, databases for storing and traversing graphs, databases that are optimized to run across multiple datacenters, databases that are designed to run in memory, databases for storing time-series data, and hundreds more.

Tomorrow's flavor of the day might not even exist now, so I can't do much more than let you know that NoSQL is a thing. So now you know. It's a thing.

For Further Exploration

- If you'd like to download a relational database to play with, SQLite (*http://www.sqlite.org*) is fast and tiny, while MySQL (*http://www.mysql.com*) and Post-greSQL (*http://www.postgresql.org*) are larger and featureful. All are free and have lots of documentation.

- If you want to explore NoSQL, MongoDB (*http://www.mongodb.org*) is very simple to get started with, which can be both a blessing and somewhat of a curse. It also has pretty good documentation.

- The Wikipedia article on NoSQL (*http://en.wikipedia.org/wiki/NoSQL*) almost certainly now contains links to databases that didn't even exist when this book was written.

## CHAPTER 24

MapReduce

The future has already arrived. It's just not evenly distributed yet.
—William Gibson

MapReduce is a programming model for performing parallel processing on large data sets. Although it is a powerful technique, its basics are relatively simple.

Imagine we have a collection of items we'd like to process somehow. For instance, the items might be website logs, the texts of various books, image files, or anything else. A basic version of the MapReduce algorithm consists of the following steps:

1. Use a `mapper` function to turn each item into zero or more key-value pairs. (Often this is called the `map` function, but there is already a Python function called `map` and we don't need to confuse the two.)

2. Collect together all the pairs with identical keys.

3. Use a `reducer` function on each collection of grouped values to produce output values for the corresponding key.

This is all sort of abstract, so let's look at a specific example. There are few absolute rules of data science, but one of them is that your first MapReduce example has to involve counting words.

Example: Word Count

DataSciencester has grown to millions of users! This is great for your job security, but it makes routine analyses slightly more difficult.

For example, your VP of Content wants to know what sorts of things people are talking about in their status updates. As a first attempt, you decide to count the words that appear, so that you can prepare a report on the most frequent ones.

When you had a few hundred users this was simple to do:

```
def word_count_old(documents):
    """word count not using MapReduce"""
    return Counter(word
        for document in documents
        for word in tokenize(document))
```

With millions of users the set of documents (status updates) is suddenly too big to fit on your computer. If you can just fit this into the MapReduce model, you can use some "big data" infrastructure that your engineers have implemented.

First, we need a function that turns a document into a sequence of key-value pairs. We'll want our output to be grouped by word, which means that the keys should be words. And for each word, we'll just emit the value 1 to indicate that this pair corresponds to one occurrence of the word:

```
def wc_mapper(document):
    """for each word in the document, emit (word,1)"""
    for word in tokenize(document):
        yield (word, 1)
```

Skipping the "plumbing" step 2 for the moment, imagine that for some word we've collected a list of the corresponding counts we emitted. Then to produce the overall count for that word we just need:

```
def wc_reducer(word, counts):
    """sum up the counts for a word"""
    yield (word, sum(counts))
```

Returning to step 2, we now need to collect the results from wc_mapper and feed them to wc_reducer. Let's think about how we would do this on just one computer:

```
def word_count(documents):
    """count the words in the input documents using MapReduce"""

    # place to store grouped values
    collector = defaultdict(list)

    for document in documents:
        for word, count in wc_mapper(document):
            collector[word].append(count)

    return [output
            for word, counts in collector.iteritems()
            for output in wc_reducer(word, counts)]
```

Imagine that we have three documents ["data science", "big data", "science fiction"].

Then wc_mapper applied to the first document yields the two pairs ("data", 1) and ("science", 1). After we've gone through all three documents, the collector contains

```
{ "data" : [1, 1],
  "science" : [1, 1],
  "big" : [1],
  "fiction" : [1] }
```

Then wc_reducer produces the count for each word:

```
[("data", 2), ("science", 2), ("big", 1), ("fiction", 1)]
```

Why MapReduce?

As mentioned earlier, the primary benefit of MapReduce is that it allows us to distribute computations by moving the processing to the data. Imagine we want to word-count across billions of documents.

Our original (non-MapReduce) approach requires the machine doing the processing to have access to every document. This means that the documents all need to either live on that machine or else be transferred to it during processing. More important, it means that the machine can only process one document at a time.

 Possibly it can process up to a few at a time if it has multiple cores and if the code is rewritten to take advantage of them. But even so, all the documents still have to *get to* that machine.

Imagine now that our billions of documents are scattered across 100 machines. With the right infrastructure (and glossing over some of the details), we can do the following:

- Have each machine run the mapper on its documents, producing lots of (key, value) pairs.
- Distribute those (key, value) pairs to a number of "reducing" machines, making sure that the pairs corresponding to any given key all end up on the same machine.
- Have each reducing machine group the pairs by key and then run the reducer on each set of values.
- Return each (key, output) pair.

What is amazing about this is that it scales horizontally. If we double the number of machines, then (ignoring certain fixed-costs of running a MapReduce system) our computation should run approximately twice as fast. Each mapper machine will only need to do half as much work, and (assuming there are enough distinct keys to further distribute the reducer work) the same is true for the reducer machines.

MapReduce More Generally

If you think about it for a minute, all of the word-count-specific code in the previous example is contained in the wc_mapper and wc_reducer functions. This means that with a couple of changes we have a much more general framework (that still runs on a single machine):

```
def map_reduce(inputs, mapper, reducer):
    """runs MapReduce on the inputs using mapper and reducer"""
    collector = defaultdict(list)

    for input in inputs:
        for key, value in mapper(input):
            collector[key].append(value)

    return [output
            for key, values in collector.iteritems()
            for output in reducer(key,values)]
```

And then we can count words simply by using:

```
word_counts = map_reduce(documents, wc_mapper, wc_reducer)
```

This gives us the flexibility to solve a wide variety of problems.

Before we proceed, observe that wc_reducer is just summing the values corresponding to each key. This kind of aggregation is common enough that it's worth abstracting it out:

```
def reduce_values_using(aggregation_fn, key, values):
    """reduces a key-values pair by applying aggregation_fn to the values"""
    yield (key, aggregation_fn(values))

def values_reducer(aggregation_fn):
    """turns a function (values -> output) into a reducer
    that maps (key, values) -> (key, output)"""
    return partial(reduce_values_using, aggregation_fn)
```

after which we can easily create:

```
sum_reducer = values_reducer(sum)
max_reducer = values_reducer(max)
min_reducer = values_reducer(min)
count_distinct_reducer = values_reducer(lambda values: len(set(values)))
```

and so on.

Example: Analyzing Status Updates

The content VP was impressed with the word counts and asks what else you can learn from people's status updates. You manage to extract a data set of status updates that look like:

```
{"id": 1,
 "username" : "joelgrus",
 "text" : "Is anyone interested in a data science book?",
 "created_at" : datetime.datetime(2013, 12, 21, 11, 47, 0),
 "liked_by" : ["data_guy", "data_gal", "mike"] }
```

Let's say we need to figure out which day of the week people talk the most about data science. In order to find this, we'll just count how many data science updates there are on each day of the week. This means we'll need to group by the day of week, so that's our key. And if we emit a value of 1 for each update that contains "data science," we can simply get the total number using sum:

```
def data_science_day_mapper(status_update):
    """yields (day_of_week, 1) if status_update contains "data science" """
    if "data science" in status_update["text"].lower():
        day_of_week = status_update["created_at"].weekday()
        yield (day_of_week, 1)

data_science_days = map_reduce(status_updates,
                               data_science_day_mapper,
                               sum_reducer)
```

As a slightly more complicated example, imagine we need to find out for each user the most common word that she puts in her status updates. There are three possible approaches that spring to mind for the mapper:

- Put the username in the key; put the words and counts in the values.
- Put the word in key; put the usernames and counts in the values.
- Put the username and word in the key; put the counts in the values.

If you think about it a bit more, we definitely want to group by username, because we want to consider each person's words separately. And we don't want to group by word, since our reducer will need to see all the words for each person to find out which is the most popular. This means that the first option is the right choice:

```
def words_per_user_mapper(status_update):
    user = status_update["username"]
    for word in tokenize(status_update["text"]):
        yield (user, (word, 1))
```

```
def most_popular_word_reducer(user, words_and_counts):
    """given a sequence of (word, count) pairs,
    return the word with the highest total count"""

    word_counts = Counter()
    for word, count in words_and_counts:
        word_counts[word] += count

    word, count = word_counts.most_common(1)[0]

    yield (user, (word, count))

user_words = map_reduce(status_updates,
                        words_per_user_mapper,
                        most_popular_word_reducer)
```

Or we could find out the number of distinct status-likers for each user:

```
def liker_mapper(status_update):
    user = status_update["username"]
    for liker in status_update["liked_by"]:
        yield (user, liker)

distinct_likers_per_user = map_reduce(status_updates,
                                      liker_mapper,
                                      count_distinct_reducer)
```

Example: Matrix Multiplication

Recall from "Matrix Multiplication" on page 260 that given a $m \times n$ matrix A and a $n \times k$ matrix B, we can multiply them to form a $m \times k$ matrix C, where the element of C in row i and column j is given by:

$$C_{ij} = A_{i1}B_{1j} + A_{i2}B_{2j} + ... + A_{in}B_{nj}$$

As we've seen, a "natural" way to represent a $m \times n$ matrix is with a list of lists, where the element A_{ij} is the jth element of the ith list.

But large matrices are sometimes *sparse*, which means that most of their elements equal zero. For large sparse matrices, a list of lists can be a very wasteful representation. A more compact representation is a list of tuples (name, i, j, value) where name identifies the matrix, and where i, j, value indicates a location with nonzero value.

For example, a billion × billion matrix has a *quintillion* entries, which would not be easy to store on a computer. But if there are only a few nonzero entries in each row, this alternative representation is many orders of magnitude smaller.

Given this sort of representation, it turns out that we can use MapReduce to perform matrix multiplication in a distributed manner.

To motivate our algorithm, notice that each element A_{ij} is only used to compute the elements of C in row i, and each element B_{ij} is only used to compute the elements of C in column j. Our goal will be for each output of our reducer to be a single entry of C, which means we'll need our mapper to emit keys identifying a single entry of C. This suggests the following:

```
def matrix_multiply_mapper(m, element):
    """m is the common dimension (columns of A, rows of B)
    element is a tuple (matrix_name, i, j, value)"""
    name, i, j, value = element

    if name == "A":
        # A_ij is the jth entry in the sum for each C_ik, k=1..m
        for k in range(m):
            # group with other entries for C_ik
            yield((i, k), (j, value))
    else:
        # B_ij is the i-th entry in the sum for each C_kj
        for k in range(m):
            # group with other entries for C_kj
            yield((k, j), (i, value))

def matrix_multiply_reducer(m, key, indexed_values):
    results_by_index = defaultdict(list)
    for index, value in indexed_values:
        results_by_index[index].append(value)

    # sum up all the products of the positions with two results
    sum_product = sum(results[0] * results[1]
                      for results in results_by_index.values()
                      if len(results) == 2)

    if sum_product != 0.0:
        yield (key, sum_product)
```

For example, if you had the two matrices

```
A = [[3, 2, 0],
     [0, 0, 0]]

B = [[4, -1, 0],
     [10, 0, 0],
     [0, 0, 0]]
```

you could rewrite them as tuples:

```
entries = [("A", 0, 0, 3), ("A", 0, 1,  2),
           ("B", 0, 0, 4), ("B", 0, 1, -1), ("B", 1, 0, 10)]
mapper = partial(matrix_multiply_mapper, 3)
```

```
reducer = partial(matrix_multiply_reducer, 3)

map_reduce(entries, mapper, reducer) # [((0, 1), -3), ((0, 0), 32)]
```

This isn't terribly interesting on such small matrices, but if you had millions of rows and millions of columns, it could help you a lot.

An Aside: Combiners

One thing you have probably noticed is that many of our mappers seem to include a bunch of extra information. For example, when counting words, rather than emitting (word, 1) and summing over the values, we could have emitted (word, None) and just taken the length.

One reason we didn't do this is that, in the distributed setting, we sometimes want to use *combiners* to reduce the amount of data that has to be transferred around from machine to machine. If one of our mapper machines sees the word "data" 500 times, we can tell it to combine the 500 instances of ("data", 1) into a single ("data", 500) before handing off to the reducing machine. This results in a lot less data getting moved around, which can make our algorithm substantially faster still.

Because of the way we wrote our reducer, it would handle this combined data correctly. (If we'd written it using len it would not have.)

For Further Exploration

- The most widely used MapReduce system is Hadoop (*http://hadoop.apache.org*), which itself merits many books. There are various commercial and noncommercial distributions and a huge ecosystem of Hadoop-related tools.

  In order to use it, you have to set up your own *cluster* (or find someone to let you use theirs), which is not necessarily a task for the faint-hearted. Hadoop mappers and reducers are commonly written in Java, although there is a facility known as "Hadoop streaming" that allows you to write them in other languages (including Python).

- Amazon.com offers an Elastic MapReduce (*http://aws.amazon.com/elasticmapre duce/*) service that can programmatically create and destroy clusters, charging you only for the amount of time that you're using them.

- mrjob (*https://github.com/Yelp/mrjob*) is a Python package for interfacing with Hadoop (or Elastic MapReduce).

- Hadoop jobs are typically high-latency, which makes them a poor choice for "real-time" analytics. There are various "real-time" tools built on top of Hadoop, but there are also several alternative frameworks that are growing in popularity.

Two of the most popular are Spark (*http://spark.apache.org/*) and Storm (*http://storm.incubator.apache.org/*).

- All that said, by now it's quite likely that the flavor of the day is some hot new distributed framework that didn't even exist when this book was written. You'll have to find that one yourself.

## CHAPTER 25

Go Forth and Do Data Science

And now, once again, I bid my hideous progeny go forth and prosper.
—Mary Shelley

Where do you go from here? Assuming I haven't scared you off of data science, there are a number of things you should learn next.

IPython

We mentioned IPython (*http://ipython.org/*) earlier in the book. It provides a shell with far more functionality than the standard Python shell, and it adds "magic functions" that allow you to (among other things) easily copy and paste code (which is normally complicated by the combination of blank lines and whitespace formatting) and run scripts from within the shell.

Mastering IPython will make your life far easier. (Even learning just a little bit of IPython will make your life a lot easier.)

Additionally, it allows you to create "notebooks" combining text, live Python code, and visualizations that you can share with other people, or just keep around as a journal of what you did (Figure 25-1).

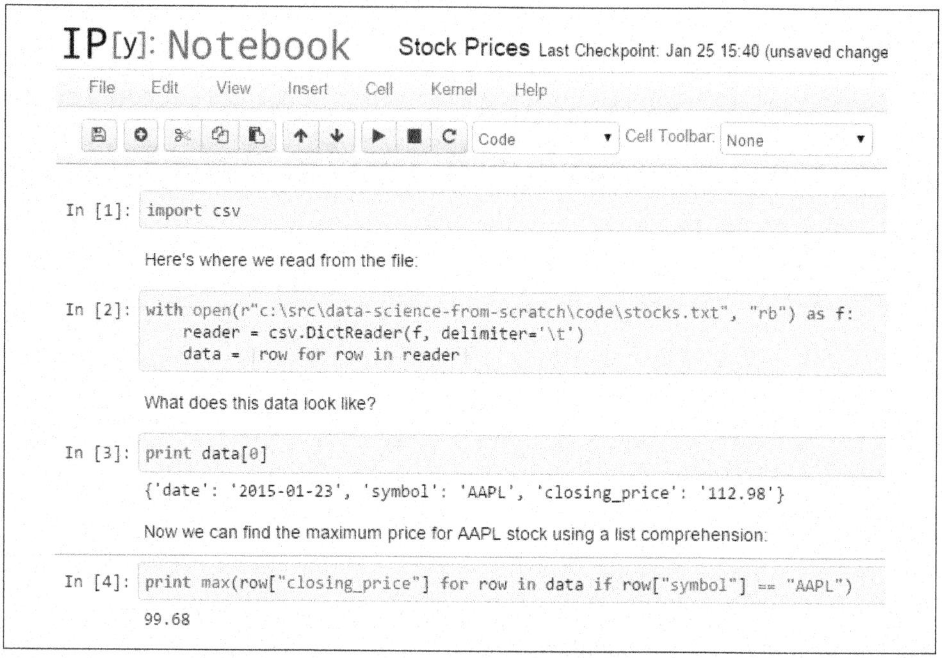
IP[y]: Notebook
Stock Prices Last Checkpoint: Jan 25 15:40 (unsaved change
File Edit View Insert Cell Kernel Help
Code
Cell Toolbar: None
In [1]: import csv
Here's where we read from the file:
In [2]: with open(r"c:\src\data-science-from-scratch\code\stocks.txt", "rb") as f:
reader = csv.DictReader(f, delimiter='\t')
data = row for row in reader
What does this data look like?
In [3]: print data[0]
{'date': '2015-01-23', 'symbol': 'AAPL', 'closing_price': '112.98'}
Now we can find the maximum price for AAPL stock using a list comprehension:
In [4]: print max(row["closing_price"] for row in data if row["symbol"] == "AAPL")
99.68

Figure 25-1. An IPython notebook

Mathematics

Throughout this book, we dabbled in linear algebra (Chapter 4), statistics (Chapter 5), probability (Chapter 6), and various aspects of machine learning.

To be a good data scientist, you should know much more about these topics, and I encourage you to give each of them a more in-depth study, using the textbooks recommended at the end of the chapters, your own preferred textbooks, online courses, or even real-life courses.

Not from Scratch

Implementing things "from scratch" is great for understanding how they work. But it's generally not great for performance (unless you're implementing them specifically with performance in mind), ease of use, rapid prototyping, or error handling.

In practice, you'll want to use well-designed libraries that solidly implement the fundamentals. (My original proposal for this book involved a second "now let's learn the libraries" half that O'Reilly, thankfully, vetoed.)

NumPy

NumPy (*http://www.numpy.org*) (for "Numeric Python") provides facilities for doing "real" scientific computing. It features arrays that perform better than our list-vectors, matrices that perform better than our list-of-list-matrices, and lots of numeric functions for working with them.

NumPy is a building block for many other libraries, which makes it especially valuable to know.

pandas

pandas (*http://pandas.pydata.org*) provides additional data structures for working with data sets in Python. Its primary abstraction is the DataFrame, which is conceptually similar to the NotQuiteABase Table class we constructed in Chapter 23, but with much more functionality and better performance.

If you're going to use Python to munge, slice, group, and manipulate data sets, pandas is an invaluable tool.

scikit-learn

scikit-learn (*http://scikit-learn.org*) is probably the most popular library for doing machine learning in Python. It contains all the models we've implemented and many more that we haven't. On a real problem, you'd never build a decision tree from scratch; you'd let scikit-learn do the heavy lifting. On a real problem, you'd never write an optimization algorithm by hand; you'd count on scikit-learn to be already using a really good one.

Its documentation contains many, many examples (*http://scikit-learn.org/stable/auto_examples/*) of what it can do (and, more generally, what machine learning can do).

Visualization

The matplotlib charts we've been creating have been clean and functional but not particularly stylish (and not at all interactive). If you want to get deeper into data visualization, you have several options.

The first is to further explore matplotlib, only a handful of whose features we've actually covered. Its website contains many examples (*http://matplotlib.org/examples/*) of its functionality and a Gallery (*http://matplotlib.org/gallery.html*) of some of the more interesting ones. If you want to create static visualizations (say, for printing in a book), this is probably your best next step.

You should also check out seaborn (*http://web.stanford.edu/~mwaskom/software/seaborn/*), which is a library that (among other things) makes `matplotlib` more attractive.

If you'd like to create *interactive* visualizations that you can share on the Web, the obvious choice is probably D3.js (*http://d3js.org*), a JavaScript library for creating "Data Driven Documents" (those are the three Ds). Even if you don't know much JavaScript, it's often possible to crib examples from the D3 gallery (*https://github.com/mbostock/d3/wiki/Gallery*) and tweak them to work with your data. (Good data scientists copy from the D3 gallery; great data scientists *steal* from the D3 gallery.)

Even if you have no interest in D3, just browsing the gallery is itself a pretty incredible education in data visualization.

Bokeh (*http://bokeh.pydata.org*) is a project that brings D3-style functionality into Python.

R

Although you can totally get away with not learning R (*http://www.r-project.org*), a lot of data scientists and data science projects use it, so it's worth getting at least familiar with it.

In part, this is so that you can understand people's R-based blog posts and examples and code; in part, this is to help you better appreciate the (comparatively) clean elegance of Python; and in part, this is to help you be a more informed participant in the never-ending "R versus Python" flamewars.

The world has no shortage of R tutorials, R courses, and R books. I hear good things about *Hands-On Programming with R*, and not just because it's also an O'Reilly book. (OK, mostly because it's also an O'Reilly book.)

Find Data

If you're doing data science as part of your job, you'll most likely get the data as part of your job (although not necessarily). What if you're doing data science for fun? Data is everywhere, but here are some starting points:

- Data.gov (*http://www.data.gov*) is the government's open data portal. If you want data on anything that has to do with the government (which seems to be most things these days) it's a good place to start.
- reddit has a couple of forums, r/datasets (*http://www.reddit.com/r/datasets*) and r/data (*http://www.reddit.com/r/data*), that are places to both ask for and discover data.

- Amazon.com maintains a collection of public data sets (*http://aws.amazon.com/public-data-sets/*) that they'd like you to analyze using their products (but that you can analyze with whatever products you want).
- Robb Seaton has a quirky list of curated data sets on his blog (*http://rs.io/100-interesting-data-sets-for-statistics/*).
- Kaggle (*https://www.kaggle.com/*) is a site that holds data science competitions. I never managed to get into it (I don't have much of a competitive nature when it comes to data science), but you might.

Do Data Science

Looking through data catalogs is fine, but the best projects (and products) are ones that tickle some sort of itch. Here are a few that I've done.

Hacker News

Hacker News (*https://news.ycombinator.com/news*) is a news aggregation and discussion site for technology-related news. It collects lots and lots of articles, many of which aren't interesting to me.

Accordingly, several years ago, I set out to build a Hacker News story classifier (*https://github.com/joelgrus/hackernews*) to predict whether I would or would not be interested in any given story. This did not go over so well with the users of Hacker News, who resented the idea that someone might not be interested in every story on the site.

This involved hand-labeling a lot of stories (in order to have a training set), choosing story features (for example, words in the title, and domains of the links), and training a Naive Bayes classifier not unlike our spam filter.

For reasons now lost to history, I built it in Ruby. Learn from my mistakes.

Fire Trucks

I live on a major street in downtown Seattle, halfway between a fire station and most of the city's fires (or so it seems). Accordingly, over the years, I have developed a recreational interest in the Seattle Fire Department.

Luckily (from a data perspective) they maintain a Realtime 911 site (*http://www2.seattle.gov/fire/realtime911/getDatePubTab.asp*) that lists every fire alarm along with the fire trucks involved.

And so, to indulge my interest, I scraped many years' worth of fire alarm data and performed a social network analysis (*https://github.com/joelgrus/fire*) of the fire trucks. Among other things, this required me to invent a fire-truck-specific notion of centrality, which I called TruckRank.

T-shirts

I have a young daughter, and an incessant source of frustration to me throughout her childhood has been that most "girls shirts" are quite boring, while many "boys shirts" are a lot of fun.

In particular, it felt clear to me that there was a distinct difference between the shirts marketed to toddler boys and toddler girls. And so I asked myself if I could train a model to recognize these differences.

Spoiler: I could (*https://github.com/joelgrus/shirts*).

This involved downloading the images of hundreds of shirts, shrinking them all to the same size, turning them into vectors of pixel colors, and using logistic regression to build a classifier.

One approach looked simply at which colors were present in each shirt; a second found the first 10 principal components of the shirt image vectors and classified each shirt using its projections into the 10-dimensional space spanned by the "eigenshirts" (Figure 25-2).

Figure 25-2. Eigenshirts corresponding to the first principal component

And You?

What interests you? What questions keep you up at night? Look for a data set (or scrape some websites) and do some data science.

Let me know what you find! Email me at *joelgrus@gmail.com* or find me on Twitter at @joelgrus.

Index

maximum likelihood estimation, 177
maximum, finding using gradient descent, 94, 99
mean
    computing, 59
    removing from PCA data, 134
median, 59
meetups (example), 227-229
member functions, 30
merged clusters, 233
minimum, finding using gradient descent, 94
mode, 60
models, 141
    bias-variance trade-off, 147
    in machine learning, 142
modules (Python), 17
multiple assignment (Python), 21

N

n-gram models, 241-244
    bigram, 242
    trigrams, 243
n-grams, 243
Naive Bayes algorithm, 165-172
    example, filtering spam, 165-167
    implementation, 168
natural language processing (NLP), 239-253
    grammars, 244-246
    topic modeling, 247-252
    topics of interest, finding, 11
    word clouds, 239-240
nearest neighbors classification, 151-163
    curse of dimensionality, 156-162
    example, favorite programming languages, 153-156
    model, 151
network analysis, 255-266
    betweenness centrality, 255-260
    closeness centrality, 259
    degree centrality, 5, 256
    directed graphs and PageRank, 264-266
    eigenvector centrality, 260-264
networks, 255
neural networks, 213-224
    backpropagation, 218
    example, defeating a CAPTCHA, 219-223
    feed-forward, 215
    perceptrons, 213
neurons, 213

NLP (see natural language processing)
nodes, 255
noise, 133
    in machine learning, 142
None (Python), 25
normal distribution, 75
    and p-value computation, 85
    central limit theorem and, 78
    in coin flip example, 82
    standard, 76
normalized tables, 283
NoSQL databases, 287
NotQuiteABase, 275
null hypothesis, 81
    testing in A/B test, 88
NumPy, 301

O

one-sided tests, 83
ORDER BY statement (SQL), 282
overfitting, 142, 147

P

p-hacking, 87
p-values, 84
PageRank algorithm, 265
paid accounts, predicting, 11
pandas, 120, 139, 301
parameterized models, 142
parameters, probability judgments about, 89
partial derivatives, 96
partial functions (Python), 31
PCA (see principal component analysis)
perceptrons, 213
pip (Python package manager), 15
pipe operator (|), 104
piping data through Python scripts, 103
posterior distributions, 89
precision and recall, 146
predicate functions, 278
predictive modeling, 142
principal component analysis, 134
probability, 69-80, 300
    Bayes's Theorem, 72
    central limit theorem, 78
    conditional, 70
    continuous distributions, 74
    defined, 69
    dependence and independence, 69

About the Author

Joel Grus is a software engineer at Google. Previously he worked as a data scientist at several startups. He lives in Seattle, where he regularly attends data science happy hours. He blogs infrequently at *joelgrus.com* and tweets all day long at @joelgrus (*http://twitter.com/joelgrus/*).

Colophon

The animal on the cover of *Data Science from Scratch* is a Rock Ptarmigan (*Lagopus muta*). This medium-sized gamebird of the grouse family is called simply "ptarmigan" in the UK and Canada, and "snow chicken" in the United States. The rock ptarmigan is sedentary, and breeds across arctic and subarctic Eurasia as well as North America as far as Greenland. It prefers barren, isolated habitats, such as Scotland's mountains, the Pyrenees, the Alps, the Urals, the Pamir Mountains, Bulgaria, the Altay Mountains, and the Japan Alps. It eats primarily birch and willow buds, but also feeds on seeds, flowers, leaves, and berries. Developing young rock ptarmigans eat insects.

Male rock ptarmigans don't have the typical ornaments of a grouse, aside from the comb, which is used for courtship display or altercations between males. Many studies have shown a correlation between comb size and testosterone levels in males. Its feathers moult from winter to spring and summer, changing from white to brown, providing it a sort of seasonal camouflage. Breeding males have white wings and grey upper parts except in winter, when its plumage is completely white save for its black tail.

At six months of age, the ptarmigan becomes sexually mature; a breeding rate of six chicks per breeding season is common, which helps protect the population from outside factors such as hunting. It's also spared many predators because of its remote habitat, and is hunted mainly by golden eagles.

Rock ptarmigan meat is a popular staple in Icelandic festive meals. Hunting of rock ptarmigans was banned in 2003 and 2004 because of declining population. In 2005, hunting was allowed again with restrictions to certain days. All rock ptarmigan trade is illegal.

Many of the animals on O'Reilly covers are endangered; all of them are important to the world. To learn more about how you can help, go to *animals.oreilly.com*.

The cover image is from Cassell's *Natural History*. The cover fonts are URW Typewriter and Guardian Sans. The text font is Adobe Minion Pro; the heading font is Adobe Myriad Condensed; and the code font is Dalton Maag's Ubuntu Mono.

Get even more for your money.

Join the O'Reilly Community, and register the O'Reilly books you own. It's free, and you'll get:

- $4.99 ebook upgrade offer
- 40% upgrade offer on O'Reilly print books
- Membership discounts on books and events
- Free lifetime updates to ebooks and videos
- Multiple ebook formats, DRM FREE
- Participation in the O'Reilly community
- Newsletters
- Account management
- 100% Satisfaction Guarantee

Signing up is easy:

1. Go to: oreilly.com/go/register
2. Create an O'Reilly login.
3. Provide your address.
4. Register your books.

Note: English-language books only

To order books online:
oreilly.com/store

For questions about products or an order:
orders@oreilly.com

To sign up to get topic-specific email announcements and/or news about upcoming books, conferences, special offers, and new technologies:
elists@oreilly.com

For technical questions about book content:
booktech@oreilly.com

To submit new book proposals to our editors:
proposals@oreilly.com

O'Reilly books are available in multiple DRM-free ebook formats. For more information:
oreilly.com/ebooks